ISLAM'S ROLE IN MODERN WORLD

Islam's Role in Modern World

M.U. Qureshi

ANMOL PUBLICATIONS PVT. LTD.
NEW DELHI - 110 002 (INDIA)

ANMOL PUBLICATIONS PVT. LTD.
4374/4B, Ansari Road, Daryaganj
New Delhi - 110 002
Ph.: 23261597, 23278000
Visit us at: www.anmolpublications.com

Islam's Role in Modern World

First Published, 2004

ISBN 81-261-1888-1

PRINTED IN INDIA

Published by J.L. Kumar for Anmol Publications Pvt. Ltd., New Delhi - 110 002 and Printed at Mehra Offset Press, Delhi.

Contents

Preface

History of mankind bears witness that most of the religions and faiths were meant for a certain nation and a certain period only. New faiths and new Prophets always appeared on the scene and discarded the previous ones. But, Islam emerged as the final faith and Prophet Muhammad (PBUH) was declared the last prophet, fulfilling God's mission.

Islam is not confined to any geographical region and not meant for any particular nation. It is also not for a certain period of time. It is a universal religion, meant for the entire humanity. That's why, Holy Quran addresses the mankind and the humanbeings as a whole. The Almighty is not the Lord of this world, He is Lord of the worlds, as per Islamic tenets.

Islam is a scientific and progressive religion, based on reasoning and logic. Hence, its relevance never exhausts. As a philosophy, ideology, faith, discipline and way of life, Islam is equally relevant in the modern world, as it was in the contemporary world, when it had come on the scene.

The modern man is fed up of materialism and its counter-effects. He needs solace and shelter, And that can be provided by a perfect heavenly discipline alone. No ideology or 'ism' can be an answer to the problems of humanity. The natural demise of Communism and failure of Marxism is a rebutting reply to the critics of religion and belief.

This 'not so bulky' book relates Islam's relevance and its role in the modern world and the new age. It also discusses Islam's contribution towards the evolution and development of culture in the civilized world.

This editor is hopeful that this humble work of his, would help scholars and students of Islamic studies in knowing Islam better.

Editor

1

Introduction

We have already exposed one aspect of the modernistic school of thought that they have made Western way of thinking and living a criterion of right and wrong. In this chapter, we are making some further submissions about the way of thinking and the method of argumentation of the modernists which are of fundamental importance to the subject under discussion.We intend to point out the reasons why all the efforts of our modern researchers have led them to the path of distortion in the name of "research".

Even a man with ordinary common sense knows that "Research" means "Search for Reality" and a researcher holds the position of a judge. It is his obligation that without forming any preconceived ideas and pre-drawn conclusions he should examine all the relevant matters thoroughly and impartially, consider all possible aspects of the problem with utmost honesty and add the weight of his judgement to the weightiest side of argument. On the contrary, if any one seeks and searches the arguments to support a preconceived idea or judgement he is certainly not the seeker of truth, nor his efforts in this direction deserve to be called a research work.

The duty of a researcher is not to collect arguments for a predetermined idea but to determine an idea in the light of arguments. He does not drag the arguments towards his judgment but the arguments drive him towards a judgement. But the process of working of our modernists is quite opposite. They believe that arguments are to serve a decision rather than the decision being dependent on arguments. This is what they think is the correct method of research and this what they teach as a methodology of research. They commonly make suggestions in their oral and written statements that:

> "We want to interpret the Qur'an and the Sunnah in a manner that it conforms to the needs of our time".

It is a clear admission to the fact that they want to bring the Quran and Sunnah to reconcile with their decisions and not make their decisions to correspond with the Quran and the Sunnah. That is they will first decide as to what are the needs of time and then in trying to find these arguments they will make such interpretations of the Qur'anic verses and prophetic traditions as to conform to their predetermined needs of the Time. This is what is termed as the "distortion of meaning". This way of argumentation can never be supported by any sensible person of the world. If the process of research is allowed to move in reverse direction then there will be no way left to protect the integrity of the truth. Because in this way every illogical claim can be supported by argument. Nothing in the world would then be devoid of argument, and as they say: "Everything can be proved by everything". Once it is decided that certain thing is to be proved through the Qur'an and Sunnah, and for this purpose you have decided to give new interpretation to the Quran and Sunnah, it would obviously mean that anything found supporting this idea would be presented as an argument no matter how weak and baseless it be and even the strongest argument against it would be thrown away being incompatible with present day life.

You probably know that the Christian missionaries, while preaching their religion in the Muslim world, always prove their beliefs through the Quran and traditions before common Muslims. For example, they say that the Quran has called Jesus as "Kalimatullah" (The word of Allah) which implies that he was Allah's attribute of "Kalam" (Speech) and the Bible of John also says the same. Also, the Quran said that Jesus was "Ruhullah" (The spirit of God) which implies that his relation with God was the same as that of Soul with body, and the same is said by Paul. They further say that the Qur'an said: "We supported Jesus with the holy spirit" and the same has been mentioned in the Bible that the holy Ghost was sent to Jesus in the form of a pigeon.

In this way they prove their concept of Trinity, and the tragedy is that they prove it through the Quran by virtue of its "new interpretation". As for the verses of the Qur'an which explicitly condemn the concept of Trinity, their "new interpretation" is that these verses condemn Trinity in the literal ' and real sense of the word, and even the Christians accept that there is only one God, and these three are only the components of one and not separate gods. Also according to their "new Interpretation" of Qur'an and its proclamation "Those who say Jesus son of Mary is god are Kafirs (unbelievers)" in fact meant to contradict the sect of monophacy. Where Qur'an has warned the Christians against the torment of Hell their "new Interpretation" is that this does not refer to Catholics but is meant for monophasics. The Qur`an says that Jesus was not crucified. The "new Interpretation is that Christians in general also believed that the third person of Trinity was not crucified and the Qur'an does not Contradict crucification of his body."

It can be seen how the magic of "new Interpretation" proved all Christians' beliefs to be in conformity witli Islam. The question arises "What is the difference between your new Interpretation and that of the Christians?" If you have a right to make "new Interpretation" of the Qur'an and Sunnah in order to amend the established laws of Islam why the Christians should not have the same right? Under what rule or regulation can you reject the Christians' "new Interpretation"?

One may argue that our comparison of "new Interpretation" of modernists with the "new Interpretation" of Christians is exaggerated, but that is not true. The readers may go through their articles on the subject and the truth of our statement will become quite apparent.

We come across numerous interesting "new Interpretations" in the book named "Islam" written by the Director of Islamic

Research, Dr. Fazlur Rehman. According to him only three daily Salahs were originally made obligatory, and two more were added in the last years of the Prophet's life. Hence their number has the possibility of accepting changes.

"Anyhow, the fact that basically there were three daily Salahs is also supported by the incidence that there is one narration according to which Prophet (PBUH) has converted the four Salahs into two". Anyway it happened in the post-prophetic era that the number of Salahs without any alternative choice, was strictly fixed as five. In this way the fact that the number was basically three got swept away in the flood of traditions reported in support of the number of five". (Monthly "Fikr-o-Nazar, vol: 5, p.259)

> This is the "new Interpretation". According to this, on one side "the flood of authentic prophetic traditions" which described the number of Salah as five from the very beginning of Islam is false and self-invented; on the other side the single narration describing the incidence of combining the two Salahs" has been considered by them as most reliable. Then again the term "combining two Salahs" has been taken to mean that the Prophet had converted four into two. This is the most interesting example of the expertise in the "new Interpretation" If you have read this narration you will definitely enjoy the fallacies of thought.' This is the way of argument about which somebody has said," you can prove everything by everything."

This is just one example that we have presented. If you go through the exegeses of these modernists you will come across many "master pieces" of their "new Interpretations." Wahy (Divine revelations) is interpreted as the Prophet's own words; Angels mean water, electricity etc.; Iblis (Satan) as the fantasy; Jinns as the savage tribes; mankind as the civilized people, Death is unconsciousness, disgrace or disbelief, life means honour and dignity, state of consciousness or embracing Islam etc.

If you keep the above exegetic points in view you will know that we have not exaggerated at all. Anyway, this was just a parenthesis. We wanted to impress that if we adopt the style of making arguments dependent on preconceived thoughts even Christianity can be proved from the Qur'an itself, and so can be Judaism, Socialism and Capitalism. Adopting the same style Dr. Pervaiz has proved Darwin's theory of evolution in his book "Iblis aur 'Adam" from the Qur'an. Also he has derived an economic system of socialist style from the Qur'anic phrase (Establish your prayers of worship). It is the same style of interpretations by which Mirza Ghulam Alimad Qadyani had pleaded that by Damishk (Damascus) the Prophet had incant Qadiy'an, the Mirza's headquarters.

Thus we see that the System of modernists is that they first fix some ideas themselves, label them as the exigencies of time and then impose the Qur'an and Hadith through their "new Interpretation" on them. This is the very first brick the angulation of which has resulted in the crookedness of entire structure of their views and thoughts, and this is the fundamental reason why their thoughts have entered the limits of 'distortion' overthrowing all principles, rules and regulations of research and knowledge.

There are some rules and regulations for research in every art and science. You cannot reach the correct conclusion unless you follow them. In the present jurisprudence also "Interpretation of statutes" is a compulsory subject. It has definite rules and regulations and unless they are given due consideration no interpretation of any legal expert can be acceptable.

In the same manner, rather more reasonable and well organised are the detailed rules and regulations for interpretation (of Quran and Sunnah and Islamic law) that have been compiled after thorough research, devoted attention and minute observations. Hundreds of books are available on the subject and each rule has been thoroughly screened. Unless the Qur'an and Hadith are interpreted within the framework of these rules and regulations no reasonable person can accept diem, exactly as such explanations of present commentators cannot be accepted that do not conform to the principles of "Interpretation of statutes".

But our modernists do not bind themselves to any such rules in their interpretations and commentaries due to their stamped way of thinking. Thus they frequently defy the established rules of interpretation of the Qur'an and Sunnah. For example, the established rule of Islamic Jurisprudence that proverbial or allegoric meaning of any word or phrase of the Qur'an or Hadith would be adopted only when literal meaning is either impossible or have become obsolete in common use. This is perfectly a reasonable rule which can not be challenged through any intellectual argument, without it no definite conclusion can ever be derived from anything said by anybody. But this rule is profusely ignored by the modernists in their writings. Wherever they find a word in the Qur'an and Hadith clashing with their concepts they unhesitatingly give it allegoric and sometimes purely imaginative interpretation. "Son" has been interpreted as "grandson", staff turned into .'argument"; death as a state of "coma or disgrace", "Satan" as "fantasy or illusion "so much so that "Allah and Messenger" have been termed as "centre of the Ummah". These are just a few examples. If these absurdities are all compiled together a voluminous book can be prepared.

It can be said by the modernists that they do not agree with the rules and regulations fixed by the Islamic jurists and that is why they do not follow them. In that case they should have pointed out those rules and given some alternate principles better than the rules of the jurists. Then they should have used their formulated rules in their writings.

But we find that their interpretations are not supported by any principle at all. At one occasion they break a rule and oppose it, but at another occasion they derive their argument for their new interpretation. They reject any tradition that appears to contradict their views, no matter how authentic chain of reporters it has, but where a tradition appears to support their views, they ignore the clear verses of the Holy Quran on the basis of a tradition which is weak and without support of authentic narrators. A recent example is the statement of Dr. Fazlur Rehman in which he has said that the meat of an animal is lawful and permissible to eat even if it is slaughtered without the name of Allah pronounced on it, while the explicit injunction of Quran is this:

> And eat not that (flesh) over which Allah's name has not been pronounced.

But since this was against the views of Dr. Fazlur Rehman, he based his arguments on a narration of Hazrat Aishah and on a saying of Imam Shafi which is perhaps the weakest argument of all his juristic inferences (as has been admitted by the scholars of my school of thought), while his own view about the application of a tradition is as follows:

> "If a tradition tells anything that is not in conformity with the apparent Qur'anic injunction I would attribute it to the specific historical era rather than to the Prophet himself'. (Monthly "Fikr-o-Nazar, p.515, vol.2)

Apart from the fact that his inference from Aishah's narration is highly misleading, Dr. Fazlur Rehman should not seek argument from this according to his own principle cited above. On what ground he attributed this tradition to the Holy Prophet (PBUH).

As far as Imam Shafi is concerned, the Doctor has commented about him as under:

The enlightened views and quick understanding of Imam Shafi did create a machinic system which undoubtedly led to stabilisation of social and religious structure of our mediaeval era, but due to it we have been deprived of modern thinking and creative intellect (Monthly "Fikr-o- Nazar", p. 3 0, vol. I)

If Imam Shafi had committed such a fundamental error bow can you quote him as authority on the validity of a religious precept? Does it not become apparent from the above examples that Dr. Fazlur Rehman and his co-workers have no set criterion for research in their mind. Not only that they have not taken into consideration any of the established rules of Jurisprudence, they do not even follow the rules framed by themselves?

There can be no other reason for this betrayal of their own principles that they form their own views and then seek arguments to support them. Obviously this method can not go along with rules and regulations, because with every new idea they have to frame new regulations. If they are requested in the name of God to let alone the "knowledge and research" and refrain from making the Qur'an and Sunnah a plaything as was done by the Jews and Christians in case of Torah and Injil, such persons are instantly labelled as "Obscurantists" and Agnorant of the exigencies of time". Their judgement about them is that they are blind to the new environment and have no knowledge of the modern demands. (Monthly "Fikr-o- p.731, vol.2)

We are conscious that in response to our sincere submissions, we shall also be rewarded with such titles but we are writing and continue to write the truth with a hope that there may be a heart in search of truth that may accept it. May be our suggestions can awake a sleeping conscience.

The million dollar questions : Who should be competent to interpret and explain the Quran and Sunnah (Prophetic traditions) and to deduce various injunctions for problems arising in new circumstances. What are the conditions and requirements necessary for this job? We find the answers to these questions in an authentic Tradition reported by Hadhrat Ali in which he said:

"I said, "O messenger of Allah! If we are confronted with a problem which has not been described in the Quran and Prophetic traditions, with no injunctions in favour or against it, what am I to do in such a situation?" He said: "Take advice of the jurists and faithful worshippers and do not employ your individual opinion".

The Holy Prophet (PBUH) has explicitly stated in this narration that two conditions must be fulfilled by a person who wants to deduce laws and injunctions from the Quran and Prophetic traditions. Firstly, he must be a jurist and secondly, he must be a devotee to worship. The importance of the first condition is obvious because objectives of the Quran and traditions can be well conceived only by those who possess vast and deep knowledge, who are fully aware of the rules laid down by the earlier jurists and who have spent their lives in understanding the intentions of divine laws. Similarly, the Prophet has made it a condition for him to be a devotee and faithfal, that is, he must have devoted himself to the practices of these laws. Anyone who can not make distinction between permissibles and forbidden in practical life and whose every day practices are in contrast of these laws can not comprehend the intentions of Islam. Deduction of the laws is, in fact, the "Search for the Truth", and the Qur'an states that Allah bestows the faculty of cognizance of the truth to the one who confides in it in his practical life. It said:

> If you foar Allah He will give you the power of discrimination between truth and falsehood.

This verse has clearly stated that "Fear of Allah" is the primary condition for a sense of discrimination between right and wrong. It is quite obvious from the above verse of the Qur'an and the Prophetic tradition that a religious and juristic solution can best be found by a person who is "jurist" and a "devotee" (or "Muttaqi". that is, the one who abstains from evil for fear of Allah).

Lately Mufti Muhammad Shafi, President, Darul-Ulum, Karachi had summarized the same thing in the following words.

> "The method of solving the problems not mentioned in the Book and the traditions is the joint consultation of jurists and devoted scholars of Islam. Imposing the personal and individual opinion on the Muslims is forbidden."

But for reasons unknown our modernists are allergic to this way of thinking. The traditional knowledge of the Qur'an and the Sunnah is not considered by them as an essential requirement for interpretation of and deductions from the Qur'an and the Sunnah, nor do they think it necessary that such a person should necessarily be fearful of Allah and devoted worshipper. For some time they have been making loud suggestion to this effect.

> "There should be no monopoly of religious scholars" on the interpretation of Quran and the Sunnah. No papacy should be allowed in Islam. No particular group, therefore, can be given the right of legislations. "The interpretation of the Qur'an and the Tradition is the right of all Muslims and not of the religious scholars alone" "Religious scholars cannot be given the power of veto in the affairs of Islam", etc., etc.

These are the suggestions that are expressed in almost all the writings of the modernists. As far as the instructions of the Qur'an and the Traditions are concerned we have already submitted that the greatest emphasis has been laid down on the fundamental requirement of knowledge and devotion for interpreting the religion. But it seems proper here to discuss real facts that are the source of these misunderstandings.

Their first suggestion is: " There is no Brahmanism or Papacy in Islam, hence the religious scholars cannot be given the exclusive rights of legislations".

Either they are totally ignorant of the real meaning of papacy and theocracy and their ills in them, or they are deliberately deceiving the simple people of the Ummah. Anyone having slightest sense of justice and the truth can understand that "knowledge" and "fearfulness of Allah" (Taqwa) is not limited to any race, colour, caste or creed which one cannot achieve through his efforts and resources. It is the name of "Eligibility and Qualification" of a specific objective which can be achieved by everyone at any time. If setting some qualifications for certain responsibilities is papacy, no section of life can be said to be devoid of it. The educational standard and moral character needed for the presidentship and ministership of a country would also be termed as "papacy". The condition of being an expert on legal affairs for a judge would also be another form of "papacy". The attainment of a law degree for legal advisor or advocate should be called papacy. The condition of having relevant academic degrees for teaching in a university, college or school should be removed. The limit of age, intellect and normal character fixed for qualifying as a candidate in elections, should all be cancelled as they are different forms of "papacy". But it is not so. How then the condition of 'knowledge' and "Taqwa" for interpreting the Qur'an and the Tradition be termed as papacy?

Anyone having a little knowledge of the term of "Papacy" and Brahmanism cannot overlook the differences between the religious scholars of Islam and the Popes and Brahmans.

(1) "Pope" and "Brahmans" are practically the titles of a specified class of colour, caste and creed. Anyone outside these jurisdictions cannot enter into their fold despite all

eligibilities and efforts. That is why we find dacoits and robbers becoming "Popes" in the history of Christian church. Contrary to this, Religious scholars of Islam (Ulema) is an attribute for which there is no restriction of caste and creed. In the fourteen hundred years of the history of Islam we find religious scholars hi every colour or creed, even the slaves have emerged as great scholars of Islamic learnings and accepted as leaders of the Ummah. The cause of their dignified status had always remained their "Knowledge" and "Taqwa" rather than their parental background.

(2) The religion of which the Pope is claimed to be a spokesman is a religion which does not provide with guidance for the most important aspects of life. That is why the word of Pope has become the word of God, and no one else can defy this. Thus he is no more an interpreter of law but a free and independent law-maker. Contrary to this, the injunctions of the Book (Quran) and the Sunnah (Prophetic traditions) are universal and the rules and regulations for their interpretation are prescribed and preserved in their original form. Any scholar saying anything against these rules and regulations will be rejected by other scholars on the ground of these principles. A number of such scholars is always present to check such misinterpretations.

(3) The process of law-making and interpretation of religion in papacy ultimately ends on one man. He alone has been regarded as the "Shepherd of the sheep of Massiah" and the Deputy of the founder of the church. Contrary to this, "Religious scholars" of Islam is not the name of any person who is the head of an organisation, but anyone who has attained religious knowledge on true lines is a Religious scholar and a heir to the Holy Prophet. Hence no individual scholar has right to impose his personal views and whims on the entire Muslim Ummah.

In the presence of such an obvious difference between the role of the Pope and of the Islamic scholar any one applying the term

Papacy to the services of the Ulema simply exhibits his loss of knowledge and common intellect.

The second demand of the modernists is that "there can be no monopoly of the Ulema on the Book and Traditions. Therefore, the right of their interpretation cannot be reserved for religious scholars alone".

Those under the charm of this propaganda are tirelessly repeating this slogan and do not stop for a while to think that thus they are making themselves similar to a person who had never seen a medical college but raises the objection as to why the treatment of diseases has been reserved for qualified doctors only or like a fool who criticises saying why the experts in law and jurisprudence alone have the right of the interpretation of law and why not others are allowed to do so?

No sensible or conscientious person can ever think on these hues. However, if one has such an imbecile approach he should know that any one has the right to perform all these duties , but to gain proficiency and elgibility for this you will have to spend years and years of hard work and labour, seeking the guidance from experts for practical experience, obtain degree and diplomas and other related experience, then, of course, you will be allowed to make interpretations.

The most sensitive and delicate work of interpreting the Quran and the Sunnah is said to require the same process how can it be termed as monopoly. Does it not require any one to get educated for it. Why the Quran and the Sunnah alone are considered to be as pitiable as to be treated by any individual at his own will? How one can be given right to interpret the Quran and the Sunnah while he has not spent even a few months in acquiring the relevant Knowledge.

They express their anger against the religious scholars all the day long as to why they alone should deserve the right to interpret the Quran and the Sunnah? But they never reflect on the amount of pain and labour they had undergone to acquire this right? How in the two hundred years of British rule in India they had remained the target of the British atrocities and aggression? With all the doors of livelihood closed on them by the British rule they preferred to live on meagre resources and devoted themselves to acquire this knowledge against all odds. They are still doing it despite the harrassment from these modernists. How they glowed their eyes in front of the dim light of oil lamps of clay? And how they attempted to shape their lives in the mould of religion? If after all that, the Holy Prophet (PBUH) gives them the right to interpret the Quran and his Sunnah, and the Muslims place their trust in them why is this resented by them?

The eagerness of modernists for interpreting the Book and the Traditions is certainly commendable; but for this they should also undergo the physical and mental strain needed for it. They, too,should spend some part of life in trodding the roads to knowledge of the Quran and learn the manners of living on that ground. If after that any one refuses to recognize them as interpreter of the Quran and the Traditions, then their complaint against the scholars would be justified.

Under the present circumstances their attitude is like what the poet said:

> Those who hold their life dear to them should not think of going to seek his beloved.
>
> Your present state of mind has been well depicted by the poet of the East, Allama Iqbal, in this poem:
>
> The knowledge of others you gained is a mere correction as if you have glowed your face with foreign cosmetics.
>
> You have given up your dignity so much that I cannot recognise you as yourself.
>
> Your mind is chained by the thoughts of others and the succession of breaths in your throat has a foreign source.
>
> The tongue is yours but the speech is borrowed from others and so are your wishes in your mind.
>
> The canaries wish to sing their own songs, the cypresses wish to be clad with their own foliage.

> You borrow the wine from others in your goblet. Even the cup you hold is not yours.

The Prophet is grieved, and the Creator asks "Am I not there?" But for you! Alas! Alas!

Under these circumstances how can the Muslim Ummah entrust you with the responsibility of interpreting the Quran and Sunnah, who, with all their shortcomings, have saved their ideological entity as Muslims.

As for the claim that Dr. Fazlur Rahman has published in the monthly "Fikr-o-Nazar" in these words:

> "In Islam the Muslim Ummah as a whole had been doing legislative work and it should still have the right to do so."

I wish they had further clarified what he meant by it. Does it mean that every individual of the Ummah should be allowed to become a legislator? Every illiterate and uncivilised person should be entrusted with legislation? Or, does it mean that the Ummah as a whole enjoys the fight to select some deserving, reliable and knowledgeable person from among them to be entrusted with this sacred job? In that case it will be a work of these selected people. Obviously even the very staunch believer in democracy does not take the term democracy to mean that every single individual can interfere with each and every affair of the state. In fact, they hold that every matter and problem is to be entrusted to the experts of that field and those who lack knowledge in that trade have to place their trust on these experts, and it is not termed as an infringement of the rights of democracy.

After this analysis of the rights of people one can easily conclude who, out of one hundred and twenty million people of Pakistan, are worthy of trust in the matter of interpretation and exegesis of the Quran and the Traditions? When any one of them really wants to understand the Quranic injunction or prophetic tradition would he seek the help of the Institute of Islamic Research or any other modernist institution or to those 'Obscurantist" scholars whom the modernists blame to have robbed the people of their democratic right? If the multitude of

Muslims turn to these scholars without any compulsion, pressure or legal restrictions, place their trust on them and their conscience get satisfied with it where does the democratic right of people get hurt? Who have injured the beliefs of the Muslim Ummah with their interpolation, the Ulema or these modernists is known to all?

Their last and biggest objection is on the condition of "Taqwa" (Fear of Allah, Piety, Abstenance from evil doings). According to them "Taqwa" like "knowledge" is not essential for interpreting the Quran We do not understand what apprehension they have against it. According to them the complication in this regard is:

"The condition of "Taqwa" is a condition that every scholar can reject the judgement of other scholar because everyone has his own standard for Taqwa". Nazis Nov.67, p.326)

We may be allowed to say that ignore for a while your individual apprehension and there will be no complication in this matter. The same 'Multitude' (Jamhur) whom they want to give the status of legislators is equally entitled to decide which of the scholars fulfils this condition of taqwa? Collectively the conscience of multitude of Muslims is never wrong. Their opinion is the will of Allah. Why should there be any hesitation in entrusting the job of interpretation of the Quran and traditions to a person whose Taqwa is accepted by the multitude?

It should be thoroughly understood that 'Taqwa' is not an ambiguous and unsettled term which can be given any meaning by anyone according to his individual liking. In Islam "Taqwa" is a legal phrase and countless religious injunctions depend on it. Whenever it is used in a legal sense it would mean "practising the permissibles, abstaining from major sins and not insisting on minor sins." In the phraseology of the Quran it is the opposite of "Fujur" (Apparent sins, Immorality). The Quran says:

Then inspired it (with conscience of) its wickedness and its piety.

Hence anyone abstaining from "Fujur" is a man of Taqwa, and therefore the people shall have no difficulty in deciding about the piety and devotion (Taqwa) of a person. With this in view there one can easily conceive that there can be no complexity or difficulty arising from imposing the condition of knowledge and Taqwa for interpretation, explication or exegesis of the Quran and Prophetic tradition."

In the end we would again like to humbly request the modernists that the use of street slogans and propaganda weapon would neither render any service to the country or the nation nor can any problems be solved with them, nor would it leave any pleasant effect on any serious mind. In the hue and cry of their slogans at the most they can suppress the voice of truth for a short while. But that can only affect the ears, but not the hearts.

2

East and West

There is an Arabic proverb according to which a fish always begins to decay from its head. This echoes the well-known Latin proverb corruptio optimi pessima: 'the corruption of the best is the worst'. What occurred in the West during the Renaissance and is now happening in so many parts of the Islamic warld is precisely the corruption of the best, the decay of the head of the fish whose body is still intact. To oppose this process and to cater to the real needs at man in both East and West, therefore, it is likewise necessary to begin from the 'head', from the teachings related to the most sublime aspect of tradition contained in its spiritual and intellectual dimensions which are the first to become inaccessible and 'veiled', rather than the social and practical dimen-sions of the tradition which usually remain more accessible. It is the decay of the best or most intellectually gifted and hence influential in the long run that must. be combated with the help of sapiential doctrines, the message from the Centre the forgetting of which is at the root of the pathetic plight of modern man now observable on such a vast scale. It is, therefore, to the metaphysical dimension of tradition contained at the heart of religion that we must turn before all else.

Methodology of Comparative Religion

A great deal has been written during the past decades on the methodology of comparative religion, on various approaches taken by Western scholars, ranging from historians to phenomenologists, in studying Eastern religions. With this already extensively debated subject we will not concern ourselves here. Rather, we shall limit ourselves to the question of Oriental and particularly Islamic metaphysics and traditional philosophy, of which the understanding in the West is sought by so many but is attained by so few, remembering that, in this domain, what holds true for the Islamic tradition to other Oriental traditions as well.

In contrast to the extravagant claims made for world-wide communication between peoples of various cultures and races, the Tower of Babel in which modern man resides makes communication of serious matters most difficult at a time when outward contact between men seems to have become easier than at any other period of human history. The common language of wisdom having been lost, there exists for Modernised men no common ground to make any meaningful communication possible, especially between the modern world and the traditions of the East. Men talk of a single humanity at a time when there has never been a little inner communication between components of the human race. Today, outwardly cut off from the umbilical cord that has always connected them to the common Divine Ground, men are reduced to islands set apart by an insuperable chasm which no amount of humanism can bridge. In no field is this as true as in metaphysical doctrines and traditional 'philosophy', or in that corpus of knowledge which determines the ultimate framework of man's other modes of knowledge as well as the values of his actions.

Because of the lack of discernment which characterizes the modern world and which is to be seen even more among Westernized Orientals, Muslim and otherwise, than among Westerners themselves, all kinds of fantastic excesses on both sides have for the most part prevented a meaningful intellectual communication and a comparative study of philosophy and metaphysics worthy of the name. The greatest gnostics and saints have often been compared with sceptics, and different levels of inspiration have been totally confused. A Tolstoy has been called a Mahatma; Hume's denial of causality has been related to Ash'arite theology on the one hand and to Buddhism on the other;

Sankara has been compared with the German idealists, and Nietzsche with Rumi. Western students of Oriental doctrines have usually tried to reduce these doctrines to 'profane' philosophy, and Modernised Orientals, often burdened by the half-hidden sense of inferiority already alluded to, have tried to give respectability to the same doctrines and to 'elevate' them by giving them the honour of being in harmony with the thought of this or that Western philosopher, who in fact is usually out of vogue by the time such comparisons are made. On both sides, usually, the relation of the 'philosophy' in question to the experience or direct knowledge of the Truth which is the source of this 'philosophy' is forgotten, and levels of reality are confused.

A first step towards a solution of this problem is to clear the ground of existing confusions in order to clarify exactly what is being compared with what. One must first of all ask what we mean by 'philosophy'. To this extremely complicated question one can provide a clear answer provided that the light of metaphysical certainty is present. But precisely because this light is lacking in most discussions, the worst kind of confusion reigns over the very attempt at a definition of the subject matter in hand. Moreover, the traditions of the East and the West have given different meanings to this term, although at the highest level of the philosophia perennis, the sanatoria dharma of Hinduism or the hikmah laduniyyah of Islam, there has always been the profoundest agreement concerning the nature of the sophia which all true philosophers 'love' and seek and in whose bosom alone can the East and West meet.

Journey of Thought

To begin with it can be said that, if we accept the meaning of the term 'philosophy' current in the West in most European languages, then it is nearly synonymous with logic—leaving aside the recent anti-rationalist movements based upon such sentiments as anxiety and fear. In the West, philosophy as usually understood has sometimes allied itself with revelation and theology or true intellectual intuition ('intellect' being understood in its original sense) as in St Bonaventure or St Thomas; at other times it has become wedded to mathematics or to the physical sciences, as in certain schools of the seventeenth century and again of the twentieth century; and at yet other times it has sought to analyze and dissect the data of the senses alone, as in British empiricism.

Also in the West, at least in its main intellectual current, metaphysics in its real sense, which is a sapiential knowledge based upon the direct and immediate experience of the Truth, has become reduced—thanks to the Occidental interpretation of Aristotle—to a branch of philosophy. As a result, men like Plotinus, Proclus, Dionysius, Erigena and Nicolas of Cusa have been treated as ordinary philosophers, whereas if we accept the meaning of philosophy given above, they cannot by any means be classified in the same category as men like Descartes and Kant, nor even with the Aristotelian and Thomist philosophers, who occupy an intermediary position between these two groups, namely the post-mediaeval European philosophers on the one hand and the gnostics and metaphysicians on the other.

Fundamental Distinction

As a result of the forgetting of the fundamental distinction between the intellect, which knows through immediate experience or vision, and reason, ratio, which can only know through analysis and division, the fundamental distinction between metaphysics as a scientia sacra or Divine Knowledge and philosophy as a purely human form of mental activity has been blurred or forgotten. Things have reached such a point that in the modern world all the different philosophical schools ranging from the purely metaphysical to the feeblest efforts of atrophied minds have been put into a single category and their content has been reduced to a lowest common denominator.

To make the problem more difficult, despite the currently accepted definition of philosophy in the West, the echo of philosophy as the doctrinal aspect of an integral spiritual way, or as metaphysics and theosophy in its original sense, still lingers on in the meaning of the word and continues to possess a marginal existence. One can in fact distinguish, at least in popular language in the West, two meanings of the term philosophy: one in the technical sense alluded to above and the other in the sense of 'wisdom'. Against this latter meaning, in fact, most professional modern European and American philosophy has rebelled more than ever before, so that these modes of thought could hardly be called philo-sophia, for they do not love but hate wisdom. Logically they should be called miso-sophia.

As far as the Oriental traditions such as Buddhism, Taoism, Hinduism and Islam are concerned, the situation is just the reverse. Except for cer tain school such as the mashsha'i or Peripatetic school of Islam, which corresponds in many ways but not completely to Aristotelianism and Thomism in the West,' certain individual Islamic figures such as Muhammad ibn Zakariyya' al-Razi, and some of the peripheral schools in India, there is nothing in the Oriental traditions which could be considered 'philosophy' in the current Western sense of the term, precisely because the major intellectual traditions of the Orient are always wedded to a direct experience of the spiritual world and intellectual intuition in the strictest sense of the term. What is usually called Oriental philosophy is the doctrinal part of a total spiritual way, tied to a method of realization and inseparable from the revelation or tradition which has given birth to the way in question. That is why to speak of rationalistic philosophy and of Chinese or Hindu philosophy in the same breath is a contradiction in terms, unless we use the word 'philosophy' in two different senses: of thought processes being wedded to spiritual experience, and of thought being completely cut off from this experience. It is a lack of awareness of this basic distinction that has made a sham of so many studies of comparative philosophy and has helped to blind to the real significance of Oriental metaphysics those in the West whose sources of knowledge are the usual academic works on the subject. Far from being the object of mental play, this metaphysics has the function of enabling man to transcend the mental plane itself.

When one has taken into consideration the above differences as well as the essential role of religion and methods of spiritual realization in the creation and the sustaining of what is usually called 'Oriental philosophy'—in contrast to what is found in modern Western philosophy—the first necessary condition for a meaningful comparative study will be complete awareness of the structure and the levels of meaning of the religious and metaphysical traditions of East and West. One can compare religions themselves; that belongs to the field of comparative religion. One can also compare the mystical and esoteric teachings of the East and the West in the field which has recently come to be called 'comparative mysticism' and which is in reality an aspect of comparative religion. These are disciplines apart from what is now becoming known as comparative philosophy, a discipline which seeks to study the intellectual heritage of various Oriental traditions and that of the Occidental through the comparative method.

Now comparative philosophy per se is either a shallow comparison of apparently similar but essentially different teachings, or, if it is to be serious, it is a comparative study of different ways of thinking and various matrices determining different sciences and forms of knowledge in reference to the total vision of the Universe and of the nature of things, a vision which is inseparable from the religious and spiritual background that has produced the 'philosophy' in question. The outward comparison of an Emerson and a Hafiz or a Sa'di will never have any meaning unless what each has said is considered in the light of Protestant Christianity and Islam respectively. Comparative philosophy without reference to the religious background, whether the religion in question has had a positive influence or has even been treated negatively, is as absurd as comparing single notes of music without reference to the melody of which they are a part.

Comparative Philosophy

Nor is comparative philosophy between East and West possible without considering the hierarchic nature of man's faculties and the modes of knowledge accessible to him. One of the most unfortunate and in fact tragic elements that has prevented most modern Western men from understanding Oriental teachings and in fact much of their own tradition is that they wish to study traditional man in the light of the model of two-dimensional modern man deprived of the transcendent dimension, the type of man with whom they are usually closely associated. The very concept of man's identity prevalent in the modern world is the greatest obstacle to an understanding of traditional man, who has been and continues to be aware of the Centre and also of the multiple levels of existence and the grades of knowledge accessible to him. If a blind man were to develop a philosophy based upon his experience of the world derived from his four other senses, surely it would differ from one based upon those four senses as well as upon sight. How much more would a 'philosophy' based upon man's rational analysis of sense data differ from one that is the result of the experience of a world which transcends both reason and the sensible world? The functioning of the eye of the heart ('ayn al-qalb or chishm-i dil of the Sufis, which corresponds to the 'third eye' of the Hindus) makes accessible a vision or an experience of reality which affects man's 'philosophy' about the nature of reality as completely as perception by the eye colours our view of the nature of material existence.

Without a full awareness of the hierarchy of knowledge—which can be reduced to at least the four basic levels of the intellectual, the imaginative (in its positive sense of imagination or khayal in Arabic), the rational and the sensible—again no meaningful comparative study is possible. When people say that Sankara said so and so, which was confirmed by Berkeley or some other eighteenth century philosopher, it must be asked whether the same means of gaining knowledge was accessible to both. Or when it is said that this or that existential philosopher has had an 'experience of being' like a Mulla Sadra or some other Muslim sage, it must first be asked whether it is possible for a philosopher who negates Being to have an experience of It, for in reality we can have an experience of Being only through the grace provided by Being Itself and by means of the paths provided by It through those objective manifestations of the Universal Intellect called religion or revelation. Whenever comparisons are to be made, it must be asked what the source of die 'philosophy' in question is, whether it comes from ratiocination, from empirical analysis or from spiritual vision, or in other words upon which aspect of the being of the knower it depends. One must always remember the saying of Aristotle that knowledge depends upon the mode of the knower.

In certain limited fields such as logic or the 'philosophy of nature', compinsons can be made for the most part legitimately without recourse to the total background alluded to above, although even here elements cannot be divorced totally from their background. But to a certain degree it is possible to compare Indian or Islamic logic with the various logical schools in the West, or atomism as it developed in India or among some Muslim's with atomism in the West, at least before the modern period. But once this limit is passed, the total background and the question of the 'source' of the knowledge in question become factors of paramount importance which one can neglect only at the expense of forsaking the possibility of true comprehension.

For example, it is possible to make serious comparative studies between Indian or Persian and Greek doctrines, or between Islamic philosophy and Western scholastic philosophy before the modern period. These studies can be meaningful because of both morphological resemblances and historical relations. But once we come to the modern period, the situation changes completely. From the point of view of Oriental metaphysics, the whole movement of thought in the West from the period after Nicolas of Cusa to Hegel, not to speak of twentieth century philosophy, is a movement toward 'anti-metaphysics' and an ever greater alienation from all that constitutes the very basis of all true 'philosophy', namely the twin sources of truth, which for traditional or perennial philosophy are none other than revelation and intellectual intuition or spiritual vision. Comparative studies made of this period should be concerned either with showing dissimilarities, conflicts and contradictions, or with the schools that have stood at the margin away from the mainstream of the history of European thought. A comparative study showing -similarities between Oriental doctrines and modern Western 'thought' could have meaning only in the case of such Western figures as those known by the collective name of the Cambridge Platonists, or Jacob Boehme, Claude St Martin, Franz van Baader and the like, who are not even generally well known in the West, to say nothing of the East. Otherwise, to say that this or that statement of Hegel resembles the Upanishads or that Hume presents ideas similar to Nagarjuna is to fall into the worst form of error, one which prevents any type of profound understanding from being achieved, either for Westerners wanting to understand the East or vice-versa.

In this order of indiscriminate comparisons without regard for the real nature of the ideas involved and for their meaning within the total context of things, Orientals have been even more at fault than the Western scholars who concern themselves with Oriental studies. In many instances found over and over again in the writings of Modernised Orientals, the nature of the experience upon which the 'philosophy' in question is based and the total world view in which alone it possesses meaning are completely overlooked. And often the sentimental desire to bring about harmony between completely contradictory and incompatible premisses—such as those upon which the traditional societies and the anti-traditional modern civilization are based—causes such writers to speak of apparent resemblances where there are in fact only the deepest contrasts and contradictions. This attitude reduces the role of comparative philosophy to that of a sentimental charity, whereas its function should be to serve the truth and to reveal contrasts and differences wherever they exist.

In speaking of differences we must also turn our glance for a moment to the question of the comparative study of doctrines, not between East and West but between the Eastern traditions themselves. One of the results of Western Colonisation of Asia during the last century has been that even today the different civilizations of Asia see each other, even if they be neighbours, in the mirror of the Occident. 'Comparative philosophy' is taken for granted to mean the comparison of ideas between East and West. Moreover, Oriental authors who undertake comparative studies usually take their own tradition and the West into consideration and nothing else. A Muslim considers only Islam and the West, and a Hindu Hinduism and Western thought, whereas the situation should be otherwise. For example, as far as relations between Hinduism and Islam are concerned, contemporary Hindu and Muslim scholars should strive to their utmost to attain today, through comparison, a degree of understanding of their respective traditions similar to what was achieved by Dara Shukuh and Mir Abu'l-Qasim Findiriski three centuries ago. Only recently, in fact, have a handful of Oriental scholars begun to take seriously comparative studies within the Oriental traditions themselves, and a few outstanding works have been composed in this domain, but a great deal more needs to be done in this fertile but almost unexplored field.

Comparing Various Oriental Doctrines

In the domain of comparing various Oriental doctrines, one finds, of course, a much firmer ground for comparison than when dealing with the modern West, seeing that Oriental civilizations are all of a traditional character, rooted in the Divine Principle which presides over and dominates them. But even here it is necessary to proceed with a spirit of discernment, avoiding shallow and sentimental comparisons and equations, and situating each school and doctrine in its appropriate place within the total matrix of its tradition. Although in a profound sense there is an East or Orient which stands vis-a-vis the Occident, a more detailed panorama of the intellectual landscape, which would give the appropriate depth to comparative studies, would reveal several Orients juxtaposed against a modern Occident whose historical tradition has, however, possessed elements and periods akin to the Orient, a term which, more than a geographical location, symbolizes most of all a spiritual reality, the world of light and illumination.

It might be asked, 'What use is the comparative study of philosophy and metaphysics?' To the West, its primary function can be to provide the criteria necessary to criticize in depth Western philosophy itself, which although outwardly critical of earlier schools of philosophy rarely turns the sharp edge of criticism against itself and is hardly ever exposed to criticism of its totality and of its basic premisses. Moreover, Oriental doctrines can fulfil that most fundamental and urgent task of reminding the West of truths that have existed within its own tradition but which have become so completely forgotten that it appears to many as if they had never existed. Today, it is in fact nearly impossible for Western man to rediscover the whole of his own tradition without the aid of Oriental metaphysics. This is particularly so because the sapiential doctrines and the appropriate spiritual techniques necessary for their realization are hardly accessible in the West, and 'philosophy' has become totally divorced from experience of a spiritual nature. In the traditional East the very opposite holds true. 'Philosophy' as a mental play or discipline which does not transform one's being is considered meaningless and in fact dangerous. The whole of the teachings of such Islamic philosophers as Suhrawardi and Mulla Sadra and all of Sufism are based on this point, as are all the schools of Hinduism and Buddhism, especially Vedanta and Zen. The very separation of knowledge from being which lies at the heart of the crisis of modern man is avoided in the Oriental traditions, which consider legitimate only that form of knowledge that can transform the being of the knower. The West could learn no greater lesson from the East than the realization of the central role of spiritual discipline in the attainment of any knowledge of permanent value.

As far as modern Easterners are concerned, one observes among most of those who are at once interested in the intellectual life and affected by the modernist spirit the most abominable lack of discernment and the dangerous tendency to mix the sacred and the profane, thus creating an eclectic conglomeration of sacred doctrines and profane and transient 'thoughts' which becomes a most deadly instrument for the destruction of all that still survives of true intellectuality and spirituality in the East. The errors committed by Easterners in this domain are perhaps even graver than those of Western scholars, because, here as in instances already cited, there is more possibility of spiritual damage in the East, where traditions have been better preserved. Some of the most destructive of those forces that have played havoc in Eastern societies during the past century are the result of shallow and facile 'syntheses' of Eastern and Western thought and superficial attempts at their unification. A more serious comparative study would therefore also serve Eastern scholars by enabling them to know better the very complex and complicated thought patterns of the modern world and the real nature of the modern world itself, so that they may be able to defend more carefully the authenticity of their own traditions while seeking at the same time to express their timeless truths in a contemporary manner without betraying their essence. In this supreme task that today stands before every genuine Oriental intellectual in general and Muslim intellectual in particular, the fruits of comparative study carried out on a serious basis can be of much value.

Finally, a comparative study in depth of Eastern doctrines and Western schools can help to achieve an understanding between East and West based not on the shifting sands of human nature nor on some form of humanism but on immutable truths, of which the attainment is made possible by the spiritual experience that is accessible to qualified men, whether of East or of West. It is intellectual intuition, and the spiritual experience of which a metaphysical doctrine is in a sense the fruit, that alone can make possible the attainment of salvation.

Science Philosophy and Logic

Unity, which, in its transcendence comprehends both the East and the West. Today, many men who have been exposed to the modern world in a sense, carry the Orient and the Occident as two poles and tendencies within themselves. A comparative study in depth can make possible, through the removal of that complex of current errors which constitutes the modern world, the vision of that 'tree that is neither of the East nor of the West', wherein alone can the East and the West be united. To seek this noble end, which would mean also the discovery of the immutable nature of man and which is the only way possible to correct the optical illusions to which the modern world is victim, must be the purpose of all serious studies of Eastern and Western doctrines and philosophies. It is a goal to the achievement of which the truly contemplative and intellectual elite of both East and West are urgently summoned by the very situation of man in the contemporary world, a situation which demands such a study, whatever be the differences in the problems faced by men living in the East and in the West.

3

Legacy of Islam

Having dealt with the problems and the significance of 'the comparative method', we must now apply this method to the Islamic universe, with which we are particularly concerned. It can be said with certainty that the comparative method, in the sense given to it in the previous chapter, is the most suitable means to explain and elucidate the Islamic intellectual and spiritual heritage for Western man. And although obviously not necessary for Muslims who wish to study their own tradition, even in their case it can be helpful to those who have received some form of modern education and whose matrix of thought and attitudes is often determined to some degree by elements drawn from the context of Western history and culture.

Studying Comparatively

In applying the comparative method to the Islamic intellectual and spiritual heritage, we must emphasize once again that the term 'philosophy' (al-falsafah or al-hikmaK) used in a traditional Islamic context must not be confused or equated with the modern use of the term, and also that the basic distinction between Oriental metaphysics and profane philosophy must be kept in mind. Moreover, the traditional Islamic 'philosophy' which is usually the subject of comparative studies fills, in fact, an intermediate position in the spectrum of Islamic intellectual life between the pure metaphysics contained in various forms of Islamic esotericism, especially Sufism but also the inner aspect of Shi'ism, and rationalistic philosophy, which through its gradual decadence in the West led to the completely profane philosophy of today. For it must be remembered that the post-mediaeval development of Western philosophy— after the Scholastic school, which is closely related to the Islamic philosophy in question—is based on the gradual decomposition of the concept of Being, which was so central to mediaeval European philosophy, and the gradual estrangement of reason, the tool par excellence of modern European philosophy, from the light of the Intellect.

With these distinctions in view, we can proceed to apply the comparative method to Islamic intellectuality and spirituality, both the 'philosophy' mentioned above, which is usually the subject, of comparative and also pure metaphysics, and gnosis (ma'rifah) in both its theoretical and its practical aspects, keeping in mind the hierarchy of knowledge that forms the basis of traditional Islamic intellectual life. In this domain, we must also be aware of the full breadth of the rich Islamic intellectual heritage which includes the several forms of gnostic doctrines contained in Sufism and various forms of Shi'ism, the school of illumination (ishraq) of Suhrawardi, the 'transcendent theosophy' (al-hikmat al-muta'aliyah) of Mulla Sadra, Isma'ili philosophy and theology, Peripatetic philosophy, later Kalam, the principles of jurisprudence (usul al-fiqh), both Sunni and Shi'ite, and many other schools, not all of which can be enumerated here. The teachings of all of these schools can be brought back to life by comparing them with metaphysical and philosophical schools of a corresponding order in other traditions and, as far as Western man is concerned, of course by comparing them with the major traditions that have dominated the West, namely the Graeco-Alexandrian and the Judeo-Christian. Moreover, the profound intellectual crisis of modern man can be brought into focus especially for Muslims through a comparison which would show the contrast between the sapiential teachings of these Islamic schools and what passes for philosophy or 'thought' in the West today. Finally, the operative and practical aspects of attaining gnosis or ma'rifah which are contained in the teachings of Sufism can be studied in the light of the current needs of contemporary man, to which we shall turn in the next chapter, as well as with respect to the present-day condition of Muslims themselves.

The application of the comparative method to the Islamic intellectual heritage can be particularly applicable for the study of metaphysics and philosophy in both the East and the West because of the special function and role of Islam in human history. Because of the integrating power of Islam and the fact that it was destined to cover the 'middle-belt' of the world, it came historically into contact with many modes of thought, including the Graeco-Alexandrian, Persian, Indian and even, to a certain extent, far Eastern. The basis of Islamic intellectual life was therefore cosmopolitan and international in conformity with the world-wide perspective of Islam itself and the universal nature of the fundamental Islamic doctrine of Unity (al-tawhid). Moreover, because it was the last revelation and therefore the synthesis of the messages of the traditions before it, Islam developed an extremely rich intellectual life into which was integrated much of the heritage of mankind that had preceded it, a heritage that became transformed by the light of Unity and converted into a building block in the new edifice of the Islamic arts, sciences and philosophy. Islamic philosophy, if considered in its totality and not only in terms of the Peripatetic school known in the West, is extremely rich and possesses schools that can be compared with most of the intellectual perspectives and traditional philosophies of the East, of the ancient Mediterranean world and of mediaeval Europe. Comparative studies would be fruitful as an adjunct to historical methods of research and would be basic in bringing out the morphological structure of the different Islamic schools by comparing and contrasting them with similar schools elsewhere. Sometimes even these two approaches, namely the historical and the comparative, can be combined, as for example a study of atomism in Kalam and a comparison of it with Buddhist schools of atomism, which could clarify the historical roots of the idea[6] and bring out the similarities and differences between the atomism of Kalam and that of the Buddhist schools. There are many pages and passages in the history of Islamic philosophy which could be clarified in this way.

Philosophical Approach

Comparative philosophy can also play an important function for Muslims themselves, not only by making the Western intellectual tradition as well as its modern deviations better known to them, but also by drawing their attention to non-Western traditions and re-establishing the balance destroyed by the unilateral domination of Western civilization over the East during the past century. As mentioned above, today for most people in the East, not only Muslims but also Indians, Japanese and others, comparative philosophy means comparing the 'philosophy' of their own civilization with that of the West and, in fact, only the modern West. Outside the small circle of traditional writers whose works are in any case still not well known in the Islamic world, it is rarely that one finds serious comparative studies made between Islamic metaphysics and philosophy and those of India and the far East. The cultivation of the comparative approach in the field of Islamic metaphysics and philosophy could make Muslims aware of the vast riches of the traditional doctrines of India and the far East, and through them could put Western philosophy in a more just perspective. Moreover, because of the nature of Oriental doctrines, the very awareness of these doctrines could help Muslim scholars discover other aspects of the Western intellectual tradition greatly neglected in the Islamic world until now precisely because of the paralyzing influence of modern European thought upon 'educated' classes in the Islamic world. The sapiential nature of Oriental doctrines and the very depth of their metaphysical teachings could be instrumental in a direct fashion in making the awareness of the Western intellectual tradition among Muslims more profound. It could thereby provide for Muslim scholars a key to the better understanding of the West and the sapiential teachings contained in the writings of such groups as the early Church Fathers, the apophatic theology of the Eastern Church, the school of Chartres, intellectual currents of mediaeval and renaissance Christian mysticism—especially of the school of Eckhardt and Angelus Silesius—and Western alchemy and Hermeticism. In any case, to introduce comparative philosophy in the serious sense into the domain of Islamic philosophy would influence the very concept of the relation of Islamic philosophy to Western thought and that of the nature of Western thought itself held by most educated Muslims today.

As far as the effect of the comparative approach upon a better understanding of Islamic philosophy itself is concerned, the extent of its possibilities is evident to anyone acquainted with the structure of Islamic thought. A few illustrations will bring out the role comparative philosophy can play in different areas. To start with the Graeco-Alexandrian tradition, we must recall that there are, of course, outstanding problems of a historical nature which deal on the one hand with the Greek roots of many facets of Islamic philosophy and on the other with the survival of important elements of the Graeco-Alexandrian heritage, particularly of the late period, in Arabic. This is a subject for historical research, and many scholars in both East and West have devoted themselves to both of its dimensions.

Morphological Comparisons

But, in addition, morphological comparisons could play an important role in bringing out the differences as well as the similarities between the Greek and the Islamic traditions and reveal how the elements of Greek thought that were accepted by the Muslims were transformed by them into elements of a new intellectual structure possessing a significance beyond what the purely historical method of tracing influences can reveal. A comparative study of Hermetic philosophy in Alexandria and alchemical philosophy in Islam, of Greek sapiential and gnostic teachings of the Middle and Neo-platonists— especially of Plotinus himself—and the masters of Islamic gnosis like Ibn 'Arabi, of the Greek Pythagorean teachings of Nichomachus and the Muslim Pythagoreans like the Ikhwan al -Safa' and many other instances would reveal the structural similarities and also the differences between doctrines of a similar or corresponding order in traditions possessing differing characteristics.

In the Graeco-Alexandrian case, comparative studies should complement the historical ones. The historical method would reveal the roots of many ideas adopted by Islamic philosophy from the Greek heritage, and the comparative method would cast light—because of the living nature of the Islamic tradition and its esoteric and gnostic teachings—upon certain forgotten features of the Graeco-Alexandrian tradition itself. It could be especially helpful in enabling Western scholars to re-evaluate their own judgment of Greek philosophy, in which they usually make no distinction between purely human philosophy and a wisdom of a supra-human inspiration. The Muslim intellectuals, thanks to the grace (barakah) of the Islamic revelation and the particular light of the 'Muhammadan' message which enabled them to penetrate into the very heart of non-Islamic traditions when necessary, discerned almost automatically the basic distinction between the sapiential doctrines of such schools as the Pythagorean, Platonic, Aristotelian and Neoplatonic on the one hand and the Sophist, the Epicurean and the like on the other. This distinction between a teaching of an ultimately divine inspiration and a purely profane philosophy was so natural for them that they separated the two immediately and did not even consider the latter type of thought to be philosophy at all. It must be recalled that Suhrawardi asserted that Aristotle was the last of the Greek philosophers and not the first, as the post-Renaissance philosophy of the West has claimed in its interpretation of the Greek heritage. The understanding of this basic distinction between a metaphysics of a purely traditional order couched in philosophical language and alone considered as philosophy, and a purely profane philosophy which the Muslims did not consider worthy of being called philosophy at all is essential for any serious re-interpretation of the Graeco-Alexandrian heritage by contemporary Western man in search of the roots of his own metaphysical heritage. If the West were to understand today the true nature of Ibn "Arabi's doctrines, which belong to a still living spiritual and intellectual tradition, these doctrines in turn could serve as a key for an understanding of a Plotinus or a Proclus, metaphysicians and gnostics who belong to a tradition the living sources of which are no longer accessible, and who are moreover usually innocently classified with modern academic philosophers. As for Muslims, the comparative method could reveal much more to them of the true structure and nature of the Graeco-Alexandrian antiquity than could facile translations of standard Western histories of Greek philosophy, works which are usually coloured by current and passing modes and fashions of thought and yet are beginning to influence the contemporary Muslim's view of the heritage of antiquity which he had viewed until now through the eyes of his own sages and metaphysicians.

Intellectual Tradition

A somewhat similar situation exists vis-a-vis the intellectual tradition of pre-Islamic Persia. Here also there are certain historical influences the understanding of which is important for a full grasp of the genesis of Islamic philosophy. But the comparative method can reveal another dimension which in this case is also a key for an understanding of the spiritual and intellectual destiny of the Persian peoples. To compare the angelology of Suhrawardi with that of Zoroastrianism or the story of Kay Khusraw with the visionary narratives of Suhrawardi is more than anything to penetrate into the way in which the universe of the pre-Islamic Persians was transformed into the Islamic one. Many of the profounder reasons for the continuation of the life of Islamic philosophy in Persia after its cessation in the Western lands of Islam can also be understood through the comparative method. Moreover, any of the deepest characteristics of the tradition of Islamic philosophy in Persia can be discovered with the help of a comparative study of Islamic shilosophy and the Weltanschauung of the pre-Islamic Persians.

The situation of the mediaeval West in relation to Islamic philosophy is somewhat similar to that of Islamic philosophy vis-a-vis the Greek heritage. There are, naturally, extensive historical relations, and the work that has been carried out during the past few decades in making better known the Latin corpus of the writings of Ibn Sina and Ibn Rushd, as well as of other Muslim authors, and in tracing their influence in the West is, of course, precious. Without it, one would not be able to understand the genesis of Scholasticism. But there are studies of a profounder nature based upon the comparative method which could enable Westerners to better understand Islam and vice-versa. As already stated, a comparative and morphological study of such figures as

Eckhardt with Ibn 'Arabi or Rumi, Erigena or other Western Diuminationists with Suhrawardi, or St Augustine with al-Ghazzali, would give a greater insight into the structure of the Islamic and Christian traditions than an attempt merely to discover lines of influence.

Oriental Scenario

As for the Asian world, it presents an arena of almost unlimited possibility for the application of the comparative method. As far as the Indian world is concerned, besides such historical influences as that of Buddhist and Hindu moral philosophy and possibly of atomism upon early Islam, and Sufism upon certain mediaeval bhaktic schools in India, there is the whole world opened by the translation of Sanskrit works into Persian, and Persian and Arabic works into Sanskrit and other Indian languages during the Moghul period. The Majma al-bahrayn of Dara Shikoh and the Persian commentary of Mir Findiriski upon that memorable expression of pwejnana, the Yoga Vasistha, are already based upon morphological and structural comparisons. Many other works of this kind also exist which need to be studied and explored. Moreover, the rich intellectual structures of Hinduism and Buddhism naturally present many resemblances to Islamic intellectuality, since all of them possess a traditional character. These resemblances can be best brought to light through the comparative method. The Advaita Vedanta school of Sankara can obviously be best understood by a Muslim by comparing it with the doctrine of wahdat al-wujud (unity of being) of Ibn 'Arabi and his followers; for a Muslim who cannot understand the doctrine of wahdat al-wujud is unlikely to comprehend the Advaita doctrine, which is like the reflection of the former doctrine in another spiritual universe. There are variations and subtle modifications of the doctrine of wahdat al-wujud and wahdat al-shuhud (unity of consciousness) developed by Indian Sufis and unknown in other Muslim lands precisely because of the challenging presence of certain Hindu metaphysical doctrines, especially Sankara's non-dualism. The correlation and the correspondence that exist on the purely metaphysical level can, moreover, be detected on the level of the cosmological sciences and of natural philosophy, and comparative studies can be made with great profit between the other darsanas such as the Sankhya and the corresponding Islamic schools.

As for the Far East, it represents a domain that in relation to Islamic philosophy should be studied almost entirely from the vantage point of comparative philosophy, for here, except for certain early alchemical ideas that reached eastern Islam from China and certain exchanges of ideas during the Mongol period, the whole relation is morphological rather than historical. For a Muslim to understand Lao-Tzu or Chuang-Tzu there is no better way than to make a comparative study between Taoism and Sufism or particular doctrines of the two traditions, such as that of the Universal Man, which present striking resemblances. This is a nearly unresearched field, which could be explored extensively to make the far Eastern tradition better known to Muslims, and the Islamic intellectual and spiritual tradition more comprehensible for the people of the far East and especially for those of Japan, where there now seems to be a genuine interest in Islamic metaphysics and philosophy.

In conclusion then, it can be said that for Muslims themselves the comparative method can play a basic role in making them aware of the great civilizations of the East and also in making the Western intellectual tradition more readily understandable in its true nature, as well as revealing to them the remarkable shortcomings and weaknesses of modern philosophy, a philosophy which many have taken much too seriously until now. It can be an instrument in combating the sense of inferiority towards the West which has developed among so many Modernised Muslims, and a necessary shock to awaken them from their hypnotic trance before the modern West. For non-Muslims interested in an understanding of Islamic metaphysics and philosophy, the comparative method can be instrumental in removing the erroneous conception of Islamic philosophy as merely a phase in the transmission of ideas to the West. This method can also help to reveal the immense treasures contained in the Islamic intellectual tradition and to make manifest the true structure of this tradition as it stands between the traditions of the Orient and those of the Mediterranean world and the West. Finally, when applied to the operative and practical aspects of Islamic spirituality, it can uncover before the eyes of modern man treasures which can provide for his profound spiritual needs. For these and many other reasons the comparative approach deserves to be applied to many aspects of the Islamic intellectual and spiritual heritage. It cannot but enrich present-day knowledge of a tradition of which many elements are still unexplored. And it cannot but provide some of the keys with which modern man can open the doors of the prison within which he has confined himself through his own ignorance and forgetfulness.

4

Relevance in Modern World

Religious scholars (Ulema) should behave according to the demands of time. This is a catchword we hear in a new style almost every day. Most of our secular minded leaders are repeating this suggestion off and on. And now we hear the echo of this suggestion even in our high level social gatherings whenever a religious subject comes under discussion. A group of people in our country is busy in surgical manoeuvres on the explicit injunctions of Islam and its established principles under the guise of modernism.They regard religious scholars as the biggest obstacle in their path. They consider that their success depends on baseless accusations and malicious propaganda against religious scholars in whichever way it is possible. For this, they have adopted the ambiguous phrase 'Demands of Time" as a hypnotiser for the modern minds, and make this a basis for their repeated appeals to the people and the government that religious scholars are the biggest obstacle in the way of progress and hence no attention should be paid to them and to what they say.

We leave them at the will of Allah from Whom no secrets of hearts are hidden. But there are some people who quite sincerely and seriously feel that religious scholars are unaware of the needs and demands of the modern age, and it is a result of this ignorance that they oppose every new thing. In these lines we wish to address this very group of people. But before this we humbly submit that if they are really well-wishers of Islam and Muslims they should give a cool thought to this matter and, for a little while, make their minds free from the grip of such hasty suggestions and try to understand what is meant by the "Demands of Time" and what is the best method of fulfilling it? With unbiased minds they should examine these allegations against the Ulema, the Islamic scholars.

The first thing to be defined is the phrase "Meeting the Demands of Time"? We feel that those who are so forcefully preaching the importance of demands of time themselves do not have a clear conception of these demands. They are simply making the ambiguous claims that religious scholars are opposed to the Demands of Time. But they never made it clear as to what those spedfic demands are which are opposed by the Ulema. If by the"Demands of Time" they mean that Muslims should endeavour to equip themselves with all the means of science and technology without which it is not possible to survive as a free nation in the world of today then indeed this is the greatest need and demand of this time. For God's sake tell us who is the single scholar who forbids this most important demand of time? Which of these scholars, and when, has issued any verdict (Fatwa) that progress in the fields of science and technology is forbidden, unlawful, meaningiess or useless? Science has made amazing progress in the recent years and it is in progress. Even in our life-time we have seen that newer inventions are coming up every day. How many of them have been opposed by the religious scholars? Electricity, Telegraphy, Telephone, Teleprinter, Wireless Radio, Transistors, Tape Recorders, Cars, Heavy Motor Vehicles, Aeroplanes, Steamers, Trains, Tanks, Mortars, Fighter Planes, Bombers, Submarines, Warships, Rockets, Missiles, Radar, Industrial Machines, Factories, Tractors, Chemical Fertilizers, Insecticide$ aind Pesticides, Surgical Instruments, X-ray & other Radiological Machines are in use with religious sanction of Islam. All sources of knowledge in Arts, Science, Commerce, Mathematics, Geography, Geology, Astronomy, Civics, and Politics are some examples of material progress. Which of these has ever been opposed by religious scholars or any obstacles been placed in their way?

The history of the past 55 years of our developing country is a witness to the fact that by the Grace of Allah our country has advanced by leaps and bounds in material and economic progress perfectly corresponding to the wishes of our righteous religious scholars and religious circles. Many of the great economic schemes have been completed during this period, large factories have been erected, vast network of roadways constructed, numerous canals dug out for irrigation, many dams were made, the old communication system was replaced with new inventions, many colleges and universities for various sciences and arts came into existence and barren land was cultivated. Only an insane person can feel unhappy about these advancements. Once again I ask our modernists to point out just one name of a religious scholar who ever opposed these achievements, or ever criticized production of expert scientists or educating people in engineering, or constructing roadways, factories, bridges, canals, river dams, using advanced technology in arms and ammunition for country's defence, or ever suggested that our army should not be trained in modern machine warfare, or that the latest telecommunication means should not be adopted, or education and training in modern arts and sciences should be stopped.

If none of the religious scholars has ever opposed it, there can be no other interpretation of this baseless accusations except malice and enmity against the righteous scholars of Islam. We know, Dot one but countless such scholars whose hopes and trust are centred around Ummah, and it is their greatest desire that side by side with its march in the straight path of Islam, they should progress by leaps and bounds in the material fields as well. That is why on the one hand they have been emphasizing on the Muslims that achievements of expertise of science and technology is an important component of our obligations, and if we fail to fulfil our obligations we shall be presented before Allah as an offender and on the other hand they are praying day and night for the prosperity and integrity of Pakistan which is best known by Allah, the All-knowing, All-aware.

We are, however, presenting below the excerpts from the writings of some of those religious scholars who are being blamed of opposing science and technology.

One of the most renowned of the religious scholars was Moulana Shabbir Ahmad Usmani. His selfless sacrifices can not be forgotten. In a conference at Dacca, in 1949, while explaining the policy of Pakistani scholars he declared in quite unequivocal terms:

> "No matter what treatment we meet from those in authority, we shall leave no stone unturned to make this new country safe and strong for the pleasure of Allah and supremacy of Islam and believers of Islam." (Presidential address Jamiat Ulem'a-e-Islam Conference, Dacca .10 February, 1949)

Further in the same speech he said,

> "We should not lag behind and show any laziness in the procurement of these material means and equipments to the last bit of our ability and competency, so that we may lower the morale of our enemy and show our supremacy on them, because this is in accordance with the Qur'anic injunction.

Continuing, he further said:

> "In my opinion the secret of all our success and prosperity lies in the four words namely, Patience and Perseverance, Fear of Allah and Purity, Unity of nation, and Numerical strength to the possible limits. In short, we must keep our relations with Allah in the right direction in our individual and collective life, so that we deserve His favour and assistance. And I pray that the entire Muslim nation should unite together and bring forth the Power that would subdue all evil forces".

The famous jurist, Mufti Muhammad Shafi, President, Darul Ulum, has written in his treatise 'Jihad' as under,

> "Indeed, the Patience, the fear of Allah and total belief in and submission to Allah is the real and unconquerable strength of Muslims. Alongwith it, however, it is also essential that equipment of war and ammunition

proper to the time and place should be acquired and stored. The Prophet (SA) always arranged for war exercises, and issued instructions to collect and acquire all those weapons that were in vogue anywhere in those days. It has been reported by Ibn-e-Katheir in his book "Al-Hidayah wan Nihayah" under the caption of Battle of Hunayn that two of the Prophets' companions could not take part in Jehad because they were in Damascus learning the techniques of manufacturing war weapons called 'Dbaba' and 'Dhabur' (The carriages that were used as Tanks in those days). Similarly, catapults were also manufactured there."

This incidence also proves that it is obligatory for the Muslims to make their countries self-sufficient in war weapons and technology and should not depend on others. Otherwise the Prophet could have purchased those carriages and catapults rather than sending his men to learn the techniques to manufacture them theirselves. We are bound to think it seriously how much our country is in need of all the equipment and weapons of war used in modern warfare so that we may not be lagging behind. We must put all our energy and resources to fulfil the aim that we become self-sufficient in the nearest possible future. ('Jihad' pp.53 to 56)"

In another of his books "Modern Weapons" the Grand Mufti has said:

"......In short the industrial products and inventions, be they new or old, if related to mankind's economic prosperity, are all benefactions of Allah that have been bestowed on human beings. Man should be wise enough to take full benefits from them and be grateful to Almighty Allah." ('Ala't- p. 15).

And Moulana Zafar Ahmad Usmani- Sheikh-ul-Hadith. Darul- Ulum-al- Islamiya, writes in one of his recent articles,

> "War weapons and technology against the enemy should be raised to the extent that the enemy is overawed with them .....our earlier Caliphs and Sultans religiously followed this rule. The companion Mu'awiyah had prepared a fleet of 500 warships during the tirne of Hadhrat Usman (RA), the third Caliph. He used to supervise personally the collection of all,defense equipments and never depended on others as we are today. The Muslim nations should join together to build up factories for ammunition and other weapons, and a continued process of research and inventions must be carried out. All these efforts are in conformity with Qur'anic injunction (Monthly Al-Balagh, p.44 J.A 1387 (H)."

Moulana Muhammad Yusuf Binouri, Sheikh-ul-Hadith Madrasah Arabiyah, New Town, writes:

> "There is no scarcity in the Islamic world, rather there is an abundance of natural resources, material reserves and wealth, but how great a tragedy it is that a major portion of their wealth is utilised by the enemies through deposits in foreign bạnks, or spent in extravagance, debauchery, undue luxuries, and immoralities. But defense stability, military training and ordnance factories are practically negligible, while the enemies of Islam are constructing airports, naval fleets, military cantonments and large ordnance factories. But the Islamic world is not only indulged in profane pursuits but has shown criminal negligence towards material progress." (Monthly Baiyyenat, R.S. 1387 (H), p. 4)

Moulana Abdul Haq, Sheikh-ul-Hadith of Darul-ulum Ilaqqania, has elaborated the same view in one of his speeches:

> "You have acquired only immorality and evil doings from Europe. They manufacture one plane in a minute and innumerable rockets and collect billions of dollars to save the Jews, and we remain asleep in our luxuries.

> If we ignore our collective problems the result can not be other than destruction." (Monthly A]-Haq, July 1967, p. 17)

Moulana Shamsul Haq Afghani has written in one of his recent articles 'Taraqqi our Islam (Islam and Progress)

> "Our deprivation from progress and our present decline is the result of our neglect towards Islam, otherwise Islam and Progress are inseparable. According to this verse it is obligatory on all Muslims that in all the modern equipments and instruments they should progress to the extent that they should be at least at par with Christian nations if not excel them. The Islamic world must use all its resources for this purpose." (Monthly 'Al-Haq', Sept 1967 p.22)

The above are the utterances of some high ranking and renowned religious scholars. These have come to our view just abruptly without any special efforts to find them. Those who had been reading the views of these scholars know it fully well that not only the religious scholars never opposed Science and Technology but they had always been indicing the Muslims to attain them. Despite this reality before their eyes there is a group of people who are beating their drums high and loud that the religious scholars are opposed to progress and advancement, they are allergic to Science and Technology, they give no importance to the demands of time, and discard every new thing.

Reality and Myths

The most clever advocate of "Falsehood" was Goebels, who spoke the Truth. when he said that if "falsehood" is spread with full force the world starts taking it as "truth". Our modernists have also been following Goebels' adage so much so that even some of the very learned and of balanced mind people regard this slogan as true while it is just a false blame, cunningly produced by propaganda machines of modern time.

If, however, these people consider music and dance, nudity and obscenity, profligacy and immodesty, co-education, free inter mixing of men and women, usury in banking and birth control as demands of time and means of progress, then indeed the religious scholars have openly opposed them, and they should have done so, they still do it and will continue doing it. We may be informed what logic and reason has ever claimed these things to be the demands of time? They must bring some logical argument to prove what relation material progress has with music and dances? Which is that progress that would stop without nudity and obscenity? What are the genuine obstacles in the way of promoting interest-free banking? How does coeducation and Free mixing of men and women help in science and technology?

The modernists may call music and dances, co-education and mixed gatherings, etc., as the demands of time, but in view of the circumstances we sincerely believe that the greatest need and demand of the present time is that the Islamic world should totally eradicate these things with full might and power. This is because, magnitude of the fatalities that has come to the forefront in the twentieth century was never witnessed before. The very Western intelligentsia itself is showing clear signs of extreme anxiety and restlessness on their premature but immoral and irrational social advancement. No literate person of the world can claim to be ignorant of this outcry that is echoing FROM the meeting chambers of Western thinkers as a result of social and moral ruin in their lives. The 'modernist' should, for God's sake, decide himself as to what really are the demands of time? Should it be that the Islamic world should march on the footsteps of the West and fall into the same abyss of moral degradation? Or should the Islamic world take lesson from the dreadful end of the West and save itself from this dangerous path forever?

Fitting in the New Role

The group of people who consider these curses of Western civilization as demands of time and means of progress call themselves as "Modernists" but it is strange that in the field of thoughts and deeds they are preaching the same outdated ideologies of the West which have not given anything but burn scars all over the body. They know it very well how rapidly the

Western style of thinking is changing about their old views, and what the latest studies of philosophy and science are proving about these subjects? Take for example the problem of population. A very substantial number of modern economists are against limiting the family size and birth control. Having been impressed by their latest arguments such economists are constantly increasing in number, but our "Modernists" are still embracing Malthus.' outdated theory that has been thrown away by the march of time some two centuries ago. I do wish to quote here the views of Philosopher-Poet, lqbal, who said:

> "Power of the West is not due to flutes and guitars, nor due to dances of veilless girls, nor due to the spell of their magical beauty, nor to their naked legs, nor to their trimmed hair styles. Their supremacy is not due to secularism, nor is their progress due to Latin script. Their power is due to science and technology. It is this fuel that is burning in their lamps. Wisdom does not lie in how your clothes are tailored, and the turban is no obstruction for science and technology".

The above is sufficient to show the nature of these accusations of our "Modernists" against the religious scholars of opposing the demands of time and Science and Technology? The question arises as to why the "Modernists" are so forcefully propagating this extremely irreasonable claim? As far as we can trace there is probably a psychological factor in action, if we rule out any specific motives behind it the fundamental error which misled these modernists is that they consider Islam analogous to Christianity and the Islamic world to the West. They had observed that at the time of revival of science and technology in the West the biggest obstacle was Christianity along with its scholars. As long as the supremacy of church prevailed in the West the whole of region was filled with ignorance and illiteracy. The Christian scholars tried to suppress every such attempt that was made to create scientific awareness among the people. People like John Hiss and Jerome were burnt alive in the city of Constance. The renowned scientist Galileo had to suffer calamities because he wanted to open new avenues in the field of science. But gradually the awareness spread and several movements came out. These tortures could not stop them, and ultimately Martin Luther, John Calone and Zongli put up a struggle that defeated Popalism and these movements got their chance to flourish. Lately Ruso, Horonic and Reman with other modernists made Futher changes and innovations in the religion and brought it in conformity to the scientific researches of that time. The situation now is that Luther, Calone, Ruso and Horonic etc. have been titled as Reformers by the religious minded people of the West. They are regarded as national heroes and people of the new generation who have not yet become totally alien to religion, regard them with a sense of honour and dignity that by making fundamental changes in Christian religion they freed the nation from the grip of Paplism which was the greatest obstacle in the way of their material progress.

Now, the modernists of Islam want to make similar amendments by considering Islam equal to Christianity and scholars of Islam parallel to popes and to themselves they regard Luthers and Rusos of the time. In this way they want to become the Reformers of Muslim nation by opposing and defaming the religious scholars. They aspire that some Henry VIII will soon appear and he will grace them by accepting their ideology and then officially implementing it for ever. Thus the coming generations will regard them in such high esteem as is the case of hero-worship with Luther and Ruso etc.

We may remark here that they are in great delusion and their dream is never going to come true. They are badly mistaken in considering Islam similar to Christianity and scholars of Islam to popes. The unnatural views of Christian religion which became common after the third century did not have adequate power to keep pace with time for all future days to come, and stand face to face with the latest scientific advancements. That was an era of dark ignorance and superstitions which could not stay in the light of knowledge. Hence science came as a great challenge and they were left with no other option than either to oppose science openly or by cutting and dipping their religion to bring it in conformity with the scientific knowledge. The popes initially adopted the first course and declared science as the forbidden tree. But Science was the real need of that time and they could not stop its progress merely by hollow claim and baseless charges against it. The result was that all their efforts faded to stop scientific advancement.

Manipulating the Religion

At this stage the modernists adopted the second course and started manipulating the religion and distorting its teachings in order that people may not mock and laugh at it. This was indeed a service to the Christianity, and if they had not done this favour Christianity would have been swept away by the torrent of Rationalism and no trace of it could be found today. The workmanship of Christian modernists helped the Christian religion to survive although its fundamental concepts were totally changed. At least its name and external structure is still existing. It is this favour of the modernists on Christianity that made them heroes of their nation and due to the major part of the Christian world holds them in high esteem.

But the case of Islam is totally different. It is a natural religion and it has come to exist till the Last Day. By virtue of this old and real interpretations it has the capability of marching forward with the researches of every era of time. Hence science has never been a danger to it nor will it ever be. Rather, we have observed that the latest inventions and researches of science generally make its beliefs and teachings more transparent. Hence it has no need either to oppose science and its progress nor to change its own concepts. That is why unlike the popes the religious scholars of Islam never opposed science, because they know the realities exposed by Islam will become more and more transparent with the advancement of science. Since the Muslim Ummah believes that Islam is the religion revealed by Allah it does not have to change at any time, and that is why this nation has always condemned and disregarded any attempts towards making any changes in its teachings.

To sum up, Islam is neither a spiritless religion like the Christianity to have any fear or danger from scientific and technological advancement, nor its religious scholars (Ulema) have ever opposed science and technology as the Popes had done, nor does need any Martin Luther, Ruso or Reman for its survival. That is why, in the history of this religion, all those who tried to amend, manipulate or modernize it, they got nothing but reproach and condemnation. In the history of this religion, the advocates of modernism have not been called Luther and Kalone, but the modernists of our history are remembered by the names of Musailmah, Abdullah bin Saba, Abu Musa Mazdar, Hasan bin Sabbah, Qaramat, Abul Fazl, Faizi and Kamal Ata-Turk. Even their children would feel ashamed of their lineage with these names. The opponents of Luther and Kalone are mentioned with great disregard by the Christians. But the opponents of modernism in Islam, namely Abu Bakr Sidiq (RA), Ali bin Abi Talib (RA), Ahmad bin Hambal (RhA) Mahmoud Ghaznawi (RhA) and Mujaddid Alf Thani (RhA) are still living with their names, and as long as the human conscience is alive the names of these sacred personalities will continue to be taken with love and allegiance. It is a pity that our present day modernists have not been able to understand the great diversity between Islam and Christianity, and as a result of this grave misunderstanding they have been busy in abusing the scholars of Islam, calling them obscurantists, accusing them of ignorance for no reason. We earnestly request them with all the well-wishes and heart-felt sympathies that they revise their attitude with cool mind and balanced thoughts, otherwise the course adopted by them is in no way beneficial for Muslims, for the country and the Ummah and even for themselves.

I hope and pray that my humble submissions leave useful impression on them.

Effects of Industrialisation

For millennia, the life is constantly on the move. Every new era is associated with new circumstances and fresh problems. But the great revolution which the world has experienced after the invention of Machine, has affected every sphere of life. It has opened the doors of research and observation for every art and science, and has created some new problems in every section of life. If we look into the teachings of religions other than Islam we find that they are not capable of absorbing the great revolution in them. The fountainhead of these teachings was human intellect rather than the Divine Revelation (Wahy), hence they had neither a full cognition of human nature nor was it based on the considerations of changing circumstances of time, nor did it have an insight on the possible future happenings. The result is that most of the original teachings of those religions have died under the loads of machines. Now there exist only two possibilities before the followers of these religions They have to say good bye to their religion if they want to keep pace with the march of time, and if their religion is more dear to them they have to turn away from the light of thought and cognition and make themselves an isolated group of people who do not belong to twentieth century. However, some people have designed an intermediary way to reshape and modify their religion in order to make it practicable for the present time. But, obviously he is the follower of his own whims and not his true religion. In this case he is deprived of the religion he followed before. But the matter of Islam is totally different. This is the only religion in the world whose guidance is ever fresh. No revolutions and circumstances make it old. It is fresh today and it will remain fresh as long as the world is existing. The reason is obvious. Its percepts and injunctions are not the product of human brain which is unaware of the coming events. The source of its teachings is the divine revelations. The Being who made it the code of life for mankind is the One who is the Creator of mankind and the entire universe. He has full knowledge of the man's nature and his needs. He is fully aware of the changing circumstances and He knows what is going to happen when and where.

It is the miracle of His words that the rules and regulations laid down by Him in the Qur'an and those preached by His last messenger Muhammad (PBUH) encircle all problems arising till the last day. The world may turn to one side or the other, these teachings will continue to provide with. The principles and laws of Islam would always suffice for all times to come.

But it is a pity that a group of people in Islamic world known as 'Modernists" has been unable to get at this reality. That is why, in taking their lead from other religions, they have started a campaign of alterations and innovations in Islam. They have made it their duty to prove that every exhibit of industrial revolution is consistent with Islam. After every such alteration and innovation they present their only argument that Islamic Injunctions must change because the world has greatly changed after the industrial revolution bringing about revolutionary changes in thought and practice.

In this connection we wish to point out two types of changes that have occurred in every walk of life as a result of industrial revolution of Europe. Some of them were inevitable for the present advancements and without them it was not possible for Science and Technology to have attained the present standard. It was due to these that the world was benefited by the latest inventions, large factories came into being, bridges have been constructed, big dams and useful additions to human knowledge have been made. This aspect of industrial revolution is indeed commendable and it is imperative for the Islamic world to progress in this field. Islam does not Place any obstacle in this direction. Rather, it looks at this achievement of power with approbation.

But, at the same time, there are some changes that are not at all essential for industrial and material progress. The West has associated them to industrial revolution for no reason, and now realising this error is sighing with grief Obscenity and nudity, free mixing of man and woman, music and dances, interest and birth control are things that have nothing to do with material and industrial progress. Experience has proved that these things have served as an obstacle rather than assistance towards progress.

Industrial Revolution

This is the evil from which the Islamic world has to save itself very diligently. Industrial revolution in the Islamic world has become a necessity, but it should be a revolution free of the profanities of Western civilization which have led them to the brink of total destruction. Unfortunately, our modernist group wants that we accept the industrial revolution of West as it is, and without an iota of change in it, and thus drown ourselves in their ideological and practical aberrances even before the Machine has taken roots in our society. That is why, instead of developing Science and Technology, this group is spending its energy in moulding Islam to bring it in conformity with Western civilisation. Supporting this new viewpoint the official spokesman of monthly 'Fikr-o-Nazar' of the Institute of Islamic Research, writes as wider:

> "The entire life style will be changed after the completion of fourth five-year plan. The rule of machine will prevail, and due to this family life will change, economy and social values will change. There will be changes in the relations between man and woman, and obviously, individual and collective thinking will be affected, and people will think more positively". (Fikro Nazar p.733, vol. 2, p. 12)

It is obvious that such people do not want to make any distinction between the industrial revolution of the Islamic World and that of the West. Our humble submission is that the "rule of machine" in the industrial sphere is not negated, what we think highly venomous are the changes in the family life, economy and social values, relationship of man and woman and the thought of general people. These "changes" do not match with the temperament of Islamic ideologies. A study of Industrial Revolution of the West itself leads us to think that we shall have to abstain from these "changes" if we want to lead a peaceful life despite the sway of machine in our lives.

The philosopher-poet of Pakistan, lqbal, bad a deep insight into the state of West, he said:

> Christianity (in Europe) is blackened with the smoke of machines

and,

> The rule of machine is the death of soul. Instruments only crush the sense of tolerance.

It will not be proper to deduce from the above that he was allergic to machines and instruments or that he opposed the progress of Technology. What he means is that the evil which the West has imposed on them alongwith the machines are detestable and should be avoided.

Present Circumstances

Under the present circumstances proper line of action for us is that in the pursuit of industrial revolution we may not blindly match on the path that has carried the West to the brink of total destruction. The industrial revolution will give rise to many difficulties and new problems, which will be resolved under the Islamic guidance and this solution will be free from the defects of the Western thought. Rather, we should acquire science and technology with deep insight and open mind in a manner that Islamic values are not injured.

On the contrary, if alteration and innovation is carried out in Islam itself to fit it into the framework of Western civilization and, somehow or the other, it is moulded to meet the requirement of the modern time, what credit goes to Islam for this? In this manner any religion can be brought in. conformity with the present time by twisting and distorting it. There are many who demonstrated such artistry in their religions. The credit of this goes to them and not to tile poor religion that became a plaything in their hands. We honestly feel that Islam cannot be matched with other religions. Treating Islam in this manner is by no means justified, and any such attempt will be an interpolation in religion and hence condemnable.

No doubt many injunctions of Islam are flexible enough to accept changes in varying circumstances, but there are certain prescribed rules which must be observed when applying these to new problems. It does not mean that every Islamic injunction can be dissolved in the readymade mixture of modern necessities. It may be understood that be Islamic injunctions prescribed by the Quran, the Sulinah and by the consensus of the Ummah are fixed and unalterable. They cannot be changed in any period. However, in the matters, which can be influenced by changes of time, the Holy Quran and Sunnah have provided us with some basic principles without giving specific commandment for a specific condition. These principles call be used as a basis for the deduction of new injunctions in every period. Had Islam permitted the people of every time to deduce Islamic injunctions according to their circumstances and in opposition to the unanimous decisions of the Muslim Ummah, it would have not provided us with so comprehensive and detailed commandments in every sphere of life. Rather, it would have said, "Keep making your own commandments according to your circumstances." On the contrary, Islam has provided us with specific and elaborate precepts with divine wisdom in order that they were to be observed upto the end of time. In short, these Islamic injunctions are fixed and cannot be changed simply because time has changed. They are not only practicable upto the Day of Judgement but they, in fact, hold the key to real material progress of the Muslims.

Quran and Traditions

There are injunctions which the Quran and traditions have themselves left to be decided by the time are alterable. They can be changed, and are being changed, according to the circumstances. But in the guise of this flexibility our modernists not only try to change those unanimously accepted injunctions that are being accepted as established for the last fourteen centuries but they desire to make amendments even in certain beliefs that are against the clear and explicit injunctions of the Quran and Sunnah, though not accepted by a single person of any significance.

In case we allow this attitude to be correct it would imply that no basic belief of Islam has been understood by any one in fourteen hundred years. It requires our serious thought if such a religion is worthy of being followed by any seiisible person?

How funny it is that our modernists feel the change of time only when they want to give religious sanction to an activity or when they want to seek approval to a thought or practice of western ideology. On the contrary, when the change of time demands labour or some hard work they do not even think of it. For example, the modernists have made loud claims that usury and interest should be made permissible because time has changed but none of them ever demanded that the concessions in the Salah

(Five daily prayers Of Worship) and Fasting during journeys should be withdrawn because the change of time has made journey far more comfortable and easy than it was in olden days. They never insisted that these facilities should be withdrawn in modern time and they were meant only for the time foregone.

The hedonistic attitude of Modernism can be well conceived with this diversity of action. In fact all its arguments are designed for their pre-conceived ideas. Since their aim is to infuse Western ideologies in Islam and any situation where this may be achieved any trivial thing they find to use it as an argument, no matter how transient and superfluous it may be. While the same argument is simply ignored when it turns against their intentions. How I wish that our Modernists think over these submissions seriously and realistically and their able efforts are spent on some constructive service instead of distorting or innovating the Islamic guidance.

5

The Modern Muslims

In the 6th century, when the world was hovering between life and death and there was no one to whom it could look for succour, the advent of Prophet Muhammad (Upon whom be peace!) gave humanity a fresh lease of life. He placed human welfare under the care of a community that was in possession of the Revealed Word and the Divine Law and in the light of these two did everything that was the symbol of purity and justice. This community had been blessed with the most harmoniously blended disposition and temperate outlook and had risen to the position of the trusteeship of mankind after going through rigorous moral training and attaining complete spiritual adjustment.

The emergence of this community marked a turning point in human history. It immediately arrested the progress of mankind towards its doom and made it safe, for centuries to come, against the moral and material hazards and calamities that were threatening to engulf it. Under its guidance humanity made a well-balanced advance towards its true goal, the various capabilities of man were called splendidly into play and an environment was created in which it was made possible for him to advance to the highest goal of progress in the shortest and the surest way.

Under the influence of this new community the lives of men, their minds and their morals were revolutionized. Unbelief and depravity of character were replaced by faith and virtuousness, false ethical values and wrong ideals gave place to high moral patterns. Politics was placed under the surveillance of ethics. In the system of Islamic civilization there was as unremitting a care for spiritual as for material prosperity. Economic development was matched with moral advancement; political expansion corresponded to spiritual uplift. A deep, inner unity of faith, an unswerving oneness of purpose, and peace and fellow-feeling had demolished all barriers between man and man in the World of Islam and made it into a society which, in spite of its being composed of diverse racial elements, was blissfully free from all social inhibitions, tensions and prejudices. The path of virtue that had been deserted for so long and had become so difficult to tread was now a smooth, even road on which people could walk in perfect freedom and security. Man's right to worship and obey God was restored. The call of religion developed great vigour that lifted millions of men from the depth of degradation to the greatest heights of glory. The spirit of man was aroused, and his genius was set to noble purposes. In short, the caravan of humanity was brought nearer to its destination and its vanguard did, indeed, arrive there.

But before the rest of the travellers could arrive at the journey's end, the caravan suddenly stopped and its leadership underwent a change. The old leader had to relinquish charge because he had not made adequate arrangements for the safety of the travellers. An unknown fellow-traveller assumed the reins of leadership at the point of dagger anti proceeded to take the caravan along a path that was tortuous and uneven and over which the nocturnal darkness prevailed even at high noon. He is engaged still in the same mad pursuit. The travellers stumble and fall headlong and groan, but the leader, in his arrogance and haste, presses heedlessly on.

In Western Europe

This, surely, is no figment of the mind, for, the Western nations, which succeeded the Muslims to the stewardship of the world, had, from the very beginning, been labouring under a serious disadvantage. They never had the good fortune to be possessed of an unpolluted source of Revealed Knowledge or an uncorrupted fund of Divine Wisdom. The insignificant part of the teachings of Jesus Christ that had reached them had got lost owing to distortions and interpolations. The Western nations tried to make up for the light of heavenly guidance with the learning of the Greeks and the Romans, and the entire Pagan legacy of Ancient Greece and Rome had fallen to their lot. They had received the worship of the perceptible, epicureanism, local patriotism and libertinism from the Greeks and the bankruptcy of religious belief, racial pride, power-worship and imperialism from the Romans.

We have seen how what was left of the religious teachings of Jesus Christ was devoured by Roman paganism. What was still left was lost in the dogmatic quarrels of the clergy. This was followed by the epidemic of monasticism and then as a reaction to it the Christian world was immersed from one corner to the other in sensual enjoyment. The depravity and luxury of the eccesiastics produced, in the European mind, a pronounced revulsion towards Christianity which was replaced in unthinking minds by religion in general. In the Middle Ages there occurred a bitter conflict between the Church and the State, which was succeeded by an even more violent clash between Christianity and science. The ghastly atrocities perpetrated by the Church officials during the course of this struggle sealed the fate of Christianity in the West, but succeeded in creating a distrust of religion is general. The Western intellectuals did the rest. They broke the remaining link with transcendental ethics. As a consequence, the West turned out and out materialistic, and power and wealth became the sole objects of its worship.

A further outcome of the peculiar development of the West was the growth of aggressive nationalism. For the preservation of national existence it became necessary to bear ill-will towards the rest of humanity. Europe, on the one hand, decided that the whole of the East was an opposite camp, and on the other, it divided itself into a number of water-tight compartments on the illusory basis of national self-determination. The world was converted into a huge market place for the sale and purchase of the weaker nations.

The coupling of moral and religious depravity with a phenomenal progress in the scientific and industrial fields led to the creation of a striking disparity between power and ethics. Men learnt to fly in the air like birds and to swim in the water like fish, but they forgot how to walk straight on the earth. Indisciplined knowledge and unenlightened wisdom furnished every highwayman with a sword. Deadly weapons were placed in untrained hands which repeatedly plunged the world into horrible blood-baths. And now science has given the atomic and Hydrogen bombs to humanity as weapons for suicide.

Under the influence of these godless nations the sciences relating to inanimate matter made great progress while the human material was brought low in every respect. Religion was ostracized and secularized; moral enthusiasm was crushed under the weight of material cravings. The religious instinct of the Eastern peoples, too, which was the Pivot of their lives, was seriously impaired.

It is a tragic fact of modern life that there exists no community worth the name in Europe, Asia, Africa, or America genuinely opposed to the pagan philosophy of materialism. The nations like the Germans in Europe or the Japanese or Indians in Asia, dre all becoming increasingly convinced of the merits of materialism. The ideological differences that one encounters in the modern world are mainly the off-shoots of an all-out struggle for political supremacy. They have no relation to moral or spiritual convictions. It is simply too much for the pride of a powerful nation that another should be in command of the international scene. No nation feels inclined to address itself to the moral regeneration of humanity should the opportunity ever come its way.

Communist Russia, though it gives the impression, at the lot that of being distinct from the rest of the Western countries, is the ripened fruit of the Western civilization. Its only distinction is that it has discarded the mask of hypocrisy and gone ahead to bring to their logical conclusion the social and ethical concepts the Western philosophers had been expounding for centuries.

The Communists were not satisfied with the speed with which the West was progressing towards the anti-religious and anti-spiritual ideals of its civilization. They accelerated the pace and attained the goal set before themselves by the Western nations and having done so, they are now trying to manoeuvre themselves into a position from which they can pull the rest of humanity to their side.

In Today's Asia

The Eastern nations are by no means in a happy position. The same urges and ambitions that rule over the West are enshrined in their hearts, too. Their leaders have only one quarrel with the West: they do not want their nations to be exploited by Western nations. They aspire to be their own masters now. Apart from this, there is no fundamental difference in the mental attitudes of the Eastern and the Western nations. What the people of the East are opposed to is that the Western ideas and ideals should be pushed through their lands by the Westerners; they want to be left free to do it themselves. They do not wish to give up the ideals of Western civilization. They only wish that they themselves should be the torch-bearers of that civilization. Further, many Eastern communities have their own traditions of paganism, together with which they are getting imbued with the pagan attitudes of the West. They are sure to! bring the characteristics of both into play in the sphere of their own influence when they come into power.

What is to be regretted is that the traditional enemy of Paganism, the Muslim, too, has become its ally and is serving as its devoted camp-follower in many parts of the world. What better proof of the universal triumph of Paganism can there be than that Muslims should regard those countries as their friends and well-wishers who are the leaders of the Pagan movement in the present age ? The modern Muslim has totally given up the idea of leadership; he has lost faith in himself. His whole mental attitude is being moulded by the under-currents of Paganism The Muslim states are exhibiting the same materialistic tendencies which are the hall-mark of the Western social system. The same enslavement to earthly longings is fast becoming the creed of the community the cornerstone of whose religious faith is the idea that'the real life is the life to come. Its solicitude for After-life is declining day by day. It is subordinating its ethical principles to material expediency with a cheerful readiness that is really astonishing. In some respects the Muslims are actually out-doing the Western races in the glorification of material wealth.

Yet, it is here alone that one sees a ray of hope. With the solitary exception of the followers of Islam all the communities in the world have lost touch with their heritage of Divine guidance. The fight of the Apostolic teachings has departed from their hearts. The passage of time has severed their connections with the real origins of their spiritual inspiration. Past experience of religious reform movements among the various nations definitely precludes the possibility of a fundamental change being brought about in their outlook by re-projecting religion into their lives. Their primary ideals are rigidly opposed to a religious conception of life.

As against this the entire spiritual inheritance of the Muslims is preserved in its pristine purity. A full record of the life and Traditions of the Holy Prophet and of the lives of his Companions, which holds the key to the understanding of the memorable rise of Islam, is still available to them without the least pollution. Moreover, a chain of religious redeemers and reformers has been continually operating among them, sustaining their spirits, nourishing their souls and guarding them against a relapse into ignorance.

The fact is that the Muslim mind, by the sheer nature of its ordering, is such that it can never be made to imbibe Pagan materialism, unless, of course, its very structure is destroyed and recast into a new form.

In an earlier chapter it has been pointed out that the Holy Prophet said of Muslims in the battle of Badr : "O God, if these (Believers) are destroyed, no one will be left on the earth to worship Thee". It is equally true of them today, because, if there is anyone who can stand up to the challenge of Paganism and offer to the world an alternative plan of life, it is they and they alone. The plan of Islam is an eternal plan. It will remain valid for all time to come. By virtue of their religion, the Muslims are the moral guardians of mankind and they will return to their duty when they will awake from sleep. That day will be a day of reckoning for the nations of the world. They certainly possess a spark which, if and when it blazes up, will burn down the whole structure of Ignorance.

'Allama Iqbal has used the medium of the presiding genius of the Order of Ignorance, the Devil himself, to give expression to this truth in his poem entitled, 'The Advisory Council of the Devil, 1936'. The evil spirits of the world are shown in it to have gathered together to ponder over the new challenges that are threatening their nefarious system. One adviser mentions Democracy as "the latest evil of the new world." Another mentions the name of Communism. He says :

> Stich an awe this budding menace has struck,
>
> That the brooks, the hills and the yonder mountains shake.
>
> The world, my Lord! is about to crumble.
>
> The world that depends upon Thy guidance alone.

The Devil allays their fears and explains to them the plans he has devised for meeting those threats. Then he speaks of what, in his opinion, is the real menace and says that though he has thought out the most appropriate line of campaign against it, too, its potentialities are so terrifying that he is constantly brooding over it. He goes on to say :

If any fear attends me, it is from the people whose ashes yet the spark of Desire contain.

Occasionally still, I see among them men who, with tears, perform the wudu in the early morn.

> He who knows the secrets of History knows
>
> That Communism is not morrow's menace, but Islam.
>
> That they from the Qur'An have departed, I know.
>
> And Capitalism is now the faith of the Believer;
>
> In the pitch-dark night that upon the East has fallen,

The wise-men of the Haram are without the light of faith, But from the exigencies of this age I fear the Law of the Prophet may re-appear.

Beware of the Law of the Prophet, a hundred times beware!

The safeguarder of women's honour, the tester of men, the Maker of men,

The voice of death for all forms of slavery.

There is no distinction of the Ruler and the ruled in its domain.

It purges wealth of foulness,

And the rich the trustees of their goods it makes.

Can a more radical thing than this there be-

That the earth belongs to God, not to the kings ?

The more this Law from the world's view is hidden the better. Luckily, the Muslim himself is devoid of faith.

Let him in meticulous interpretations of the Book his energies waste

And a helpless groper in the gloom of Theology be.

Satan then gives the following advice to his council :

Whose mighty 'takbirs' the spell of time and space can break,

May his night of decay no day-break see.

You keep him a stranger to the world of deed, I say,

That all his movements on the life's chess-board be frustrated.

For him such poetry and mysticism are, indeed, the best,

Which from his eyes life's broad spectacle conceal.

Every moment do the thought of their awakening tremble,

'Me real purpose of whose faith is the supervision of the Universe.

Philosophy and Ideology

The World of Islam can still give the message of faith and life to the disillusioned humanity. It is the message the Holy Prophet

(Peace be on him!) had imparted to it about 1,400 years ago. It is a simple, dynamic, radiant message, a grander and more majestic message than which the world cannot hope to receive.

It is the same message which prompted the Muslims of Medina to come out of their homes and spread over the whole world; it is the same message which was so exquisitely summed up by a spokesman of the Muslims before the Emperor of Iran who had asked the followers of Islam as to what had brought them to his land: "We have been sent by Allah to deliver whom He pleaseth from the overlordship of His slaves to His Overlordship; and from the narrowness of this world to the boundlessness of the Hereafter; and from the oppression of other religions to.the equity and fairness of Islam."

Not one word of this message can be altered even to-day, more than thirteen hundred years after it was first delivered. It is just as capable of moving the minds and filling the hearts of men in the 21st century as it was in the 6th.

Today, too, humanity is prostrated before false deities, sculptured and unsculptured, the worship of One Transcendent God is getting rare, the animal in man has got loose and the ecclesiastics, the rulers, the capitalists and the political leaders have lifted themselves to the dizzy heights of godhood.

The world with all its vastnesses has become more constricted, murky and suffocating to-day than ever before. Being the devotee of material power the man of to-day refuses to admit the existence of any other power. He has been captivated by his own material achievements. He finds himself deceived, and frustrated and is growing increasingly petty, exclusive, selfish and skeptical. Everyone believes that he alone has the right to live, the rest may go and hang themselves; who cares ? Politicians and national leaders have made life still more narrow and difficult by erecting artificial barriers in society. They have laid bold of the wells of life, and bound up the structures of economic and political forms with the wishes and necessities of the privileged classes. Lands which, in the past, were renowned for richness and fertility, have been rendered barren. Entire populations have been placed, like helpless children, under the trusteeship of aliens. The modern mode of life is forging constantly new fetters for the spirit of man, the levies and imposts are getting heavier day by day, peace is assailed from all sides, and mental stress, dissensions, riots and strikes have become the inevitable constituents of daily existence.

To-day, again, it is necessary to "deliver men from the oppression of other religions to the equity and fairness of Islam." Even in the 21st century there are religions abounding in superstitious beliefs and fantastic teachings, that tyrannize over their followers and drive them like deaf and dumb animals. Then there are the new-political and economic-religions like collectivism, nationalism and socialism that are a step ahead of the ancient pagan faiths in fanatical intolerance and coercion. The last two World Wars were the "gifts" of these very dogmas to humanity, beside which the sanguinary religious strifes of old Rome and the bitter conflicts between the Church and the intelligentsia of Europe in the Middle Ages recede into insignificance.

To-day, too, the Message of Islam is an open invitation to the worship of, and surrender to, One God and belief in the Apostleship of the prophets, particularly that of Prophet Muhammad (Upon whom be peace!) and in Resurrection and Final judgement. In return for submitting to this call the world will emerge from the darkness of Ignorance and the spirit of man will be set free. Man will re-discover his equilibrium and from the narrow confines of the world of matter he will come out into a world which, although enclosed within himself, stretches beyond time and space.

There never was a clearer appreciation of the need and the utility of this Message as now. The civilization of Ignorance has been publicly disgraced, its shame is being flagrantly exposed. People are disgusted with life; they are despaired of the intellectual and cultural leaders. Modern civilization is seriously ill. From all indications the psychological moment has arrived when a radical change in the leadership of human affairs is called for. So far, changes in leadership have only been in the nature of a change of personnel. There has been no major shift in thinking. It does not matter much to the ship of human destiny whether Britain is at the helm of affairs or America or Russia, because their moorings are basically the same and they are subject to identical intellectual impulses.

The only thing that can cure the world of its present ills and ailments is that its leadership should pass from the hands that are coloured with the blood of humanity to those that were destined to guide, humanity, i.e., from the hands of Britain, America and Russia to the hands of the followers of the Prophet Muhammad (Peace and blessings of God be upon Him).

Awakened at Last

To attain this objective the World of Islam will have to find its spiritual roots. It will have to re-dedicate itself to Islam, There is absolutely no need of a new religion, a new Canonical Law or a new set of moral teachings for the Muslim. Like the sun, Islam was, is and will never be old. The Apostleship of Prophet Muhammad (Peace be on him!) is endowed with the quality of timelessness. No other Apostle of God is to be raised now. His religion is everlasting, his teachings are immortal. But the Muslims do require a renaissance of faith. One cannot face new hazards and meet new challenges with a dilapidated faith and unauthorized practices. A decaying building cannot stand through a flood. One must have a living, glowing and unbending faith in the cause one seeks to uphold. If the Islamic World aspires to inject a new enthusiasm and a new life into humanity, to give it the courage to resist and revert the torrents of materialism and religious disbelief, it will first have to produce that enthusiasm and that life in itself.

The Muslims will have to regenerate themselves internally. They cannot brave the onslaught of the ungodly West by imitating its empty cultural norms customs, and social concepts, for these things have no place in the growth and rise of nations. All cultural imitations are bound to make a people small. The Muslims can exert themselves only by means of that inner force, in respect of which the West is growing insolvent day after day.

The secret of a Muslim's strength lies in his faith in the Divine recompense and reward in the After-life. If the Muslim World, too, sets up the same worldly ideals before itself and gets caught in the same web of material desires as the West, the latter with its larger fund of material knowledge and power evidently has a prior claim to superiority.

History speaks of times when Muslims grew indifferent to the value of the inner force and the wells of spiritual vigour within them ran dry owing to distrait. Then arose, occasions calling for great feats of faith and the Muslims tried to draw upon that force, but to them dismay they learnt that it had deserted them long ago. It then dawned upon them that they had done themselves great injury by neglecting it, and they made frantic efforts to work it up artificially but it proved futile.

During such times there also occurred events in the course of which the honour of Wani seemed to be at its height and it was hoped that the entire Muslim World would be set ablaze with fury and Muslims would rush forth front every (quarter to defend their sacred rights but nothing happened beyond a ripple hue and a wavelet there. Under the surface everything remained (dead and motionless).

The major task before the Muslim leaders and thinkers to-day is to rekindle the flame of faith in the hearts of Muslims. They should do in this respect all that the early preachers of Islam did, and at the same time avail themselves fully of all the opportunities the modern age has put into their hands.

The Qur'an and Um Sumah can still re-vitalize the withered arteries of the Islamic World. Their study and influence still fire, one with the desire to smash the citadel of Ignorance. They have it rousing quality about them that can spur a slumbering people into a new life. Under their inspiration deadly struggles can once again ensue between belief and unbelief, faith and perfidy, the heart and the intellect. The world can once again be made to ring to the battle between the tranquillity of mind and the ease of body—a battle which all the prophets had to wage, and without which no vital change in the moral make-up of men can be brought about. There will then be born in every Muslim home high-souled men who will fully correspond to the description contained in the following verses of the Qur'an :

> "They were youths who believed in their Lord, and We advanced them in guidance. We gave strength to their hearts; behold, they stood up and said : ' Our Lord is the Lord of the heavens and of the earth; never shall we call upon any god other than Him; if we did, we should indeed have uttered an enormity.'
>
> (Al-Qur'An, XVIII : 13-14)

The world will then see again living specimens of the religious earnestness and sacrificial spirit of Bildi and 'Ammar, Khabbab and Khubaib, Suhaib and Mus'ab bin 'Umair and 'Usman bin Maz'fln and Anas bin an-Nadhr; the gentle breeze of faith will once again Kiss the face of the earth and a new World quite different from the one we know will come into existence.

Today, the Muslim society is a victim of self-complacency and readiness to compromise with the circumstances. The perils which are so relentlessly closing in on it from all sides leave it unmoved. It is drifting and it does not know to what end. Its heart is without the warmth of desire.

There is a dire need of disturbing the complacency of this Community of the Faithful; it must be persuaded to care for human welfare more than for its own interests.

Rising to the Occasion

No matter how well provided with material resources a nation may be, it cannot hope to go far in the world without maturity of thought. It will always be playing in the hands of adventurers and exploiters.

Unfortunately the followers of Islam cannot distinguish between good and bad and will as willingly place their trust in a foe as in a freind. Often, indeed, it turns out to be easier for their enemies to win their confidence than for their well-wishers. The Holy Prophet (Upon whom be peace!) once said, "A Muslim is not bitten twice from the same hole." It is just the reverse of it now. 'The Muslims may be bitten from a hole, not once or twice, but a hundred times, yet will they put their finger into it again and again. The political awakening among them is almost nil.

They are constantly acting so as to invite the foreigners and their own selfish leaders to exploit them.

On the contrary, the Western nations, in spite of all their moral and spiritual shortcomings, are characterized by keen political consciousness. No one can lead them by the nose where their own interests are involved. They choose their leaders with care. However glorious a leader's record might be, if they feel that he has done his job and a new man is called for, they will replace him without hesitation. That is why these nations are, on the whole, safe from the machinations of professional politicians and dishonest leaders. Their rulers know that an enlightened public opinion keeps a watchful eye on them.

The Muslim World cannot afford to lose time in catching up with the West in inculcating proper consciousness among its masses and educating them in the responsibilities of good citizenship. It goes without saying that mere education is no proof of consciousness in a community, though it is a necessary condition thereof. Deliberate and systematic steps will have to be taken in this direction. It is for Muslim leadership to realize that persons who cannot do their own thinking cannot constitute a reliable people, whatever enthusiasm they may show for a cause. There is no stability in their thoughts and emotions. They have a weakness for catch words; they are prone to think with their hearts rather than with their brain. Any slogan can lure them away, any juggler can fool them.

In spite of being a revealed religion, having its roots in Divine Revelation and Apostleship, Islam had worked out a typical consciousness among its people—a consciousness that was deeper; stronger and wider than what we mean by it to-day. It had developed a frame of mind that was stoutly anti-Pagan and an understanding which, with all its breadth and flexibility, could not for a moment accommodate beliefs and notions which were inconsistent with its own basic pattern.

Take, for example, the following incident. Owing to the teachings of the Prophet (Peace be on him!) it had got fixed firmly in the minds of the Companions that injustice was an evil which was not to be permitted in any circumstances. They had given up their ancient family and tribal predilections, believing that there was no place for such things in Islam. Then one day they heard the Prophet (Peace be on him !) say:" Stand by your brother, be he the aggressor or the aggrieved." Had there been the slightest weakness in the development of their new understanding, they would have readily accepted the command in its apparent meaning, firstly, because of the background of their native traditions and, secondly, because they believed as a matter of faith that what the Holy Prophet (Peace be on him !) said was not out of his own volition but due to Divine inspiration. Their loyalty to the Prophet (Peace be on him!) was unmatched. Yet, they could not resist speaking out, " Helping the aggrieved is all right, O Prophet of God, but how can one help the aggressor?" The Prophet (Peace be on him !) explained that the way to help the aggressor was to restrain him from committing aggression. This gave them a new understanding and enlightenment. But until they had heard it, they were not disposed to accept even the advice of the Prophet (On whom be peace !) in spite of their implicit faith in him. This was because Islam had taught them to exercise their judgement and they learned how to use it.

Similarly, the Prophet once despatched an army under the command of a Companion and enjoined on it to remain obedient to its Commander. On the way it so happened that the Commander got upset with his men for some reason and had a big fire kindled. He ordered the soldiers to march into the fire. The soldiers refused. They said that they had embraced Islam to save themselves from fire and not to march into it. When the incident was reported to the Prophet (Peace be on him !), he commended the action of the soldiers and said that had they stepped into the fire, they would never have come out of it (meaning that they would have gone straight to hell).

The Companions did not hesitate even to challenge the Caliph publicly if they suspected him to be guilty of a wrong act. Once, as the mighty Caliph 'Umar arose to Mess a gathering Imams cut short by Aman who said that he would "neither listen to, nor obey" the Caliph unless he explained how he happened to be wearing a garment made of two pieces of cloth while to others he had allotted only one piece each. Hazrat 'Umar advised him to hold pewit and then called upon his son,, 'Abdullah. At the first instance there was no response. Hazrat 'Umar called again, "O 'Abdullah, the son of 'Umar!" This time 'Abdullah got up. Hazrat 'Umar said to him, "Tell them whether the hulla I am wearing is mine own or one borrowed from you". 'Abdulla affirmed that it was his ('Abdullah's) and that he had lent it to his father for use. On hearing it, Salman said, "Proceed Amir-ul-Mu'minin, we will now listen to you."

This powerful awakening proved to be the strongest bulwark against the imperialistic ambitions of the Umayyads. It was not until the whole of the generation that had been brought up under the influence of the Prophet (Peace be on him !) had passed away that the Umayyads could have a sigh of relief.

Every movement has an intellectual background. No revolution can succeed unless minds of the people have been prepared for it. A study of the French Revolution will show how irresistible the masses can become, once their minds are aroused. The French Revolution was not the outcome of a sudden impulse. Its leaders, had patiently prepared the minds of Frenchmen much in advance. There was an army of intellectuals who had given a meaningful content to the popular urges that ultimately found expression in the three-word slogan of "Liberty, Equality and Fraternity." Though its leaders could not make the revolution beneficial for humanity, it proved to be a mighty force in human history because it had sprung from the minds of the people.

If the West is still alive and powerful, it is due to the stout political consciousness and the keen civic sense of its people. One hears but rarely of anyone there violating his allegiance to his country or subordinating national interests to personal considerations.

The leaders in the Muslim countries on the other hand, can a, day mortgage the destiny of their people and walk away with it. Their people will still swell their ranks and dance to their tunes. In a number of Muslim countries the conditions are extremely deplorable—the common man there leads a sub-human existence, the authority of God is brazenly violated and all sorts of shameful things are done, and it calls up no indignation and arouses no pain among the Muslims. This is so because the process of thinking among Muslims is stagnant and their social consciousness is almost dead.

It is essential for the revivification of Islam that conscious efforts should be made for the development of an enlightened and responsible public opinion in the Muslim countries. Without it all manifestations of religious enthusiasm or political fervour will be of little significance.

The famous book of fiction, the Arabian Nights, tells the story of an age when the State or the Empire was the lengthened shadow of one man—the King or the Caliph, who held sway over society like a huge tree that sends out enormous branches in all directions and robs the tiny plants growing under it of sunshine and air. The wheels of the nation's life moved for him alone, for him alone did the farmers till the soil, the traders ply their trade and the workmen work with their tools; for him alone did the authors write, the poets sing, the soldiers march into the battlefield, the mothers give birth to children, the earth open up its bowels and the seas dish out their treasures.

Enormous Influence

This exerted enormous influence. on the Muslim social organization whether in Baghdad, Cairo or Damascus. The stories of the Arabian Nights and the literary masterpieces of "The Book of Aghani" are a living proof of the strength of this influence. But, for all that, the spirit of this age was diametrically opposed to the spirit of Islamic civilization. Islam had come to bring the structure of such a civilization to the ground. The Holy Prophet (Upon whom be peace!) had dubbed it as the "Age of Ignorance" and foretold the end of the reign of all imperial rulers.

This age has now forfeited its right to continue any more. The very idea of such an age is revolting to our mind. Who in the current context of things would like a state of society to exist in which a few individuals were permanently sick with indigestion due to over-eating, while the rest of them were permanently in the threat of death due to starvation ? Such a situation is illogical, unnatural and unjust. It should not have been tolerated even for a day. If it flourished in the past, it was because Islam had not yet acquired enough strength to expose its hypocrisy. As the Islamic movement spread and people learnt to distinguish clearly between right and wrong, they progressively emerged out of it. The age of the Arabian Nights has quit the stage of History for all time to come.

Islam can have nothing to do with egotism and self-conceit, individual or collective. Whether these sentiments take the form of family or sectarian pride, as in the Eastern and the Islamic countries, or of British Imperialism, American Capitalism or Russian Communism, as in the Western world, they are patently un-Islamic. These systems may succeed in putting off their doom for some time, but they are bound ultimately to go. The conscience of humanity cannot be cheated indefinitely. The future of the world is inseparably linked with the social justice of Islam.

The work of the regeneration of Islam, does not end here. If the Muslim World really wants to turn its way upwards and make Islam once again the instrument of realizing human destiny as has already happened, it cannot afford to ignore any more its educational, scientific and industrial development and the organization of its military strength. It must quickly make itself independent of the West and attain a position wherein it can work its natural resources, manufacture its weapons and feed and clothe its people without having to look to others for assistance. It must build up its economic and military strength so that it may not have to join this or that power bloc for security and protection.

So long as the Muslim countries continue depending on the West for economic and military aid, the West will not cease to suck their blood and keep them weak and disorganized. In the past, the Muslims were neglectful of their duty to themselves and to the rest of the world, and they were condemned to a long period of servitude and misery. The rule of the West was clamped down upon them, which proved to be the starting point of the degeneracy of man in modern times. If they do not pay immediate attention to their intellectual and economic re-birth, the period of their suffering will be extended and the world will be damned indefinitely.

The educational set-up of the Islamic World will have to be thoroughly over-hauled in the light of the Islamic ideals and precepts. To learn from the Western countries which are scientifically and technologically advanced is one thing, but the moment Muslims forget that their roots are in Islam, and become the intellectual camp-followers of others, their creative energies are damped. In former times the intellectual leadership of the Muslims was accepted all over the world. Their culture and learning had made their way into every sphere of human life all over the globe. For a long time the world continued to think in the Islamic way and draw inspiration from Islamic life. Arabic was the vehicle of learning in the Western world and every writer of note used this language to say what he had to say. Sometimes the original book was brought out in Arabic and a summary of it was produced in another language like Imirn Ghazzilis Kimiya-i-Saadaf. Though the educational system introduced by the Arabs was more Greek and Iranian in its essence than Islamic, and had a number of defects from the academic point of view, it had gained currency almost everywhere.

Then the time changed, and there dawned the epoch of Western ascendancy. It brought with it a new attitude towards learning, which was the product of Europe's own cultural experiences and implities. The world began to follow the new structure. The Muslim countries, too, on account of their intellectual sluggishness succumbed to the illusion their salvation lay only in a slavish submission to the west and to its educational system.

Ground was thus prepared for not merely intellectual adoration but also for actual imitation of the Western civilization by the Muslim intelligentsia. Religious skepticism, self-conceit, discontent and all other characteristics of the modern Western mode of living began steadily to replace the cultural ideals of the rising generations of the Muslims. The spiritual civilization of Islam began systematically to be replaced by the material culture of Europe.

Regaining of World Leadership

It is vital for the regaining of world-leadership for Islam now that the Muslim should re-establish their intellectual superiority over the West. For this the Islamic culture will, have to re-assert itself. Crusading endeavours will have to be made in all branches of learning. This, obviously, is not the work of a few individuals or associations. The Muslim states should take the task of intellectual regeneration seriously in hand. High-powered committees and institutions should immediately be set up for the purpose of evolving an educational structure that should fully conform to the spirit of the Qur'ãn and the Sunnah without overlooking the requirements of modern learning and scientific research. Muslim educationists and scientists ought to apply their own force of speculative reasoning to the empirical sciences so that they can save the coming generations of Muslims from developing a feeling of contempt for their own past and a despair for their future.

This is the way in which an Islamic revival can be brought about. This is the way in which the Muslims can spread the light of Islam to lands far away and save mankind from the stark ruin that is staring it in the face. Leadership is not an easy job. It calls for tremendous faith, labour and sacrifice.

6

Modernity under Religion

Religion is generally understood to mean the recognition of the existence of a supernatural ruling .power, the creator and controller of the universe, who has given to man a spiritual nature which continues to exist after the death of the body, and of man's duty to be obedient to this power. As a concept of life, it is all-encompassing. Science, on the other hand, is the study of the perceptible world. Both are extremely broad-ranging subjects, and their respective spheres are in many aspects quite separate from each other. It is not intended here to go into the details of these two subjects, but to deal only with the clash — real, or unreal — which has taken place between science and religion on an academic level, and certain of its consequences. One of the reasons for this clash is the claim that scientific discoveries have proved religion baseless, and it is principally this point on which attention has been focused here.

Traditional Conflict

The traditional conflict between science and religion made itself felt in the eighteenth and nineteenth centuries. It was during this period that, in the light of new scientific discoveries, many came to feel that there was no further call to believe in God. One of the most compelling reasons for believing in God, amongst others, was that without this belief, the universe was inexplicable. The antagonists of religion were quick to point out that we no longer required the 'God' hypothesis when there was no aspect of the universe which could not be explained quite easily by the findings of scientific research. To them, the idea of God was redundant and, therefore, baseless.

This claim was quite flimsy from the academic or logical point of view even at the time it was made, and now science itself has admitted, directly or indirectly, that it had no satisfactory ground for making such a claim.

Of what nature was this discovery of science which attempted to convince people that there was no further need for the concept of God? It was no more than the discovery that the universe is bound by certain laws. In ancient times, man had simply believed that all happenings in the world were directly attributable to God. But modern findings revealed that behind every event there was a cause which was discoverable by observation. For instance, Newton observed that all the stars and planets in the vastness of space are bound by certain immutable laws and move in strict accordance with those laws. Darwin's research showed that man had not come into existence through an act of special creation but had evolved, in-consonance with general material laws, from the lower species and had gradually developed into *homo sapiens*, i.e. man as we now know him. Similar observational studies showed that all events seemed to occur as part of a known system called the 'Law of Nature.' Significantly, this law of nature functioned with such effective regularity that it was considered entirely predictable.

These discoveries were taken to mean that the universe, which we had regarded as God's domain, was actually subservient to a set of material and physical laws. When these laws were applied, they yielded consistent results, and this further convinced members of the educated elite that they were right in embracing atheism. The German philosopher, Kant, declared: 'Give me matter and I shall demonstrate how the world is made out of matter.' Haeckel even went so far as to say that, given water, chemical elements and time, he would be able to create a man. Nietsche proclaimed with triumphant finality, 'God is dead.' Another belief had it that the creator and sustainer of this universe was not an alive, intelligent being possessing power; that the universe, from beginning to end, was material. All movements and all manifestations of the universe, whether related to life or to lifeless matter were nothing but blind material processes. The world discovered by science evinced no signs whatsoever of the hand of God — which is surely the basis of all religions. Then how could it be considered rational to believe in God?

Laws of Nature

All the heroes who had discovered the laws of nature were believers in God, but, ironically, when their research was brought before the public, it was thought that their discoveries had rendered meaningless the very existence of God. Since, in order to explain events, one had only to have recourse to the causes and laws of the material universe, there seemed to be no need to postulate the existence of a God who was extraneous to that universe. It was said, for example, that the rising and setting of the sun had not been properly understood until telescopes had been made and mathematics developed. The former ascription of these phenomena to the will and power of supernatural beings had been due merely to man's poor comprehension of these matters. And now that astronomy had proved that there was a universal system of gravitation which controlled the movements of the sun, moon and stars, there was no further need to believe in God. Gradually, all those happenings in nature, which were supposed in ancient times to have invisible superhuman forces at work behind them, were shown to be the results of the action and reaction of the forces of nature. It was as if, after the natural causes of events had been described in modern scientific terms, belief in God should automatically cease. Julian Huxley, in his book, *Man in the Modern World,* says:

If the rainbow is generated by the refraction of the sun's rays on falling rain, it is not set in the sky as a sign by God. If the plague is inevitably generated by the Bacillus pestis and spread by rat-fleas, an outbreak of plague can no longer be looked on as sign of divine wrath. If animals and plants have slowly evolved through hundreds of millions of years, there is no room for a creator of animals and plants, except in a metaphorical sense totally different from that in which the word was originally and is normally used. If hysteria and insanity are the natural results of disordered minds, there is no place remaining in them for possession by devils.

After presenting this piece of 'reasoning' with great conviction, he says that the ascription of such events 'to supernatural beings is merely due to man's ignorance combined with his passion for some sort of explanation.' He then sums up with: 'If events are due to natural causes, they are not due to supernatural causes' (pp. 18-19).

Serious Weakness

There is a serious weakness inherent in such arguments of the anti-religionists, which can be best understood through illustrations. Think of the railway engine speeding along the track. How do its wheels revolve? If we attempt to answer this question by studying the different parts of the engine and their movements, we shall arrive at the conclusion that the movement of the wheels is an extension of the functioning of the locomotive's mechanism. But would we be justified in believing that the reason for their movement is the engine and its various parts? Obviously, we would not. We should first have to consider the respective roles of the engineer who designed the engine and the engine driver who set it in motion. Without their instrumentality, the engine could neither exist, nor move. The engine and its parts are not then the final reality. The final reality is the mind which has brought the engine into existence, and runs it at will. A Christian scholar, Cecil Boyce Hamann, has aptly said: "Nature does not explain, she is herself in need of explanation." This is because, as he puts it, nature is a fact, not an explanation.

Let us consider, for example, how a chick comes into this world. In embryo, it develops inside the smooth, hard shell of an egg, then it emerges when the shell breaks up. How does it come about that the shell breaks up at the right moment and the fledgling, which is no more than a small lump of flesh, finds its way into the outer world? In the past, the obvious answer was: "It is the hand of God." But now, microscopic studies have shown that on the completion of twenty-one days, when the chick is ready to emerge, there appears on its beak a small, hard horn with which this 'lump of flesh' is able to break through the walls of its cell. The horn, having done its job, falls off a few days later. This observation, from the point of view of the anti-religionists, contradicts the old concept that it is God who brings the chick out of the shell, because the microscope has clearly shown that a 21-day law exists which is responsible for creating conditions which make it possible for the chick to emerge from the shell. This is a mere fallacy. What modern observation has done is to add a few more links to the chain of factors which lead up to an event. It does not tell us the real cause of the occurrence. It has just shifted the problem of the breaking up of the shell to the development of the horn. The breaking of the shell by the chick is simply an intermediate stage in the occurrence rather than its cause. Will the cause of the event be understood only when we learn what made the horn appear on the chick's beak? In other words, when we have traced the event back to its primary cause, the cause which 'knew' that the chick required some hard instrument to break through the shell and, therefore, in exactly twenty-one days, compelled a hard substance to appear on the beak in the form of a horn and to fall off after having discharged its function?

'How does the shell break?' was the question that faced man previously. Now, in the light of recent observations, instead of an answer, we have another question: 'How does the horn develop?' In the context of perceived phenomena, there is no difference in the nature of these two questions. At the most, questions of the type that lead us from one link to another in the chain of cause and effect demand an extension of the observation of facts, if they are to be answered at all. On this basis, they do not elicit any valid explanation.

Explanation of Nature

The discoveries held by the atheists to be an explanation of nature and, as such, an alternative to God, can just as easily be thought of as being the way nature works. We can, quite rationally, say that God implements his will through these laws, only parts of which man, with his limited skills, has been able to discover. Let us suppose that religious-minded people, who believe that it is God who causes the ebb and flow of the tides, are confronted with the scientific explanation that the tides are actually caused by the gravitational pull of the moon and vary according to the geographical configuration of the seas and land surfaces. There would be no need for them to deny this explanation in order to uphold their belief in God's instrumentality. They could accept it without causing the slightest harm to their religious beliefs. It is true that tides do occur in consonance with geographical configuration and as a result of gravitational pull. But, after all, what are these things? They too are God's creations. It is through these phenomena that God acts. As John Wilson observed: This does not destory my belief. It is still God (working through these things') who is responsible for the tides.'

Similarly, in the field of biology, the theory of evolution implies that biological processes no longer demand the existence of metaphysical realities. In other words, in order to understand the nature of life, we do not need to believe in a conscious God, modern studies having 'proved' that life automatically patterns itself along certain material lines: reproduction, variation and selective survival. That is, through reproduction, living creatures continue to be born, certain congenital variations go on developing, then after a long and complicated process of mutation, an altogether new species comes into being. Thus, according to the antagonists of religion, the application of Darwin's principle of natural selection in biology has made it not only possible but imperative to reject outright the concept of God's hand in life's development.

Various Species

The supposition that the various species of living creatures have come into being through a gradual process of evolution has yet to be established as a fact, but even were we to give credence to this theory, it could still be said with equal conviction, that this is God's chosen way of creation, rather than its being the result of a blind, automatic force. Mechanical evolution can easily be proved to be a creational evolution. This being so, those anti-religionists who refer to science for support have no genuine basis on which to reject this argument of creational evolution.

This is far from being all that there is to the matter. The truth is that twentieth century science has lost its ability to convince. Today, Newton has been replaced by Einstein, and the theories of Planck and Heisenberg have overthrown those of Laplace. Now the anti-religionists, at least on an academic level, can no longer claim that science has arrived at the ultimate truth. Indeed, the theory of relativity and the quantum theory have led scientists to the conclusion that it is impossible in science to separate the observer from the observed. This means that we can see only certain external manifestations of reality; we cannot apprehend it in its essence. The revolution that has occurred in science in the twentieth century has itself proved the importance of religion from the scientific point of view.

In his book, *The Limitations of Science,* J.N. Sullivan states the case thus:

What is called the modern "revolution" in science consists of the fact that the Newtonian outlook, which dominated the scientific world for nearly two hundred years, has been found insufficient. It is in process of being replaced by a different outlook, and, although the reconstruction is by no means complete, it is already apparent that the philosophical implications of the new outlook are very different from those of the old one. We are no longer taught that the scientific method of approach is the only valid method of acquiring knowledge about reality. Eminent men of science are insisting, with what seems a strange enthusiasm, on the fact that science gives us but a partial knowledge of reality.

This change in the scientific outlook seems to have taken place suddenly. It is not yet sixty years since Tyn-dall, in his Belfast Address, claimed that science alone was competent to deal with all man's major problems. But, in truth, so far as these remarks sprang from the conviction that the sole reality is 'matter and motion,' their foundations had already been undermined. The attempt to represent nature in terms of matter and motion was already breaking down. That attempt was at its most triumphant by the end of the eighteenth century, when Laplace was emboldened to affirm that a sufficiently great mathematician, given the distribution of the particles in the primitive nebula, could predict the whole future history of the world. The fundamental concepts isolated by Newton had proved themselves so adequate in the applications that had been made of them that they were regarded as the key to everything.

Newtonian Concepts

The first indication that the Newtonian concepts were not all-sufficient came when men tried to fashion a mechanical theory of light. This endeavour led to the creation of the ether, the most unsatisfactory and wasteful product of human ingenuity that science has to show. For generations this monster was elaborated. Miracles of mathematical ingenuity were performed in the attempt to account for the properties of light in terms of the Newtonian concepts. The difficulties became ever more heartbreaking until, after the publication of Maxwell's demonstration that light is an electromagnetic phenomenon, they seemed to become insuperable. For it had dawned on men of science that there was, after all, nothing sacrosanct about the Newtonian entities. After a certain amount of hesitation, and a few last desperate efforts to make electricity mechanical, electricity was added to the list of irreducible elements.

This may seem to have been a simple step to take, but it was, in reality, of profound significance. For the Newtonian concepts were all of a kind that one seemed to understand intimately. Thus the mass of a body was the quantity of matter in it. Force was a notion derived from our experience of muscular effort. Nevertheless, we supposed that we knew the nature of what we were talking about. But in the case of electricity its nature is precisely what we did not know. Attempts to represent it in familiar terms — as a condition of strain in the ether, or what not — had been given up. All that we knew about electricity was the way it affected our measuring instruments. The precise description of this behaviour gave us the mathematical specification of electricity and this, in truth, was all we knew about it. It is only now, in retrospect, that we can see how very significant a step this was. An entity had been admitted into physics of which we knew nothing but its mathematical structure.

Since then other entities have been admited on the same terms, and it is found that they play precisely the same role in the formation of scientific theories as do the old entities. It has become evident that, so far as the science of physics is concerned, we do not require to know the nature of the entities we discuss, but only their mathematical structure. And, in truth, that is all we do know. It is now realized that this is all the scientific knowledge we have even of the familiar Newtonian entities. Our persuasion that we knew them in some exceptionally intimate manner was an illusion.

With this realization it is no long step to Eddington's position that a knowledge of mathematical structure is the only knowledge that the science of physics can give us. Leaving out all aesthetic, ethical, or spiritual aspects of our environment, we are faced with qualities such as massiveness, substantiality, extension, duration, which are supposed to belong to the domain of physics. In a sense they do belong; but physics is not in a position to handle them directly. The essence of their nature is inscrutable; we may use mental pictures to aid calculations, but no image in the mind can be a replica of that which is not in the mind. And so in its actual procedure physics studies not these inscrutable qualities, but pointer-readings which we can observe. The readings, it is true, reflect the fluctuations of the world-qualities; but our exact knowledge is of the readings, not of the qualities. The former have as much resemblance to the latter as a telephone number has to a subscriber.

Knowledge of Structure

The fact that science is confined to a knowledge of structure is obviously of great "humanistic" importance. For it means that the problem of the nature of reality is not prejudged. We are no longer required to believe that our response to beauty, or the mystic's sense of communion with God, have no objective counterpart. It is perfectly possible that they are, what they have so often been taken to be, clues to the nature of reality. Thus, our various experiences are put on a more equal footing, as it were.

Our religious aspirations, our perceptions of beauty, may not be the essentially illusory phenomena they were supposed to be. In this new scientific universe even mystics have a right to exist (pp. 138-42).

Such explanations from scientific philosophers now abound. Morton White in his book *The Age of Analysis,* points out that 'the philosophically-minded scientists of the 20th century have started a new crusade, the names of Whitehead, Eddington and James Jeans are the most prominent among them.' He then bears out this notion of a 'crusade' with highly pertinent quotations from each of them.

'Nature is alive' (p. 84). Such was the interpretation of modern information by the English mathematician and philosopher, A.N. Whitehead (1861-1947).

The stuff of the world is mind stuff (p. 134). So said the English astronomer, Sir Arthur Eddington (1882-1944), deriving this conclusion from his studies in science.

The English mathematical physicist, Sir James Jeans (1877-1946), interprets modern research thus: The universe is a universe of thought' (p. 134).

The views of the most perceptive scientists, can be summed up in J.W.N. Sullivan's words: 'The ultimate nature of the universe is mental' (p. 145).

The thoughts of these scholars clearly negate any material interpretation of the universe, their special virtue being that they have been advanced in the context of modern findings in the field of physics and mathematics. That the proponents of such ideas have had to make courageous, herculean efforts to overcome the materialistic outlook is aptly expressed by Morton White with reference to Whitehead: 'He is a heroic thinker who tries to beard the lions of Intellectualism, Materialism and Positivism in their own bristling den' (p. 84). Morton White may have said this only about Whitehead, but this applies to all the scientists mentioned above.

This philosophical question as to the final reality being mind or matter is actually concerned with the question of whether the universe has developed independently and spontaneously through some material process, or whether there is a non-material being who has created it at will. If we accepted the former proposition, it would be just like saying that, in the last analysis, a machine is simply a fortuitous compound of iron and petrol. That is to say, that the machine started off as iron and petrol, but owing to some blind, automatic process, it took on the form of a machine. All a pure accident! A machine, as we all know, is the product of an engineer's mind. That mind, quite distinct from the matter, existed before the machine. It conceived it, designed it, and brought it into being. The machine's existence was clearly consequent upon the exercise of mind and will.

In determining the nature of the mind, differences can be found among those who believe the mind to be the final reality, just as believers in God have diverse concepts of God. Even so, the conclusion arrived at by academic study that the final underlying reality of the universe is mind, testifies by its very nature to the truth of religion and amounts to a rejection of atheism. The truly significant change in modern science is not to be found in its increased powers to aid man's religion and science progress, but in the change in its metaphysical foundations.'

The best exposition of this viewpoint is to be found in *The Mysterious Universe,* by Sir James Jeans. By pure scientific argument, the writer has come to the conclusion that in the light of modern physics, 'The universe cannot admit of material representation, and the reason, I think, is that it has become a mere mental concept.'

He later goes on to say that "if the universe is a universe of thought, then its creation must have been an act of thought" (pp. 133-34).

He holds that the modern concept which interprets matter in terms of waves of electrons is quite unconceivable to human thought, because these 'waves' could be only the 'waves of probabilities' without having any material existence. Such reasons have compelled Jeans to conclude that the substance of the universe is thought, not matter. Now where is this thought situated? His answer is that it exists in the mind of a great 'mathematical thinker? Because the structure of this thought that comes to our mind is a completely mathematical structure. The 'great Architect of the Universe thus begins to appear as a pure mathematician,'

Sir James Jeans then states the entire case with great precision: It seems at least safe to say that the river of knowledge has made a sharp bend in the last few years. Thirty years ago, we thought, or assumed, that we were heading towards an ultimate reality of a mechanical kind. It seemed to consist of fortuitous jumble of atoms, which was destined to perform meaningless dances for a time under the action of blind purposeless forces, and then fall back to form a dead world. Into this wholly mechanical world, through the play of the same blind forces, life had stumbled by accident. One tiny corner at least, and possibly several tiny corners of this universe of atoms had chanced to become conscious for a time, but was destined in the end, still under the action of blind mechanical forces, to be frozen out and again leave a lifeless world.

Measure of Agreement

Today there is a wide measure of agreement, which on the physical side of science approaches almost to unanimity, that the stream of knowledge is heading towards a non-mechanical reality; the universe begins to look more like a great thought than like a great machine. Mind no longer appears as an accidental intruder into the realm of matter; we are beginning to suspect that we ought rather to hail it as the creator and governor of the realm of matter — not of course our individual minds, but the mind in which the atoms out of which our individual minds have grown exist as thoughts.

The new knowledge compels us to revise our hasty first impressions that we had stumbled into a universe which either did not concern itself with life or was actively hostile to life. The old dualism of mind and matter, which was mainly responsible for the supposed hostility, seems likely to disappear, not through matter becoming in any way more shadowy or insubstantial than heretofore, or through mind becoming resolved into a function of the working of matter, but through substantial matter resolving itself into a creation and manifestation of mind. We discover that the universe shows evidence of a designing or controlling power that has something in common with our own individual minds — not, so far as we have discovered, emotion, morality, or aesthetic appreciation, but the tendency to think in the way, which, for want of a better word, we describe as mathematical.

In spite of this complete about-face in science from the academic point of view, it is a fact that, in practice, there have been no noticeable changes in the attitudes of anti-religionists. On the contrary, they are engaged in seeking new arguments to support their theory. The reason for this is not to be found within any academic framework. No, the reason is to be traced, alas! to a biased mentality. How often have we seen educated people refuse to accept the truth when ample proofs have been offered to them, simply because of deeply-rooted preconceived ideas. It was just such a prejudiced attitude, in the seventeenth century, which had prevented Italian scholars from accepting Galileo's theory as an alternative to Aristotle's, although a ball thrown from the Leaning Tower had demonstrated quite conclusively that Galileo was right. Again, it was this bias which caused scholars at the end of the nineteenth century to ridicule Berlin Professor Max Planck when he gave a physical explanation of light,— the quantum theory, — which proved the Newtonian concept wrong. Planck's theory was not accepted for many years, but today it is considered one of the most important principles in physics.

There is a common belief that it is only laymen who are guilty of prejudice and not scientists; we should do well, therefore, to mark the words of A.V. Hills, himself a scientist: 'I should be the last to claim that we, scientific men, are less liable to prejudice than other educated men.

Sir James Jeans underscores this when he says, 'Our modern minds have, I think, a bias towards mechanical interpretation.'

Now, in a world where prejudice holds sway, how can we hope that a concept will be accepted only because it has been proved academically? The often-repeated experiences of history show that man has all along been governed by his emotions rather than by his intellect, in spite of the fact that academically and logically, reason occupies the higher position. More often than not, reason has played into the hands of emotion. It has seldom happened that it has gained a positive control over the emotions. Indeed, the intellect has always coined arguments to support the emotional and thus tried to prove that emotional attitudes were rational. Man finds it a psychological necessity to cling to his emotional being, even at the cost of remaining blind to reality. We must remember, therefore, that we are not dealing with machines, which ought to respond to the mere flicking of a switch. What we have to address ourselves to is man, and man accepts something only when he himself is willing to do so. If he is not, no argument, however sound it may be, will convince him. Arguments are not, sad to say, electric switches. That man, with all his capacity for reasoning, should so seldom, himself, be amenable to reasoning, is perhaps the greatest tragedy of human history.

Religion to Protect

Modern scholars have come to the conclusion that we may have succeeded in making great discoveries about inanimate matter, but that we cannot be certain of having been successful in discovering the facts of man's nature and existence, for there exists a strange disparity between the sciences of inanimate matter and those of life. The sciences which concern themselves with the inanimate part of our world differ from the biological sciences in that the former are subject to definite laws whereas the latter are, to quote Dr. Alexis Carrel, inextricably lost 'in the midst of a magic forest whose countless trees unceasingly change their place and shape.' Unlike material phenomena, biological phenomena cannot be defined in terms of algebraic equations. The sciences of the material world are confined to description, a lower form of science altogether, because they do not unveil the ultimate nature of things, but only convey certain qualities such as weight and spatial dimensions. They do give us the power to predict future events, and often to determine at will their occurrence; in learning the secret of the constitution and properties of matter, we have gained the mastery of almost everything which exists on the surface of the earth — excepting ourselves. The science of living beings in general, and of the human individual in particular, has not made such spectacular progress. It still remains at the descriptive stage, while the elucidation of the real nature of living beings requires much more than mere description.

The Nobel prize winner, Dr. Alexis Carrel, who achieved unique fame in biological research at the Rockfeller Institute in New York, elaborates at some length in his book, *Man, the Unknown,* on what is meant by man:

Man is an indivisible whole of extreme complexity. No simple representation of him can be obtained. There is no method capable of apprehending him simultaneously in his entirety, his parts, and his relations with the outer world. In order to analyze ourselves we are obliged to seek the help of various techniques and, therefore, to utilize several sciences. Naturally, all these sciences arrive at a different conception of their common object. They abstract only from man what is attainable by their special methods. And those abstractions, after they have been added together, are still less rich than the concrete fact. They leave behind them a residue too important to be neglected. Anatomy, chemistry, physiology, psychology, pedagogy, history, sociology, political economy do not exhaust their subject. Man, as known to the specialists, is far from being the concrete man, the real man. He is nothing but a schema, consisting of other schemata built up by the techniques of each science.

He is, at the same time, the corpse dissected by the anatomists, the consciousness observed by the psychologists and the great teachers of the spiritual life, and the personality which introspection shows to everyone as lying in the depth of himself. He is the chemical substance constituting the tissues and humours of the body. He is the amazing community of cells and nutrient fluids whose organic laws are studied by the physiologists. He is the compound of tissues and consciousness that hygienists and educators endeavour to lead to its optimum development while it extends into time. He is the homoaconomicus who must ceaselessly consume manufactured products in order that the machines, of which he is made a slave, may be kept at work. But he is also the poet, the hero, and the saint. He is not only the prodigiously complex being analyzed by our scientific techniques, but also the tendencies, the conjectures, the aspirations of humanity. Our conceptions of him are imbued with metaphysics. They are founded on so many and such imprecise data that the temptation is great to choose among them those which please us. Therefore, our idea of man varies according to our feelings and our beliefs. A materialist and a spiritualist accept the same definition of a crystal of sodium chloride; but they do not agree with one another upon that of the human being. A mechanistic physiologist and a vitalistic physiologist do not consider the organism in the same light. The living being of Jacques Loeb differs profoundly from that of Hans Driesch. Indeed, mankind has made a gigantic effort to know itself. Although we possess the treasure of the observations accumulated by the scientists, the philosophers, the poets, and the great mystics of all times, we have grasped only certain aspects of ourselves. We do not apprehend man as a whole. We know him as composed of distinct parts. And even these parts are created by our methods. Each one of us is made up of a procession of phantoms, in the midst of which strides an unknowable reality.

In fact, our ignorance is profound. Most of the questions put to themselves by those who study human beings remain without answer. Immense regions of our inner world are still unknown. How do the molecules of chemical substance associate in order to form the complex and temporary organs of the cell? How do the genes contained in the nucleus of a fertilized ovum determine the characteristics of the individual deriving from that ovum? How do cells organize themselves by their own efforts into societies, such as the tissues and the organs? Like the ants and the bees, they have advance knowledge of the part they are destined to play in the life of the community. And hidden mechanisms enable them to build up an organism both complex and simple. What is the nature of our duration, of psychological time, and of physiological time? We know that we are a compound of tissues, organs, fluids, and consciousness. But the relations between consciousness and cerebrum are still a mystery. We lack almost entirely a knowledge of the physiology of nervous cells. To what extent does will power modify the organism? How is the mind influenced by the state of the organs? In what manner can the organic and mental characteristics, which each individual inherits, be changed by the mode of life, the chemical substances contained in food, the climate, and the physiological and moral disciplines?

We are very far from knowing what relations exist between skeleton, muscles, and organs, and mental and spiritual activities. We are ignorant of the factors that bring about nervous equilibrium and resistance to fatigue and to diseases. We do not know how moral sense, judgement, and audacity could be augmented. What is the relative importance of intellectual, moral, and mystical activities? What is the significance of aesthetic and religious sense? What form of energy is responsible for telepathic communications? Without any doubt, certain physiological and mental factors determine happiness or misery, success or failure. But we do not know what they are. We cannot artificially give to any individual the aptitude for happiness. As yet we do not know what environment is the most favourable for the optimum development of civilized man. Is it possible to suppress struggle, effort, and suffering from our physiological and spiritual formation? How can we prevent the degeneration of man in modern civilization? Many other questions could be asked on subjects which are to us of the utmost interest. They would also remain unanswered. It is quite evident that the accomplishments of all the sciences having man as an object remain insufficient, and that our knowledge of ourselves is still most rudimentary.

This passage more than adequately demonstrates that we still have not formulated a true science of man. About the material part of human existence we are fairly well informed, but we are completely ignorant of who or what controls it. Life is still a mystery to us, and until it is unveiled, there can be no proper apprehension of what, in essence, it is. Alexis Carrel's book, *Man, the Unknown,* is an attempt to make scientific approach to its discovery.

Today man can split an atom; he can make icy lands habitable; he has walked on the moon and sent probes into outer space. Such instances of advanced technological progress give the impression that if man can learn so much about his material environment that he is able to exploit it at will, he should certainly be able to discover himself and, in the process, set right whatever ails him. But there are strong indications in our known world that man can never be understood in the same way that matter can.

Let us look at this entity, called man, on a purely physiological basis. He is composed of millions and millions of cells of protoplasm. And what is protoplasm? We can say with certainty that it is a viscous, translucent, homogeneous, structureless substance endowed with contractility and a chemical composition allied to that of albumen: it is the physical basis of life and, clearly, we know a great deal about it as such. Yet we have to concede that we do not know why it should have this unique property of life, or how this came to be so. Moreover, it is a fact that the methods we employ to study the material world cannot be applied to protoplasm in any way which should elicit an answer to these awesome questions. All that is visible to us is a compound of certain things.

Means and the Resources

If we had the means and the resources, we should be able not only to destroy but also to create such compounds. Indeed, science has discovered the elements of which protoplasm is composed and the particular proportion of those elements have also been learnt. But it is in vain that we join together the two distinct forms of protoplasm, the nucleus and the cytoplasm, albeit in the correct proportions, for no protoplasm is thus formed which has the property of life. While other chemical compounds can be formed by combining their elements in the correct proportions, (e.g. one molecule of water is made up of one atom of oxygen and two atoms of hydrogen) the life-giving matter which is the main constituent of a human being's body can in no way be brought into existence by human agency. Our powers of creation extend only to inanimate matter, never to living entities.

This is the area in which we are the most helpless, and we have no option but to admit it. The greatest irony is that although all our physiological studies are concerned with the living man, the results they yield bear more relevance to this cadaver. Science has discovered both the elements which constitute protoplasm and their correct proportions, yet the particular order or arrangement which is responsible for the life-property of protoplasm has still to be revealed. The moment this arrangement disintegrates, the protoplasm is rendered lifeless. It is as if a particular arrangement was responsible for the existence of soul in the protoplasm. But the difficulty that confronts us is that so long as we keep this arrangement intact, the protoplasm cannot be chemically analysed. The moment we break it, life vanishes. Whenever protoplasm is subjected to chemical analysis, the soul has already left it. And this will always be the case. Science will always remain in the dark regarding the reality of life. But this is not the end of our problem. It goes much deeper than this.

Unveil Reality

Let us suppose someone sets out to unveil reality, thus disclosing to man the law of life, and, to this end, he begins the study of human settlements. After prolonged examination of different societies, he comes to the conclusion that, since society is composed of human beings, he had best concern himself with the individual, the better to understand the group. So he reduces his focus accordingly. His first preoccupation then is with psychology. But he soon realizes that no single philosophy emerges, because there are several schools of thought on the subject, all arriving at different conclusions. One school claims that the senses are central to all human actions while others say that all man's responses are reactions to impressions received consciously or unconsciously from the external world. Yet others say that it is sexual desires which provide the stimulus for all of man's actions. A different type of study shows that an unrecognized urge to realize a certain set of ideals keeps man active. Some schools of thought take consciousness to be a reality and explain the whole of man's being in relation to this; others hold that the mind and intellect, have no existence, and that there is no central power commanding the various parts of the body. Rather the parts which receive most attention are better developed and that is what makes it possible, for example, for one man to be highly skilled in dancing, another in archery and yet another in profound reflection. These differences in thinking in the field of psychology go to such extremes that one might be led to wonder if there was any such unified science as psychology.

On seeing this jungle of ideas, our inquirer thinks of studying another aspect of human existence — biology — in order to come to more cogent conclusions. But in this discipline he finds that man is treated as an amalgam of the metabolism, the respiratory system, the blood circulation, and so on. These systems are based on certain chemical changes and, judging from their action and reaction, it would appear that the different parts of the whole bodily system are sub-functions of the metabolism.

After deep reflection, he comes to the conclusion that since the existence of the human body and its development are related to chemical actions and reactions, the principles according to which chemical changes take place should first of all be properly understood, failing which no really satisfactory information about man could ever be discovered. So he engrosses himself in the study of physics and chemistry and, indeed, devotes the major part of his life to it. This branch of study leads him on to an investigation of the molecule and the atom, from which he proceeds to study the electrons and protons of which the atom is composed. The realization then comes to him that the whole universe is nothing but electric waves, and he becomes immersed in the study of the latest discoveries in nuclear science. He thus collects a huge mass of facts, but at the end of it all, he fails to arrive at any firm conclusions about the reality of man. He has become lost in a world which, in spite of being visible, has remained impenetrable. According to Dr. C.E.M. Joad, matter is something unreal which cannot be grasped. It is a part of the four dimensional space-time continuum, a network of electric waves, or a wave of probability which perished on being looked at; and it has even been considered an extension of the observer's consciousness instead of something solid and tangible.

This pathetic end to the quest for the secret of life in the material sciences shows that the secret of life is not discoverable by man. Now just as a sick man cannot treat his disease himself and is forced to consult a doctor, so a man who is in need of spiritual sustenance cannot provide this for himself without turning to God. The fact that he cannot discover the secret either of life or of his own nature is a sure indicator that he is in need of the God who created him in the form in which he exists. Just as God has created man in such a way that he needs oxygen and then has given him oxygen in abundance, He has made him yearn to know the secret of life and then sent His messengers to him so that all veils should fall from reality. And so the world went on.

7

Muslims in Dilemma

> And it (the resurrection) will not take place until you see affairs which will cause you to ask one another whether your Prophet has mentioned anything concerning them, and until the mountains will be displaced from their stations.
>
> (Prophet's Hadith)

When we turn to the contemporary Muslim as he finds himself in today's world, we discover that although his problems are not identical with those of Western man, he too lives in a situation which presents him with numerous difficulties, one which puts his faith *(iman) to* the most arduous test possible. One can find in the Islamic world today a full spectrum of people ranging from purely traditional elements, through those who are caught between traditional values and modernism, to the blatant modernists who nevertheless still move within the Islamic orbit, and finally to the few who no longer consider themselves to belong to the Islamic universe at all.[1] With this latter group we are not concerned, for they can no longer be considered as the representative of *homo islamicus* who is the subject of our present discussion, although they, too, often return finally to the Islamic pattern of things. It is the *iman* of the other groups, who already possess faith in one degree or another, that is put to the test in a world which makes the real appear illusory and the illusory real, a world which seduces men into believing that spiritual reality—the only reality there is—is out-moded in comparison with a supposedly 'real' world which is dissolving before the bewildered eyes of modern man like sand running through his fingers.

Departure from Normal Course

'The major difference between the contemporary Muslim and his Western counterpart is that the former, in contrast to the latter, lives in a society where the Centre is still visible and therefore the rim can also be seen for what it really is. He lives in a world where the transcendent dimension is still present, where the majority of men still perform their religious rites and duties, where the Divine Law or SharVah is still considered to be the ultimate law, even if not fully practised by everyone, and where the figure of the saint and sage is still a living one, although now perhaps less easy to find than before. There is also the basic difference that the contemporary Muslim knows less about the modern world than does Western man, that his intelligence has been tested in fewer ways and that he has not in general developed the kind of discernment found among those in the West who have re-discovered tradition and by the same token come to know the real nature of the modern world. The situation of contemporary Muslims, like that of other Orientals in general, is also in one aspect more difficult than that of Western man is that changes now taking place in the East are more rapid and often more devastating. In a sense, the West has little more to lose to the onslaught of modernism, whereas there are still many things of spiritual value in the East which are being threatened every day, whether by means of books, the radio or the bulldozer. The contemporary Muslim must and cannot but wage a continuous holy war (jihad), not only within himself to keep his mind and soul healthy and intact, but also outwardly to protect what he can of the marvellous spiritual and artistic heritage his forefathers have bequeathed him in the expectation that he too will preserve and transmit it to the next generation. In this sense then, that he is being pulled by the forces of the Islamic tradition on the one hand and of secularism and modernism on the other, the contemporary Muslim, especially of the class thoroughly influenced by the modern world, may also be said to be situated between the rim and the axis, although his 'existential' situation differs from that of Western man in secularized post-industrial society because of the different elements which have conditioned his mind and soul.

Islamic World

The contemporary Muslim who lives in the far corners of the Islamic world and has remained isolated and secluded from the influence of modernism may be said to live still within a homogeneous world in which the tensions of life are those of normal human existence. But the Muslim who lives in the centres of the Islamic world touched in one degree or another by modernism lives within a polarized field of tension created by two contending world views and systems of values. This tension is often reflected within his mind and soul, and he usually becomes a house divided against itself, in profound need of re-integration. If he is of an intellectual bent, he sees on one side the rich intellectual heritage of Islam as a still-living reality, a heritage which is precisely a message from the Centre and a guide for man in his journey from the rim to the Centre. It is a world view based on the supremacy of the blinding reality of God before whom all creatures are literally nothing, and then on the hierarchic Universe issuing from His Command (Amr) and comprising the multiple levels of being from the archangelic world to the l'evel of material existence. It is a Weltanschauung based on viewing man as the 'image of God' (khalaqa'llahu Adama 'ala swatihi), as God's vice regent (khalifah) on earth but also as His perfect servant ('abd) obeying His every command. It is based on the idea that all phenomena in the world of nature are symbols reflecting divine realities and that all things move according to His Will and their spiritual nature (malakiit), which is in His Hands. It is based on the conception that only the law of God, the Sharfah, has ultimate claim upon the allegiance and respect of men and that it alone can provide for their felicity in its true sense.

On the other side and in contrast to this world view, the contemporary Muslim sees the basic assumptions of modern Western civilization, nearly all of which are the very antithesis of the Islamic principles he cherishes. He sees philosophies based either on man considered as a creature in rebellion against Heaven or on the human collectivity seen as an ant-heap in which man has no dignity worthy of his real nature. He sees the Universe reduced to a single level of reality—the spatio-temporal complex of matter and energy—and all the higher levels of reality relegated to the category of old wives' tales or—at best—images drawn from the collective unconscious. He sees the power of man as ruler upon the earth emphasized at the expense of his servanthood so that he is considered to be not the khalifatallah, the vice regent of God, but the khalifah of his own ego or of some worldly power or collectivity. He sees the theomorphic nature of man either mutilated or openly negated. He reads the arguments of Western philosophers and scientists against the symbolic concept of nature, a concept which is usually debased by being called 'totemistic' or 'animistic' or some other term of that genre, usually loaded with pejorative connotations. He is, in fact, made to believe that the transformation from seeing the phenomena of nature as the portents or signs (Sy&t) of God to viewing these phenomena as brute facts is a major act of progress which, however, only prepares nature for that ferocious rape and plunder for which modern man is now beginning to pay so dearly. Finally, the contemporary Muslim is taught to believe that the law is nothing but a convenient agreement within a human collectivity and therefore relative and ever-changing, with the implication that there is no such thing as a Divine Law which serves as the immutable norm of human action and which provides the measures against which man can judge his own ethical standards objectively.

These and many other intellectual and philosophical questions beset constantly the mind of that contemporary Muslim who is touched in one degree or another by the influence of modernism. Not all the questions present themselves with the same force to everyone, nor is every Modernised Muslim Modernised to the same degree. For this reason the dilemma of every contemporary Muslim is not the same. But, nevertheless, the tension between two world views of a contradictory nature is to be observed widely, the kind and degree of tension differing, of course, from one milieu and even one individual to another.

Clash of Approaches

The same confrontation of world views and the same dilemma is also to be observed in other domains. In education—in its universal sense as the most important means of transmitting the tradition from one generation to another —again two contending systems vie with each other, with the contemporary Muslim caught in between. On the one hand, there are the classical channels of education ranging from the laps of grandparents and parents to Quranic schools (maktabs) to traditional universities (madrasahs) to Sufi centres (khanaqahs or zdwiyahs), not to speak of ateliers and guild centres where the arts and crafts are taught. On the other hand, there are radio and television programmes mostly dubbed from European languages, and on the formal level the modern educational systems of various Muslim countries, nearly all of which consist of poor imitations of various Western models at a time when the Western educational system itself is undergoing a crisis of unparalleled dimensions. The difference between the relation of parent to child or teacher to student in the two systems, as well as the content of the subject matter taught, is as great as can be imagined. In the more Modernised circles of the 'Islamic world, even small children face this tension, as on the one hand they still learn the various traditional stories which contain the profoundest wisdom in simple language from the mouth of a grandparent or a nanny and, on the other hand, they watch murder stories and the like on television screens. Among the adults, the opposition and the tension are even more evident, with two contending educational systems providing a natural battlefield upon which the contemporary Muslim, both as an individual who wishes to receive education and as a parent wanting to select a school for his or her child, stands bewildered. The transition from the traditional educational system to the modern ones has in most cases been abrupt and disruptive and one of the major causes of the confusing state which the contemporary Muslim now faces.

Pressure of Modernism

It might be thought that the dilemma of the contemporary Muslim under the influence and pressure of modernism is limited to the intellectual and educational realm, but this is far from true. Actually, a crisis of the same intensity, and perhaps of an even more direct effect, exists in the world of forms with which art is concerned. In this domain, the remarkably homogeneous yet diversified world of Islamic art, which has succeeded in creating an Islamic ambience for the Muslim within which he has lived and died, is threatened from every direction. Traditional Islamic architecture has been at a peak during nearly all of its long history and can be cited as a supreme example of that architecture which Goethe referred to as 'music grown silent'. Today, in many Islamic cities, architecture is no longer music grown silent but sheer noise and cacophony petrified. An art which was a direct call from the Centre and which reflected the Centre and the Transcendent in nearly everyone of its forms" is now threatened by an 'art' of the most debased and opaque nature whose source of inspiration is revealed by the veil of ugliness with which it shrouds the environment.

The same conflict is to be seen in the auditory arts. Classical Arabic, Persian and North Indian music, all of which are among the highest expressions of Islamic art, have to compete with music of a much lower order of inspiration, to put it mildly, not only on a particular programme but sometimes even within the same composition. Classical poetry likewise has to contend with an army of young poets often cut off from their own traditional roots but bent on imitating at all costs not only the content but even the form of modern European and American poetry. Even the chanting of the Holy Quran, that supreme form of Islamic sacred art, is sometimes mutilated beyond recognition in many city centres where indiscriminate use is made of loudspeakers as if people wished to compete with the traffic noise through sheer volume. Altogether, in the realm of forms as. in the realm of ideas, there remains an acute tension and confrontation between two contending worlds within which the contemporary Muslim has to live and to make daily decisions.

Conflicts and Tensions

As far as political, social and economic life are concerned, the conflicts and tensions are so many and at the same time so evident that there is no need to delve into them here. Numerous studies have already been devoted to them in the East and the West. The general trend in these domains as elsewhere is towards the secularization of the economic and political life of the Muslim peoples in total contrast to the Islamic conception, which has sacralized man's daily life including, of course, his political and economic activities and institutions.

As an example of the contrasts created within these fields and the dilemmas brought into being for the present-day Muslim who is aware of the world about him may be mentioned the concept of freedom. In the traditional Islamic view, absolute freedom belongs to God alone and man can gain freedom only to the extent that he becomes God-like. All the restrictions imposed upon his life by the Shari'ah or upon his art by the traditional canons are seen not as restrictions upon his freedom but as the indispensable aids which alone make the attainment of real freedom possible. The concept of hurriyyah (the word into which 'freedom' is usually translated today in modern Arabic) is taken from the post-Renaissance idea of individual freedom, which means ultimately imprisonment within the narrow confines of one's own individual nature. This totally Western idea is so alien to traditional Islam that this word cannot be found in any traditional text with the same meaning it has now gained in modern Arabic. In the Islamic world-view, freedom to do evil or to become severed from the source of all existence is only an illusory freedom. The only real freedom is that which enables man to attain that perfection which allows him to approach and ultimately become unified with the One who is at once absolute necessity and absolute freedom. How far removed is this concept from the current Western notion of freedom, and what confusions are created within the mind of a man who is attracted by the pull of both ideas! These confusions affect nearly all of his daily decisions and his relations with nearly all the institutions of society from the family to the state. And they reflect upon art as well as morality, influencing individual patterns of behaviour in matters as far apart as sex and literary style.

These are only some of the dilemmas the contemporary Muslim in contact with the modern world faces. Many more could be added in nearly every domain of life. Together these contending factors have succeeded in converting the life and thought of most Modernised Muslims into a patchwork of conflicting thoughts and actions whose contradictory nature remains often hidden from themselves. It might, of course, be asked why this dilemma must exist at all. Why cannot Muslims simply evaluate modern civilization according to the principles of their own tradition and simply reject what is opposed to these principles? The answer lies in the state of mind of most Modernised Muslims, who, having been witness to the superior power of the modern West in the economic and military fields, fall under the spell of everything else that comes from the West, from philosophy to ethics, from social theories to canons of beauty. Moreover, many of them display a sense of inferiority vis-a-vis the West which is truly amazing. They take much too seriously the various currents that issue forth from the West and usually last but a short time, and they make every effort possible either to conform to them or to distort the teachings of Islam to appear in harmony with these currents. The source of the tension that exists within the soul of the Modernised Muslim is precisely the strong pull of the modern world upon a segment of the Islamic ummah (Islamic community) whose hold upon its tradition and whose roots within the tradition have been weakened during, and as a result of, that very historical process which has enabled modernism to spread throughout the Islamic world.

Segment of the Islamic World

It must, however, be added that there is also a vast segment of the Islamic world which, although touched by the storm of modernism, has its roots firmly grounded in the Islamic tradition and, in fact, sees in the events that pass over the surface of the earth today a confirmation rather than a denial of Islam, for these very events concerning the latter days were predicted long ago in traditional Islamic sources. The Holy Prophet (upon whom be peace) spoke more than once of conditions arising at the end of time about which men would question whether the Prophet had mentioned anything concerning them, that is, events which would break the mould of traditional Islamic life completely. He spoke of mountains being moved from their station, alluding to the devastation brought upon the natural environment. He spoke through his God-given knowledge of these and many other events to which the modern world is now becoming witness.

These confirmations cannot but strengthen the faith of those contemporary Muslims who are firmly rooted in their own tradition, while those whose faith has become shaken as a result of the corroding influence of modernism are suspended within a field of tension, between the rim and the axis, between secularism and modernism on the one hand and the sacred and the traditional on the other. Such people are therefore also in profound need of a message from the Centre, a message that would be authentic and at the same time reinterpreted in a fresh manner to save them from their particular condition of animated suspension and intellectual paralysis. Although their condition differs from that of Western man both psychologically and mentally, their need for a return to the Centre is as urgent, for they, like Western man who in an earlier period of his history became cut off from his spiritual traditions, are faced with the uncertainties of life and death, with a vacuum which cannot but be saved by the sacred. However, in contrast to modern Westerners, contemporary Muslims belong to a tradition which is still fully alive and needs only to be re-lived and to have its immutable principles applied again to existing conditions for them to be saved from the whirlpool of doubt and uncertainty into which they have cast themselves almost with the innocence of children imitating a 'sophisticated' adult, but without being truly innocent. Far as the Quran has asserted so often, man is responsible for his actions before God, and the Modernised Muslim is certainly no exception to this divinely ordained principle.

8

Thoughts in Practice

An hour of meditation is better than sixty years of acts of worship.

(Prophet's Hadith)

Knowledge without action is like a tree without fruit.

(Arabic proverb)

Having dealt with the role that Sufism can play in fulfilling the spiritual needs of modern man in general, we now turn to a particular aspect of the Islamic tradition, namely the relation between contemplation and action, which concerns so directly the present-day plight of Western man to which brief reference has already been made in the previous chapter (pp. 58-9). One of the basic problems of modern man is the divorce between contemplation and action, and in fact the almost complete destruction of the former by the latter, even in religious circles which were always devoted to the contemplative life. This loss of balance between these two primordial modes of human existence is itself another consequence of the loss of the Centre and the attempt made by modern man to remain content with the periphery, with dispersive action independent of the vision and message from the Centre which alone can prevent human action from becoming meaningless dissipation. It is, therefore, of particular importance, as an instance of bringing the doctrinal and practical cachings of the Islamic tradition to bear upon the existing problems of Western man, to turn to the message of Islam concerning the contemplative and active lives as possibilities for man to follow in his terrestrial journey.

The two quotations at the beginning of this chapter, if interpreted in the light of the question of the relation between contemplation and action, express their just relationship in Islam, a religion which, as already stated, has never allowed the'contemplative and active lives to become totally divorced from each other or to be separately institutionalized. For the modern world, which is immersed so completely in a way of acting and doing bound to purely terrestrial ends that it has lost sight of the meaning of contemplation, let alone its primacy over action, it is hardly conceivable that in a civilization such as that of Islam action and contemplation should exist side by side harmoniously and, in fact, complement each other. Today it is difficult to imagine a universe of thought, action and being in which contemplation leads to action, and action on the spiritual plane becomes the way of access to the inner garden of contemplation.

Contemplation in Islamic spirituality, as in other integral traditions, is essentially a knowledge that relates the knower to higher modes of being. It is identified with shuhud (vision) and ta'ammul (literally 'to regard attentively') and is related to tafakkur (meditation) in traditional Islamic sources. It is referred to constantly in the Quran, which commands man to contemplate the beauties of the Universe and their divine prototypes. The essentially gnostic character of Islamic spirituality lends a contemplative air to all the authentic manifestations of Islam, including, of course, its sacred art, and causes the soul of the Muslim to tend towards contemplation as that of a Christian tends toward sacrifice. There lies deep within the texture of the soul moulded by the message of the Quran a tendency to uproot itself from the world of multiplicity and to establish itself at the centre of that 'void' which symbolizes Divine Unity and whose reflection is to be found in both virgin nature and in Islamic sacred art. There is the tendency within the soul of the Muslim to be satisfied with the contemplation of a single flower, a blade of wheat, a solitary bush or tree, which, being epiphanies of the Divine, all provide even more than the contemplative eye needs to behold, and all serve as the gateway to the Infinite. For as the Persian poem states,

> If thou dissectest the heart of any atom thou shalt behold a sun within it.
>
> (Hatif of Ispahan)

Moreover, in the Islamic context, this contemplation has always been wedded to action understood in its traditional sense. The contemplative form of Islamic spirituality has never been opposed to correct action and has in fact often been combined with an irresistible inner urge to action. It is this inner unity that made Islamic civilization at the height of its power one of the most virile and active in human history at the same time that it harboured within itself a most intense contemplative life.

Here again the message of the Quran expresses the rapport between contemptation or knowledge and action, between al-'ilm and al-'amal, which was divinely ordained for the Islamic community. Throughout the Quran the injunction to contemplate God's wisdom in creation as well as in its meta-cosmic reality is followed by injunctions to act correctly and according to principles derived from that wisdom. The call to daily prayer in its Shi'ite form, based on formulae drawn from the Quran, serves as a good example of this principle, for it summarizes the hierarchic relationship between God's wisdom, man's knowledge of it and the action which issues from this knowledge. The second part of the call to prayer (adhan) consists of three phrases: *hayy 'ala'l-salat*, hurry to prayer, *hayy 'ala'l-falah*, hurry to salvation, *hayy 'ala khayr al-'amal*, hurry to the best act, good works or correct action. Prayer, which in its highest form is contemplative and unitive, leads to salvation or deliverance of the soul from all bondage and imperfection and this in turn leads to correct action. Without prayer or contemplation one cannot be in a state of grace or goodness and without being good one cannot do good. Correct action depends on the correct mode of being, which in turn issues from the correct relation with the source of all existence through prayer, which in its most exalted mode is pure contemplation. How often is this simple truth forgotten in the modern world where men want to do good without being good, to reform the world without reforming themselves, to exalt action and belittle contemplation, unaware that without observance of the above hierarchy no action can ever yield completely fruitful results, especially so far as human welfare in its broadest sense is concerned.

Contemplation and Action

In the light of the innate relationship between contemplation and action contained in the formulae of the *adhan* it can be said that although Contemplation and action are complementary, they are not on an equal footing. Contemplation and meditation, which is closely related to it, stand above action, as the hadith about an hour of meditation being more worthy than sixty years of acts of worship reveals. At the same time, correct action follows from contemplation and is related to the realized aspect of knowledge which contemplation in fact makes possible. The Arabic saying that knowledge without action is like a tree without fruit can be interpreted to mean precisely that theoretical knowledge is incomplete if it is not actualized through contemplation into realization, which in turn leads to a transformation and, in fact, to the 'death and resurrection' of man and thus to the correct mode of action, which issues effortlessly from the newly acquired mode of being. It means that such theoretical knowledge has not fulfilled its proper function. Contemplation alone can turn this theoretical knowledge into concrete realization leading in turn to correct action, which may be inward or outward, depending on the conditions chosen for the man by the hand of destiny. It can turn the theoretical metaphysical doctrine, which is like a purifying snow within the mind, to a fire in the centre of the heart, a fire which not only melts the heart but also enlivens the limbs and provides them with a new vitality.

Relating Two Views

The relationship between contemplation and action in human life thus described is an echo, in the matrices of time and space, of the principial domain, and an image, although in reverse, of the cosmogonic act itself. In the Quran, the act of creation, the fiat lux, is expressed in the majestic verse

> But His command, when He intendeth a thing, is only that he saith unto it: 'Be!' and it is.
>
> (XXXVI; 82, Pickthall trans.)

Creation is related to an act which at the same time bestows existence and knows all things in principle. The act of God is at once the Word or Logos (al-kalimah) and the Intellect (al-'oql). Therefore, not only does God utter the word kim (Be!), but also the spiritual root (malakut) of all things resides in His presence, as the Quranic verse immediately following the one above confirms:

> Therefore glory be unto Him in Whose hand is the dominion (malakut or 'spiritual root') over all things! Unto Him ye will be brought back. (XXXVI; 83)

The Divine Act, therefore, is inextricably related to the Divine contemplation of the essences of things, of their a'yan, or to use the terminology of the Quranic verse just cited, their malakut, which means at once 'dominion' and the higher planes of reality or the spiritual world.

Furthermore, in Sufi metaphysics and cosmology, which are based directly on the Quranic revelation, the creation of the Universe is conceived as a 'breathing' by God upon the immutable archetypes (al-a'yan al-thabitah), which are God's knowledge of all things as well as their spiritual essence. The 'breath of the Compassionate' (nafas al-Rahman) externalizes the Divine possibilities in the form of external objects. The Divine Act creates the cosmos through contemplation, a cosmos which itself is the result of God's contemplation of Himself for it was in order to contemplate His own Beauty that God created the Universe.

Islamic Philosophers

Likewise, according to the Islamic philosophers such as Ibn Sina, the very substance of the Universe is the result of God's contemplation of Himself. By contemplating Himself, the Necessary Being (viajib al-wujud)' causes to exist the First Intellect, and the First Intellect in turn the Second Intellect, down to the world of generation and corruption in which man resides. Contemplation and existence, knowledge and being, are interrelated, and on the highest plane God's act and self-knowledge are ultimately the same.

Spiritual Realization

In the process of spiritual realization, which is in a way the reversal of the cosmogonic act, namely a journey by means of the arc of ascent (al-qaus al-su'udi) through all the degrees that have been brought into being by the cosmogonic act in the stages of the descending are (al-qaws al-nwsuli) of cosmic manifestation, contemplation and action are once again interrelated. Contemplation leads to correct action, and action, conceived as inner spiritual travail as well as external acts which put the soul in the right state to undergo the inner alchemy, leads to the doors of contemplation. But because man must know in order to act, contemplation, as already stated, always precedes action in a principial manner. Thus the contemplative man is held in higher esteem in traditional Islamic society than the man of action, as the famous hadith testifies:

> The ink of the man of knowledge is more worthy than the blood of the martyr.

Yet precisely because there is no monasticism in Islam; because Islam is a society of 'married monks' ; because the Divine Law of Islam (the Shari'ah) is at once a code of action and a way of preparing the soul for the flights of contemplation in the spiritual world; and because of many other factors, the ink and the blood have never been totally divorced, and the Islamic order has preserved a remarkable balance between the contemplative and the active lives, a balance which cannot be fully understood by a merely theoretical discussion of the subject from the outside. As long as man does not participate in tradition in an operative manner and does not benefit from the grace or barakah issuing from its rites and other sacred forms, the complementarity of the contemplative and the active lives is most difficult to conceive. It happens often in the Western world today that both contemplation and action are thought about abstractly and categorized logically, but rarely are they lived and practised correctly, with the result that their inner complementarity is rarely appreciated or understood. How often in the modern world does one hear from men who have only a theoretical knowledge of tradition without actual participation in it, that such and such a way of life corresponds to the way of action and such and such another to contemplation; that one must do such a thing according to one particular traditional source and contemplate in such a way according to another, as if one were collecting art pieces from various parts of the world for a museum exhibition. Yet, although all authentic traditional sources speak with authority, they cannot be understood by a simply theoretical grasp of the teachings they contain nor can selections be made from their teachings by men who do not follow one tradition themselves and who ultimately place their own selves as the judge of God-given traditions.

So, many modern men, therefore, who rely only on books and simply speak about tradition without practising it, are never able to perform correct action in the spiritual sense, not to speak of reaching states of contemplation which in their pure form, alone possessing spiritual efficacy, belong only to the traditional universe. The man who does not practise a spiritual way cannot experience that inner certitude, that inner attachment of one's being to the Divinity, which makes of action an application of immutable principles and the gateway to the world of contemplation, which brings about a state of unity whereby contemplation and action are wedded in an indissoluble union. In fact, what is invocation (dhikr), that central practice of Sufism, but such a wedding between action and contemplation at their highest level? There is an immeasurable difference between the man who does not practise a tradition and does not live 'existentially' attached to a traditional world and one who participates in such a world, especially if he be one whose participation is active, if he be one who lives in the awareness of being motivated and moved at every moment of life by the 'hands' of God according to the Quranic verse

> The Hand of Allah is above their hands. As the Alexandrian Sufi Ibn 'Ata'allah al-Iskandari states:
>
> (XLVIII; 10)

> He who is negligent awakens in the morning by considering what he is going to do,

And he who is wise by considering what God will do with him.

There is an immense, difference between the two, even in the context of the traditional world. How much greater is the difference in a world such as the modern one in which many men live in a state of total amnesia or at best a simply theoretical and cerebral understanding of tradition, a state which hides from them the possibilities of practising the traditional life in an active way and of opening inner doors to the world of contemplation amidst external circumstances and situations which, seen only from the outside, appear opposed to such possibilities and incongruent with the spiritual life.

Effects on Society

When we turn to the actual possibilities of practising the contemplative life within the Islamic tradition, we are faced at first sight with a situation which seems to leave out the possibility of a contemplative life, if this form of life is identified with one form or another of monasticism, as in Christianity or Buddhism. Monasticism is banned according to the famous dictum,

> 'There is no monasticism in Islam', but this institutional ban does not by any means imply the closing of the door to the life of contemplation. On the contrary, Islamic spirituality, being gnostic in nature, is based directly upon contemplation and, as stated above, there is in the Muslim soul a tendency toward contemplation which is combined with combativeness (jihad), understood in its esoteric sense of removing all the obstacles which veil the Truth and make it inaccessible. As we have seen in the previous chapter, Sufism, the main manifestation of Islamic esotericism, contains within itself the possibility of the most intense contemplative life, not because it is a monachisme errant as some orientalists have called it, but because such a perspective lies by nature within the Islamic revelation and constitutes its essence.

The unitary principle of Islam, however, could not permit this contemplative way to become crystalized as a separate social organization outside the matrix moulded by the injunctions of the Divine Law or SharVah. It had to remain as an inner dimension of that Law and institutionally as an organization integrated into the Islamic social pattern and inseparable from it. As a result, contemplatives of the highest order have often combined their life of contemplation with the most intense forms of activity, and throughout Islamic history outstanding Sufis have been known to be scholars, artists, teachers and even administrators and rulers. In such cases, the inner contemplative life has intensified and given meaning to their acts rather than in any way diminishing their efficiency or appropriateness.

In the case of women, people with a Christian background familiar with the distinction between Mary and Martha, and aware of the figures of such outstanding Christian women contemplatives and saints as Hildegard of Bingen and Catherine of Sienna, often find it difficult to understand how the possibility of the contemplative life could exist for a woman in Islam. Putting aside certain female ascetics like Rabi'ah, who is one among many female saints and mystics in Islam, most contemplative Muslim women have, like men, found the possibility of the contemplative life within the matrix of the Muslim social order itself. To accept one's destiny as the wife and mother who is of necessity concerned with daily problems, and to submit oneself to one's social position and duties with the awareness that this is in reality submitting oneself to the Divine Will have led many Muslim women to an intensely contemplative inner life amidst, and integrated into, the type of active life imposed upon her by the hands of destiny. The Muslim woman's acceptance of her role and duty as specified by Islamic teachings echoes the state of spiritual poverty or/ay and even offana', or 'annihilation', in God, and can lead, when combined with true piety and devotion to spiritual practices, to these states. For both men and women in Islam, the contemplative life lies not outside but within the active norms of life specified by the Shari'ah, exceptional cases and circumstances as willed by God being, of course, always possible.

Essential Rapport

The most essential rapport between contemplation and action in Islam is to be found in prayer, especially in quintessential prayer or invocation (dhikr) as practised by the Sufis. Therein contemplation and action become unified. Perfect action, which is the dhikr, leads to contemplation (shuhud or mush-Shadah), while contemplation is itself the dhikr inasmuch as the dhikr is unified with 'Him who is invoked' (madhkw). In perfect invocation, he who invokes or performs the act of invocation (dhiikir) becomes united with the dhikr and the madhkw in a supreme union which transcends the dichotomy between action and contemplation, knowledge and existence, the knower and the known, and in which all polarities are embraced within the essential and at the same time primordial Unity.

One can, moreover, distinguish in the dhikr, or unitive prayer, a contemplative action and an active contemplation. The incantatory methods of Sufism, if practised under the direction of a master and within the protective matrix of traditional orthodoxy, are all forms of contemplative action at the highest level, leading ultimately to union with God. Inasmuch as the process of realization is, as already asserted, in a sense the reversal of the cosmogonic act, the traversing of the ascending are (al-qaws al-fu'udt) on the path of return to the Source and Origin by means of the contemplative act results in going from a state in which knowledge and existence are separated to a state in which they are united. As a result, in a mysterious fashion the agent who performs the contemplative act is able to transcend his own limited existence as agent through his very action. The secret of this paradox lies in the fact that in the dhikr man performs an act, but an act that is preceded by contemplation, an act which is also a state of being, an act which is ultimately not the act of man but the act of God. Hence, in the same way that through the Word God created the world, again through His Word—the dhikr, which is mysteriously the act of man participating in the eternal and immutable act of God—creation ascends in the scale of being and finally returns to its Source. Quintessential prayer is a contemplative act which leads to pure contemplation and finally union.

As for active contemplation, it too is nothing but the dhikr seen from another point of view. Sufism is not a passive form of mysticism. It is a journey (suluk) in search of Divine Knowledge, the attainment of which leads to union and to the overcoming of the separation between man in his fallen state and man as the Universal and Perfect Man (al-insan al-kamil), who is in eternal union with God because he is the perfect mirror in whom the Divine Names and Qualities are reflected. There is, then, in the very method of Sufism or the dhikr, as it is combined with various forms of meditation (fikr), an active contemplation of the spiritual realities. For those who actually tread the path, the salikun, in contrast to the stationary members of Sufi orders who remain satisfied with being simply blessed with the grace of initiation (the mutabarr-ikun), the whole of the spiritual work is continuously combined with the element of active contemplation in which progress upon the spiritual path is achieved through an active participation of the whole being of the adept.

All this explains why, in Islam, one of the symbols of the Universal Man, who embodies the full realization of the truth and in whom the dhikr has become fully operative, is the Seal of Solomon. The triangle with its base toward heaven symbolizes contemplation, and the other, in the reverse position, symbolizes action. It is this perfect harmony and wedding between the two that makes the act of the contemplative at once the sword that discriminates between truth and error and establishes harmony and justice, and the brush that paints upon the canvas of time and space the beauties of the spiritual world and opens thereby the gate for the return to that world through the very contemplation of the forms of beauty thus created.

The relationship between action and contemplation described on its most essential level as quintessential orison is reflected also on the plane of the study of nature and of the creation of art. Islamic science certainly enabled man to gain knowledge of nature and also to act upon nature, as we see in agriculture, medicine and the like. But the final goal of this science was to enable man to contemplate nature and to aid him to act upon himself and to remake himself with the help of the contemplative knowledge thus gained. Islamic science was concerned with a process which also implied the possibility for nature, considered as the theophany (tajalli), to act upon the soul of man, as well as the possibility for men to 'act' upon nature through the contemplation of its epiphanies. Islamic science thus began with an objectivization of nature which made it an 'object' of study to achieve a unitive knowledge which finally integrated man with his own prototype as well as with the prototype of nature, so that nature became a 'thou', an intimate witness to the Divine Presence. Moreover, action upon nature has always been regulated and kept within limits in the Islamic perspective because the traditional Muslim knows fully that ultimate happiness comes not from endless action turned outward toward the plundering and devastating of nature but from acting inwardly upon oneself to tame one's own lower nature and to 'Islamize the Satan of one's own being', as the Sufis would say.

Modern Science

In direct contrast to this perspective, modern science, which is marked by the complete lack of a contemplative dimension, has sought since the seventeenth century to drive a wedge between man and nature by extending further and further 'the edge of objectivity', with the result that this 'objectivity' has finally led to the total alienation of man from his natural environment, an alienation which, combined with a theory of action as an aggressive externalization of human energy with the aim of indiscriminately raping and plundering nature, has led the world to its present environmental crisis. The relation between contemplation and action in the Islamic sciences of nature, which is derived from the principial relation already delineated, contains a message of the utmost importance for modern man in search of a means to save himself from the catastrophe brought about by his own folly.

Likewise, in Islamic art there is an intimate relation between action and contemplation which recaptures in the world of forms the complementarity existing between the two in the principial order. The artist obviously makes something: that is, he acts in one way or another upon matter. But because he follows traditional patterns, norms, regulations and procedures which are themselves derived from and are the fruit of contemplative vision, his action is subsequent to contemplation and follows in its wake. In the case of many a traditional artist who is himself engaged in spiritual practice, the phase of making or acting is based upon the direct fruit of his own contemplation as well as the fruit of contemplation of previous masters handed down to him through traditional channels. As a result, the various manifestations of Islamic art themselves serve as an aid to contemplation. Whether it be the courtyard of a mosque, an arabesque design, a verse of Sufi poetry or a traditional musical composition, various forms of Islamic art serve the function of strengthening the wings of the soul for its contemplative flight into the heavenly empyrean. Their beauties are, in fact, so many reminiscences of the beauties of paradise which man can taste even here on earth on the wings of contemplation and spiritual vision. They are beauties which do not externalize the soul but draw it to its own Centre. In Islamic art, as in the Islamic sciences of nature, contemplation and action are intertwined and complementary, while the hierarchic relation according to which contemplation precedes action is always preserved. The relation seen in these domains is, moreover, nothing other than the application to these fields of the principial relation existing between them in the spiritual life, one which is so basic and fundamental that it can be seen in every authentic manifestation of Islam itself and also of its arts and sciences.

Operative and Practical Aspects

As far as the operative and practical aspects of man's spiritual life are concerned, the perfect and exemplary relation between contemplation and action is to be found for every Muslim in the life of the Holy Prophet, who is of necessity the model for every form of spiritual life in Islam. If there are those who, as a result of the influence of modernism, seek to belittle the importance of the contemplative life in Islam, they need only study the life of the

Prophet both before the commencement of his prophetic mission and during the twenty-three years when he lived on earth as a prophet. In both periods, he was devoted intensely to contemplation and spent much time in solitude, while at the same time he transformed human history through a series of actions of such far-reaching consequences that they cannot be gauged in ordinary human terms and are beyond the domain of imagination. Likewise if there are those who wish to over-emphasize the importance of external action and to extol action pure and simple as an end in itself, again they need only study the actions of the Prophet, which were always the applications of principles rooted in contemplation and derived from knowledge of the Divine Order.

Of course, no one has the right to claim or to hope to achieve the perfection of a prophet, but the very harmony between contemplation and action, between a heart that was always at peace in the Divine Presence and a mind and body that acted with the utmost determination combined with resignation to the Divine Will—as seen in the exemplary life of the Prophet of Islam—is the perfect embodiment of the ideal relationship and the complementarity between contemplation and action for Muslims. The Prophet thus remains the perfect model (uswah) to follow, and in him is to be seen, in a blinding fashion, perfect contemplative action and active contemplation, and the union of action and contemplation in that coincidental opposition which transcends all duality and opposition. The end of human life according to Islam is to act according to the Divine Will and finally to reach, through self-purification, such a state of knowledge and vision or contemplation as to see God everywhere. The Prophet was that perfect being who acted according to the Divine Will at every moment of his life, his gaze fixed on the Divine realities, contemplating God both beyond manifestation and in every speck of His creation. If the Prophet is thus to be found the perfect manifestation of the complementarity of contemplation and action which lies at the heart of the Islamic way of life and which characterizes, at its highest level of meaning, the central method of realization in Islamic spirituality. His example not only remains supreme for Muslims but is also of the utmost importance for those in the modern world in search of harmonizing once again the contemplative and the active lives and bringing unity to the life of man, whose total submersion in multiplicity and surrender to dispersive action has already drained his life of spiritual quality and meaning and threatens even to destroy the just equilibrium between the soul and the body upon which all human life depends and without which the essential human nature of man becomes devoured by his accidental animality.

9

Islam vs Western World

It is also necessary to turn to the specific challenges of an intellectual and spiritual order which the modern West has placed before the contemporary Muslim and to the role that the Islamic tradition can play in providing the means to answer these challenges. As already mentioned, it is in the nature of things in the present-day situation that if one wishes to discuss the challenges to Islam of the West and in fact of modern civilization in general, one must begin by using the sword of discrimination and by embarking on a kind of 'intellectual iconoclasm' to clear the ground of all the 'idols' which clutter the contemporary scene. Modern civilization, whether in the West or in its overflow in the East, takes pride in having developed the critical mind and the power of objective criticism, whereas in reality it is, in a fundamental sense, the least critical of all known civilizations and the one farthest removed from a true sense of discernment, for it does not possess the objective criteria to judge and criticize its own activities. It is a civilization which fails in every kind of basic reform because it cannot begin with the reform of itself.

There is a traditional Islamic saying according to which Satan hates sharp points and edges. This old adage contains a most profound truth, which applies directly to the present-day situation. The Devil, being everywhere, manifests his influence by dulling all sharp points and edges which are accessible to him, so that sharp distinctions disappear in the milieu dominated by his influence. The edges of doctrines become corroded and their sharp form gradually fades away. Truth and error become ever more confused, and even sacred rites and doctrinal formulations, which are the most precious gifts of God to man, become hazy and indefinite as a result of this corroding influence which makes everything appear indistinct and ambiguous. To discuss the challenge of the modern world to Islam requires, therefore, that this haze be dispelled through a rigorous application of intellectual discernment based ultimately upon thė shahadah, whose first stroke when written in Arabic is, in fact, in the form of a sword. This sword must be used to break the false idols of the new age of ignorance (jdhiliyyah), idols which so many Muslims accept without even bothering to question their nature. It must be used to cut away and remove all the false ideas and "isms' that clutter the mind of Modernised Muslims. It must help to chisel the soul of the contemporary Muslim from an amorphous mass into a sharp crystal which glows in the Divine Light, for a crystal glows precisely because of its sharply defined edges.

Criticism of the Modern World

It should never be forgotten that in the present situation any form of criticism of the modern world based upon metaphysical and religious principles is an act of charity in its profoundest sense and in accordance with the most central virtues of Islam. Also one should never forget—considering a certain attitude prevailing among some Muslims who are afraid of being critical for fear of seeming discourteous, or lacking in adab (which in the traditional Islamic languages means at once courtesy, correctness of manners, culture and literature)—that the Prophet of Islam (upon whom be peace) not only possessed adab in its most perfect form but also asserted the Truth in the most straightforward and naked manner. There were moments of his life when he was extremely categorical, and he never sacrificed the Truth for the sake of adab. Islam has never taught that one should accept that two and two make five in order to display adab. In fact, adab has always been the complement to the perception and assertion of the Truth in every situation and circumstance. Once, an eminent spiritual authority from North Africa said, 'Do you know what adab is? It is to sharpen your sword so that when you have to cut a limb it does not hurt.' It is this type of attitude that is needed by Muslims in their discussion of the West and its challenges to Islam. The Truth not only has a right to our lives and our beings but also has the prerogative to ask us to make sense to others and to express and expound it whenever and wherever possible. Today we need to be critical, even to the degree of stringency, precisely because such an attitude is so rare and so much in demand.

What is lacking in the Islamic world today is a thorough examination and careful criticism of all that is happening in the modern world. Without such a criticism nothing serious can ever be done in confronting the West. All the statements of Modernised Muslims which begin with the assertion, 'The way to harmonize Islam and . . .'—whatever may follow the'and' are bound to end in failure unless what follows is another divinely revealed and inspired world-view. Otherwise, attempts to harmonize Islam and Western socialism or Marxism or existentialism or evolution or anything else of the kind are doomed at the start by the very fact that they begin without exposing the system or 'ism' under question to a thorough criticism in the light of Islamic criteria, and also because they consider Islam as a partial view of things to be complemented by some modern ideology rather than as a complete system and perspective in itself, whose very totality excludes the possibility of its becoming a mere adjective to modify some other noun which is taken almost unconsciously as central in place of Islam. The rapid change in fashions of the day which makes Islamic socialism popular one day and liberalism or some other Western 'ism' the next is itself proof of the absurdity and shallowness of such an approach. He who understands the structure of Islam in its totality knows that it can never allow itself to become reduced to a mere modifier or contingency vis-a-vis a system of thought which remains independent of it or even hostile to it.

Defensive and Apologetic Attitude

The defensive and apologetic attitude adopted by so many Modernised Muslims towards various fashionable modes of thought that issue from the West almost with the rapidity of seasonal changes is closely allied to their lack of a critical sense and of a discerning spirit. Usually, obvious shortcomings and that which is easy to criticize are criticized, but few have the courage to stand up and criticize the basic fallacies of our times. It is easy to point out that the life of students in traditional madrasahs is not hygienic, but it is much more difficult to take a firm stand and assert that much of what is taught in modern educational institutions is far more deadly—for the soul of the students—than the physically unhealthy surroundings of some of the old madrasah buildings. There are too few people in the Islamic world who can confront the West and criticize and answer with the sword of the Intellect and the Spirit the very basis of the challenge with which the West confronts Islam. Such is the case today—but it does not have to be so. There is no logical reason why a new intellectual elite could not develop in the Islamic world, an elite which would be able to provide an objective criticism of the modern world from the point of view of the eternal varities contained within the message of the Islamic revelation, applying the God-given treasures of Islam to the wretched situation of modern man and the ever more serious plight he faces.

Various Angles

As already discussed there are today essentially two main classes of people in the Islamic world concerned with religious, intellectual and philosophical questions: the *'ulama'* and other religious and traditional authorities in general (including the Sufis), and the modernists still interested in religion. Only now is a third group gradually coming into being which is traditional like the *'ulama'* but also knows the modern world. As far as the 'ulama' and other traditional spiritual authorities are concerned, it has already been shown that they usually do not possess a profound knowledge of the modern world and its problems and complexities. But they are the custodians of the Islamic tradition and its protectors, without whom the very continuity of the tradition would be endangered. They are usually criticized by the modernists for not knowing European philosophy and science or the intricacies of modern economics and the like. But this criticism, which is again of the facile kind, is for the most part ill-directed. Those who possessed the financial and political power in the Islamic world during the past century rarely allowed the madrasahs to develop in the direction of making it possible for the 'ulama' to gain a better knowledge of the modern world without becoming corrupted by it. In the few places where attempts were made to modify the madrasah curriculum, the hidden intention was more often to do away with the traditional educational system by deforming it beyond hope, rather than to really extend its programme to embrace courses which would acquaint the students with the modern world as seen in the light of Islamic teachings. Furthermore, few attempts have been made to create institutions which would provide a bridge between the traditional madrasahs and modern educational institutions. In any case, the modernists have no right to criticize the 'ulama' for a lack of knowledge of things which they never received the opportunity to master.

As for the second class, whose attitudes have been analyzed in previous chapters, they are the product of either Western universities or universities in the Islamic world which more or less ape the West. Now, universities in the Islamic world are themselves in a state of crisis which stems from the question of identity, for an educational system is organically related to the culture within whose matrix it functions. A jet plane can be made to land in the airport of no matter which country in Asia or Africa and be identified as part of that country. But an educational system cannot be simply imported; the fact that modern universities are facing a crisis in the Islamic world of a different nature from that which is found in the West is itself proof of this assertion. The crisis could not but exist because the indigenous Islamic culture is still alive. Moreover, this crisis affects deeply those who are educated in these universities and who are usually called the 'intelligentsia'. This term, like that of 'intellectual', is a most unfortunate one, in that often those so characterized are the farthest removed from the domain of the intellect in its true sense. But, by whatever name they are called, most of those who are products of

Western-oriented universities have one feature in common: a predilection for all things Western and a sense of inferiority relative to things Islamic. This sense of inferiority vis-a-vis the West among so many Modernised Muslims, which is, moreover, shared by Modernised Hindus, Buddhists and other Orientals in general who are affected by the psychosis of modern forms of idolatry, is the greatest malady facing the Islamic world, and afflicts most deeply the very group which one would expect to face the challenge of the West. The encounter of Islam with the West cannot therefore be discussed without taking into consideration that mentality which is in most cases the product of a modern university education, a mentality which, during the past century, has been responsible for most of the apologetic Islamic works concerned with the encounter of Islam and the West.

Modernised Approach

This apologetic, Modernised approach to the crisis of the encounter of Islam and the West has tried to answer the challenge of the West by bending over backwards to show in one way or another that this or that element of Islam corresponds to just what is fashionable in the West today, while other elements, for which there could not be found a Western equivalent by even the greatest stretch of the imagination, have been simply brushed aside as unimportant or even extraneous later 'accretions'. Endless arguments have been presented for the hygienic nature of the Islamic rites or the 'egalitarian' character of the message of Islam, not because such things are true if seen in the larger context of the total Islamic message, but because hygiene and egalitarianism are currently accepted ideas and norms in the West—or at least they were before the Hippie movement. By affirming such obvious and too-easily defensible characteristics, the apologists have evaded the whole challenge of the West, which threatens the heart of Islam and which no attempts to placate the enemy can avert. When surgery is needed there must be a knife with which to remove the infected part. Also, when error threatens religious truth nothing can replace the sword of criticism and discernment. One cannot remove the negative effect of error by making peace with it and pretending to be its friend.

The apologetic attitude is even more pathetic when it concerns itself with philosophical and intellectual questions. When one reads some of this apologetic literature, which issued mostly from Egypt and the Indian subcontinent at the beginning of this century and which tried to emulate already very stale and dead debates between theology and science in Victorian England or in France of the same period, the weakness of such works, which were supposed to answer the challenge of the West, becomes completely evident, even more so against the background of the decades that have since gone by. Of course at that time one could also hear the strong voice of the traditional authorities, who, basing themselves on the immutable principles of the Islamic revelation, tried to answer these challenges on a religious level, even if they were not aware of the more abstruse and hidden philosophical and scientific ideas involved. But this voice gradually diminished, without of course ceasing to exist altogether, while the other, that of the modernists, became ever more audible and invasive.

This phenomenon has led to the rather odd situation today in which, among the educated classes, practically the most ardent defenders of modern Western civilization in the world are Westernized Orientals. The most intelligent students at Oxford or Harvard are far less confident in the West and its future than those Modernised Orientals who for some time have sacrificed everything at the altar of modernism and are now suddenly faced with the possibility of the total decomposition of their idol. Therefore, they try ever more desperately to cling to it. For the Modernised Muslims, especially the more extreme among them, the 'true meaning' of Islam has been for some time now what the West has dictated. If evolution is in vogue, 'true Islam' is evolutionary. If it is socialism that is the fashion of the day, the 'real teachings' of Islam are based on socialism. Those acquainted with this mentality and the works it has produced are most aware of its docile, servile and passive nature. Even in the field of law, how often have completely non-Islamic and even anti-Islamic tenets been adopted with a bismillah added at the beginning and a bihi nasta'in at the end, while the substance of the material contained in between has been derived or even copied from some Western code?

Western Civilization

Now suddenly this group, who were willing to sell their soul to emulate the West, see before their eyes the unbelievable sight of the floundering of Western civilization itself. What a painful sight it must be for such men! Therefore they try, in the face of all evidence, to defend the Western 'value system' and become ferociously angry with those Westerners who have themselves begun to criticize the modern world. Probably, if the obvious decomposition of modern civilization, which became gradually evident after the Second World War, had become manifest after the First World War, when the traditions of Asia were much more intact, a great deal more from these traditional civilizations could have been saved. But the hands of destiny had charted another course for mankind. Nevertheless, even in the present situation, there is a great deal that can be done, for as the Persian proverb says, 'As long as the root of the plant is in water there is still hope.' On the plane of true activity, according to traditional principles, the possibility of doing something positive always exists, including the most obvious and central act of stating the truth, and acting accordingly. Despair has no meaning where there is faith (iman). Even today, if in the Islamic world there comes to be formed a true intelligentsia at once traditional and fully conversant with the modern world, the challenge of the West can be answered and the core of the Islamic tradition preserved from the paralysis which now threatens its limbs and body.

To realize exactly how much can still be saved in the Islamic world, it is sufficient to remember that for the vast majority of Muslims even now, Islamic culture is still a living reality in which they live, breathe and die. From Indonesia to Morocco, for the overwhelming majority, Islamic culture must be referred to in the present tense and not as something of the past. Those who refer to it in the past tense belong to that very small but vocal minority which has ceased to live within the world of tradition and mistakes its own loss of centre for the dislocation of the whole of Islamic society.

Paradoxical Situation

The irony of the situation resides, however, in the fact that it is precisely such a view of Islam as a thing of the past that is held by most of those who control the mass media in many countries in the Islamic world and who therefore exercise an influence upon the minds and souls of men far beyond what their number would justify. In many lands, those who control such means as radio, television and magazines live in a world in which Islamic culture appears a thing of the past precisely because they are so infatuated with the West that no other way of seeing things than the Western one seems to have any reality for them, even if that other way be a still living reality existing on their very doorsteps.

Strangely enough this Westernized minority in the Islamic world has gained a position of ascendancy at the very moment when the West has lost its own moorings completely and does not know what it is doing or where it is going. If a simple Arab or Persian peasant were to be brought to one of the big Middle Eastern airports and asked to observe the Europeans entering the country, the contrast in nothing more than the dress, which varies from that of a nun to practically nude, would be sufficient to impress upon his simple mind the lade of homogeneity and harmony of the products of Western civilization. But even this elementary observation usually escapes the thoroughly Westernized Muslim, who, though usually well-meaning if nothing else, does not want to face the overt contradictions in the civilization he is trying so avidly to emulate.

Of course, despite the predominance and continuation of this attitude in many circles the situation has changed somewhat during the past three decades. Muslims who went to Europe between the two world wars thought of the trees along the Seine or the Thames practically as Shajarat al-tuba and these rivers as the streams of Paradise. Whether consciously or unconsciously, most members of this generation of Modernised Muslims transferred almost completely their image of Paradise and its perfections to Western civilization. But today this homogeneity of reaction and blind acceptance of the West as an idol is no longer to be observed. The inner contradictions of the West that have become ever more manifest during the past three decades no longer permit such an attitude. The present-day generation of Modernised Muslims is much less confident about the absolute value of

Western civilization than their fathers and uncles who went to the West before them. This in itself can be a positive tendency if it becomes the prelude to a positive and objective evaluation of modernism. But so far it has only added confusion to the ranks of Modernised Muslims, and only here and there has it resulted in the appearance of a handful of Muslim scholars who have awakened to the reality of the situation and have ceased to emulate the West blindly. But alas! The main problem, which is the lack of a profound knowledge of the real nature of the modern world based upon the criteria of Islamic culture, remains. There are still too few 'occidentalists' in the Islamic world who could perform for Islam the positive aspect of the function which 'orientalists' have been performing for the West since the eighteenth century.

Weakening of the Confidence

Despite the weakening of the confidence in the West on the part of Modernised Muslims, the Muslims are still on the receiving end in the realm of both ideas and material objects. Lacking confidence in their own intellectual tradition; most-Modernised Muslims are like a tabula rasa waiting to receive some kind of impression from the West. Moreover, each part of the Islamic world receives a different kind of baggage of ideas, depending on the part of the Western world to which it has become closely attached. For example, in the domain of sociology and also, as mentioned above, in philosophy, the Indian sub-continent has closely followed English schools for the past century, and Persia has followed French schools. But everywhere the Modernised circles are sitting and waiting to adopt whatever comes along. One day it is positivism and the next structuralism. Rarely does anyone bother to adopt a truly Islamic intellectual attitude which would act from an immutable centre and in a positive manner with discernment toward all that the wind blows our way. The intellectual situation is as bad as the domain of women's fashion, where in many Islamic lands, women remain completely passive as obedient consumers and emulate blindly whatever a few Western fashion-makers decide for them. In dress fashion as in philosophical and artistic fashion, Modernised Muslims have no role to play at the source where decisions are made.

It is, of course, true that even Western people themselves are hardly aware of the deeper roots of the movements that sweep the West one after another, and that twenty years ago no one foresaw that such an extensive movement as that of the Hippies would become widely spread in the West. But Modernised Muslims are even farther removed from the current in that they are unaware not only of the roots but even of the stages of incubation and growth of such movements and wait until they occupy the centre of the stage, and then react either with surprise or again in a state of blind surrender.

The ecological crisis is a perfect example of this state of affairs. Muslims have waited until the crisis has become the central concern of a vast number of Western people before even becoming aware of the presence of the problem. And even now, how many people in the Islamic World are thinking of this crucial problem in the light of the extremely rich tradition of Islam concerning nature which, in fact, could provide a key for the possible solution of this major crisis, were men to make use of it?

To study in a more concrete fashion the challenges of the West to Islam, it is necessary to take as example some of the 'isms' which are fashionable in the modern world today and which have affected the cultural and even religious life of the Islamic world. Let us start with Marxism, or more generally speaking, socialism. Today in many parts of the Islamic world there is a great deal of talk about Marxism, which, although it does not usually attack Islam directly, has an important indirect effect upon religious life—not to speak of economic and social activity. Many who speak of Marxism or socialism in general in the Islamic world do so with certain existing problems of society in mind for which they are seeking solutions. But very few of them actually know Marxism or theoretical socialism in a serious sense. In spite of all the young Muslim students speaking about Marxism in so many university circles, one wonders how many have actually read Das Kapital, or even important secondary sources, or could defend the Marxist position seriously on a purely rational plane. The Marxist fad has become an excuse for many young Muslims to refuse to think seriously about the problems of Islamic society from the

Islamic point of view and within the matrix of their own social situation. It is enough to accept the label of this black box with its unknown contents to have one's ego inflated and one's mind fall into the illusion that one has become an 'intellectual' or a member of the liberated 'intelligentsia', but an intelligentsia who, following the already established Marxist solutions to all kinds of problems, thought out in a completely different socio-cultural context in other lands, no longer have any responsibility to think in a fresh manner about the problems of Islamic society as an Islamic society. It is precisely this blind following of Marxism as a package whose content is never analyzed, or as an aspirin to soothe every kind of pain, that prepares the ground for the worst kind of demagogy. Instead of discussing problems in a reasonable and meaningful manner,' those who have fallen under the influence of what is loosely called Marxism, develop a blind and unintelligent obedience which leads to a senseless confrontation and finally a mental sclerosis resulting in untold harm to the youth of Islamic society—not to speak of its obvious harm to the life of faith.

Unfortunately, the response given by Islamic authorities to the challenge of dialectical materialism has for the most part consisted until now of arguments drawn from the transmitted (naqli) or religious sciences rather than from the rich intellectual tradition of Islam contained in the traditional intellectual ('aqli) sciences. Now, religious arguments can be presented only to those who already possess faith. Of what use is it to cite a particular chapter of the Quran to refute an idea held by someone who does not accept the authority of the Quran to start with? Many of the works written by the 'ulama' in this field can be criticized precisely because they address deaf ears and present arguments which have no efficacy in the context in question. This is especially saddening considering the fact that the Islamic tradition possesses such a richness and depth that it is perfectly capable of answering on the intellectual level any arguments drawn from modern European philosophy. In reality, what is all modern philosophy before traditional wisdom but a noise that would seek in its self-delusion to conquer Heaven? So many of the so-called problems of today are based on ill-posed questions and on ignorance of truths, and are of a nature which traditional wisdom alone can solve, a traditional wisdom found from ancient Babylonia to mediaeval China, and found, in one of its most universal and certainly most diversified forms, in Islam and in the vast intellectual tradition which Islam has brought into being during its fourteen centuries of existence.

Dead Communism

The danger of Marxism for Islam became aggravated by the appearance in certain Islamic countries, especially within the Arab world, of a Marxism with an Islamic veneer, creating a most tempting trap for certain simple souls. This insidious use of religion, often with direct political aims in mind, is in fact more dangerous than anti-religious and at least 'honest' Marxism, and corresponds to the thought and attitude of that class of men whom the Quran calls the munafiqun (hypocrites). In this case also there is no way to give an Islamic response to answer such pseudo-syntheses intellectually and to demonstrate clearly that Islam is not just anything at all provided a bismillah is added at the beginning, but a total vision of reality which cannot compromise with any half-truths whatsoever.

Another 'ism' of great danger to Islam, one with a longer history of intrusion into the Islamic world than Marxism, is Darwinism or evolutionism in general, whose effect is particularly perceptible among the Muslims of the Indian sub-continent, obviously because of the strong British influence in education in that area. We have already had occasion to speak of the works of outstanding European biologists against evolution and to allude to the proofs brought forth by contemporary anthropologists to show that whatever may have occurred before, man himself has not evolved one iota since he first set foot upon the stage of terrestrial history. But, unfortunately, almost no contemporary Muslim thinker has taken note of these sources and made use of their arguments to support the traditional Islamic view of man. For a notable segment of Modernised Muslims, evolution remains practically like a religious article of faith whose overt contradiction with the teachings of the Quran they fail to realize.

Darwinian Theory of Evolution

In fact, the Darwinian theory of evolution, which is metaphysically impossible and logically absurd, has been subtly woven in certain quarters into some aspects of Islam to produce a most unfortunate and sometimes dangerous blend. We do not mean only the shallow Quranic commentators at the turn of the century, but have in mind even a thinker of the stature of Iqbal, who was influenced by both the Victorian concept of evolution and Nietzsche's idea of the superman. Iqbal is an influential contemporary figure of Islam but, with all due respect to him as a poet, his ideas should be studied in the light of the ijtihad which he himself preached so often. He should certainly not be put on a pedestal. If we analyze his thought carefully we see that he had an ambivalent attitude towards many things, including a love-hate relationship with Sufism. He admired Rumi yet expressed dislike for a figure like Hafiz. This is due to the fact that he was drawn, on the one hand, by the Sufi, and more generally speaking Islamic, idea of the Perfect Man (al-insan al-kamil) and on the other by the Nietzschean idea of the superman, two concepts which are, in fact, the very antipodes of each other. Iqbal made the great mistake of seeking to identify the two. He made this fatal error because, despite his deep understanding of certain aspects of Islam, he had come to take the prevalent idea of evolution too seriously. He demonstrates on a more literate and explicit level a tendency to be found among the many modern Muslim writers who, instead of answering the fallacies of the theory of evolution, have tried to bend over backwards in an apologetic manner to accept it and even to interpret Islamic teachings according to it.

General Tendency

The general tendency among Muslims affected by the evolutionist mentality is to forget the whole Islamic conception of the march of time. The later Quranic chapters about eschatological events and the latter days of mankind are forgotten or passed over in silence. All the hadiths pertaining to the last days and the appearance of the Mahdl are laid aside or malconstrued, either through ignorance or by ill intention. Just the one hadith of the Prophet that asserts that the best generation of Muslims are those who are his contemporaries, then the generation after, then the following generation until the end of time, is sufficient to nullify, from the Islamic point of view, the idea of linear evolution and progress in history. Those who think they are rendering a service to Islam by incorporating evolutionary ideas, as currently understood, into Islamic thought are, in fact, tumbling into a most dangerous pitfall and are surrendering Islam to one of modern man's most insidious pseudo-dogmas, one created in the eighteenth and nineteenth centuries to enable men to forget God.

Moreover, accepting the evolutionary thesis brings into being overt paradoxes in daily life which cannot be easily resolved. If things are going to evolve for the better, then why bother to spend one's effort on improvement? Things are going to get better by themselves anyway. The very dynamism preached by modernists stands in opposition to the usually accepted idea of evolution. Or, seen from another point of view, it can be argued that if the effort, work, movement and the like preached in the modern world are effective, then man can influence his future and destiny. And if he can affect his future then he can also affect it for the worse, and there is no guarantee of an automatic progress and evolution to say the least. All of these and many other paradoxes are brushed aside in certain quarters because of an enfeebled intellectual attitude which has as yet to produce a serious and widely known Islamic response of a metaphysical and intellectual nature to the hypothesis of evolution. The challenge of evolutionary thought has been answered in contemporary Islam in nearly the same way as has the challenge of Marxism. There have been some religious replies based upon the Holy Book, but not an intellectual response which could also persuade the young Muslims whose faith in the Quran itself has been in part shaken by the very arguments of the evolutionary school. Meanwhile, works of evolutionary writers, even of the nineteenth century such as Spencer, who are no longer taught as living philosophical influences in their own homeland, continue to be taught in universities far and wide in the Islamic world, especially in the Indian subcontinent, as if they represented the latest proven scientific knowledge or the latest philosophical school of the West. Few bother even to study the recent anti-evolutionary developments in biology itself or the reassertion of the pre-evolutionary conception of man—views which are gaining ever greater adherence in many circles in the West itself today. And what is worse, there are too few efforts on the part of the Muslim intellectual elite to formulate from Islamic sources the genuine doctrine of man and his relation to the Universe which would act as a criterion for the judgment of any would-be theory of man and the cosmos, evolutionary or otherwise, and which would also provide the light necessary to distinguish scientific facts from mere hypotheses and scientific evidence from cross philosophical materialism parading in the dress of scientific fact or even religious belief.

Another important 'philosophical' challenge to the Islamic world concerns the Freudian and Jungian interpretation of the psyche. The modern psychological and psychoanalytical point of view tries to reduce all the higher elements of man's being to the level of the psyche, and moreover to reduce the psyche itself to nothing more than that which can be studied through modern psychological and psychoanalytical methods. Until now, this way of thinking, in its scientific form, has not affected the Islamic world as directly as has evolutionism, and we do not know of any important and influential Muslim writers who are Freudian or Jungian, but its effect is certain to increase soon. It must therefore be remembered that Freudianism, as well as other modern Western schools of psychology and psychotherapy, are the by-products of a particular society very different from the Islamic. It needs to be recalled also that Freud was a Viennese Jew who turned away from Orthodox Judaism. Few people know that he was connected to a messianic movement which was opposed by the Orthodox Jewish community of Central Europe itself, and that therefore he was opposed to the mainstream of Jewish life, not to speak of Christianity. Many study Freudianism but few delve into its deeper origins which reveal its real nature.

Sufism from the East

Recently one of the outstanding figures of Sufism from the East wrote a series of articles on Sufism and psychoanalysis in

French, making a comparison between the two. With all due respect to him it must be said that he has been too polite and lenient towards psychoanalysis, which is truly a parody of the initiatic methods of Sufism. Fortunately for Muslims, until now the influence of psychoanalysis has not penetrated deeply among them, nor have they felt the need for it. This is due most of all to the continuation of the practice of religious rites such as the daily prayers and pilgrimage. The supplications, 'discourses' and forms of pleading that are carried out in religious centres by men, women and children open the soul to the influx of Divine Grace and are a most powerful means of curing the soul's ailments and untying its knots. These forms of prayer achieve a goal which the psychoanalyst seeks to accomplish without success and moreover often with dangerous results, for he lacks the power which comes from the Spirit and which alone can dominate and control the soul.

But psychoanalytical thought, which is agnostic or even in certain cases demonic, is bound to penetrate gradually into the Islamic world, probably mostly though the translation of Western literature into Arabic, Persian, Turkish, Urdu and other Islamic languages. The effect of such translations will be to bring into being, and in fact is already bringing into being, a so-called 'psychological literature' opposed to the very nature and genius of Islam. Islam is a religion which rejects individualistic subjectivism. The most intelligible material symbol of Islam, the mosque, is a building with a space in which all elements of subjectivism have been eliminated. It is an objective determination of the Truth, a crystal through which radiates the light of the Spirit. The spiritual ideal of Islam itself is to transform the soul of the Muslim, like a mosque, into a crystal reflecting the Divine Light.

Islamic Literature

Truly Islamic literature is very different from the kind of subjective literature we find in the writings of Franz Kafka or at best in Dostoevsky. These and similar writers are, of course, among the most important in modern Western literature, but they, along with most other modern Western literary figures, nevertheless present a point of view which is very different from, and usually totally opposed to, that of Islam. Among older Western literary figures who are close to the Islamic perspective, one might mention first of all Dante and Goethe who, although profoundly Christian, are in many ways like Muslim writers. In modern times, one could mention, on of course another level, T. S. Eliot, who, unlike most modern writers, was a devout Christian and possessed, for this very reason, a vision of the world not completely removed from that of Islam.

In contrast to the works of such men, however, the psychological novel, through its very form and its attempt to penetrate into the psyche of men without possessing any criterion with which to discern Truth as an objective reality, is an element that is foreign to Islam. Marcel Proust was, without doubt, a master of the French language and his In Search of Time Past is of much interest for those devoted to modern French literature, but this type of writing cannot under any conditions become the model for a genuinely Muslim literature. Yet it is this very type of psychological literature that is now beginning to serve as a 'source of inspiration' for a number of writers in Arabic and Persian. It is of interest to note that the most famous modern literary figure of Persia, Sadeq Hedayat, who was deeply influenced by Kafka, committed suicide because of psychological despair and that, although certainly a person of great literary talent, he was divorced from the Islamic current of life. Today, in fact, his ideas are opposed by Islamic elements within Persian society. Nevertheless, such writers, who often deal with psychological problems and disturbances found in Western society, problems which the Muslims have not experienced until now, are becoming popular among the Muslim youth who thereby become acquainted, and even inflicted, with these new maladies.

Worst Tragedies

One of the worst tragedies today in the Muslim world is that there has appeared recently a new type of person who tries consciously to imitate the obvious maladies of the West. Such people, for example, are not really in a state of depression but try to put themselves into one in order to look modern. They compose poetry that is supposed to issue from a tormented and depressed soul whereas they are not depressed at all. There is nothing worse than a state of nihilism except its imitation by someone who is not nihilistic but tries to produce nihilistic literature or art only to imitate the decadence of Western art. The influence of psychology and psychoanalysis, combined with an atheistic and nihilistic point of view and disseminated within the Islamic world through literature and art, presents a major challenge to Islam which can be answered only through recourse to traditional Islamic psychology and psychotherapy contained mostly within Sufism, and also through the creation of a genuinely Islamic literary criticism which would be able to provide an objective evaluation of so much that passes for literature today.

Degree of Penetration

The degree of penetration of anti-Islamic psychological as well as philosophical Western ideas through literature into the Islamic World can be best gauged by just walking through the streets near universities in various Middle Eastern cities. Among the books spread on the ground or on stands everywhere one still observes traditional religious books, especially of course the Quran. But one observes also a larger number of works in Islamic languages dealing with subjects ranging all the way from Marxism and existentialism to pornography, presented usually as 'literature'. There are, of course, rebuttals and answers as well, for Islam and its spirituality are still alive. But the very presence of all this writing itself reveals the magnitude of the challenge.

As far as nihilism is concerned, the Islamic answer is particularly strong and, putting pretenders aside, the Muslims, even the Modernised ones, have not experienced nihilism in the same way as have Westerners, for whom nihilism has become an experience of almost central importance. The main reason for this is that in Christianity the Spirit has been almost always presented in a positive form, as an affirmation, as the sacred art of Christianity reveals so clearly. The void or the nihil has not usually been given a spiritual significance in Christian theology and art, as it has been for example in Islam and also in the Far East. Therefore, as a result of the rebellion against Christianity, modern man has experienced the nihil only in its negative and terrifying aspect, while some have been attracted to Oriental doctrines especially because of the latter's emphasis upon the Void.

In contrast to Christianity, where the manifestation of the Spirit is identified always with an affirmation and a positive form, Islamic art makes use of the 'negative' or the 'Void' itself in a spiritual and positive sense in the same way that metaphysically the first part of the shahddah begins with a negation to affirm the vacuity of things vis-a-vis Allah. The space in Islamic architecture is essentially a 'negative space'. Space in Islamic architecture and city-planning is not the space around an object or determined by that object. Rather, it is the negative space cut out from material forms, as for example in traditional bazaars. When one walks through a bazaar one walks through a continuous space determined by the inner surface of the wall surrounding it, and not by some object in the middle of it. That is why what is happening architecturally in many Middle Eastern cities—such as the building of a large monument in the middle of a square to emulate what one finds in the West— is the negation of the very principles of Islamic art and is based on a lack of understanding of the positive role of negative space and the nihilism in Islamic architecture.

To return to the question of psychology and psychoanalysis, it must be added that the presence of this perspective in so much art criticism in the West has permitted this kind of thinking to seep into the mind of a small but significant portion of Islamic society through art as well as literature— significant because it wields influence and often forms the taste of the psychologically passive masses of traditional Muslims. Traditional Islamic literary tastes are thereby being influenced by the completely anti-traditional ideas emanating from Jungian and Freudian circles and threatening one of the most central and accessible channels of Islamic norms and values. It might, furthermore, be added that, as already mentioned, Jungian psychology is more dangerous than

Freudian in this respect in that it appears to be dealing with the sacred and the noumenal world whereas in reality it is deforming the image of the sacred by confusing the spiritual and the psychological domains and subverting the luminous and transcendent source of archetypes into a collective unconscious which is no more than the dumping ground for the collective psyche of various people and their cultures. Islamic metaphysics, like all true metaphysics, stands totally opposed to this blasphemous subversion as well as to the methods of profane psychoanalysis which are, as already stated, no more than a parody of Sufi techniques. But how many contemporary Muslims are willing to stand up and assert their basic differences rather than try to glide over them in order to placate the modern world with all its fundamental errors and subsequent evils?

Another challenge to Islam which has come to the fore only since the Second World War is the whole series of movements of thought and attitudes loosely bound together under the title of existentialism, which is the latest wave of Western thought to reach the Muslims following various forms of positivism. There are of course many branches of existentialism, ranging from the Existenz Philosophic of the German philosophers to the theistic philosophy of Gabriel Marcel and finally to the agnostic and atheistic ideas of Sartre and his followers. This type of philosophy, which developed on the European continent early in this century, still holds the centre of the stage in many continental countries. Although it has not, as yet, had a serious effect upon the Muslim world, during the past few years its influence—which can be characterized categorically as negative—is beginning to make itself felt, again through art, and more directly through philosophical works as such, which are beginning to influence some Muslims concerned with philosophy and the intellectual life. Because of the anti-metaphysical attitude of much of what is taught in this school and the fact that it has forgotten the meaning of Being in its traditional sense, which lies at the heart of all Islamic philosophy, the spread of existentialism, especially in its agnostic vein, is a most insidious danger for the future of Islamic intellectual life.

Furthermore, there is the tendency in certain quarters to interpret Islamic philosophy itself in the light of Western modes of thought, the latest being the existential school. Muslim 'intellectuals' are directly to blame for this dangerous innovation (bid'ah), which, strangely enough, is also the most blind and unintelligent type of imitation (taqlid). If this type of interpretation continues it will cost the new generation of Muslims very dearly. Today, one sees everywhere in various Muslim countries people learning about their own intellectual and philosophical past from Western sources, many of which may contain useful information and may be of value from the point of view of scholarship, but nearly all of which are of necessity written from a non-Muslim point of view. In the field of thought and philosophy in its vastest sense the countries that have suffered most are those which use English or French as media of instruction in their universities: countries such as Pakistan, the Muslim sectors of India, Malaysia and Nigeria, or the Islamic Maghrib such as Morocco and Tunisia. It is certainly long overdue, with all this talk of anti-colonialism, for Muslims to overcome the worst type of colonialism possible—the colonialism of the mind—and to seek to see and study their own culture, especially its intellectual and spiritual heart, from their own point of view. Even if, God forbid, there are certain Muslims who want to reject some aspect of their intellectual heritage, they would first of all have to know that heritage. Both acceptance and rejection of anything must be based upon knowledge, and there is no excuse for ignorance, no matter what direction one wishes to follow. One cannot reject what one does not know any more than one can accept something in depth without true knowledge. Nor can one throw away what one does not possess. This is a very simple truth, but one that is too often forgotten today.

Some years ago a famous Zen master visited a leading Western university. After his lecture on Zen, a graduate student asked, 'Don't the Zen masters believe that one should burn the Buddhist scrolls and throw away the Buddha images?' The master smiled and answered, 'Yes, but you can only burn a scroll which you possess and throw away an image which you have.' This was a most profound answer. The master meant that you can only transcend the exoteric dimension of religion if you practice that exotericism and subsequently penetrate into its inner meaning and transcend its forms. He who does not practice exotericism cannot ever hope to go beyond it; he merely falls below it and mistakes this fall for a transcending of forms. The same applies on another level to man's traditional intellectual heritage. One cannot go 'beyond' the formulations of the sages of old when one does not even understand them. He who tries to do so mistakes his pitiful ignorance and 'expansion' and apparent 'freedom' from traditional norms of thought—an ignorance which is in reality the worst kind of imprisonment within the limitations of one's own nature—for the true freedom which comes solely from the illimitable horizons of the world of the Spirit and which can be reached only through the vehicle provided by religion and its sapiential doctrines.

Contemporary Muslims should be realist enough to understand that they must begin their journey, in whatever direction they wish to go, from where they are. A well-known Chinese proverb asserts that 'the journey of a thousand miles begins with a single step.' Now this first step must of necessity take place where one is located, and that is as much true culturally and spiritually as it is physically. Wherever the Islamic world is to 'go', it must begin from the reality of the Islamic tradition and from its own real, and not imagined, situation. Those who lose sight of this fact actually do not travel effectively at all. They just imagine that they are journeying. A Pakistani or a Persian or an Arab 'intellectual' who wants to be a leader of thought for the Muslim people must remember who he is, if he wishes to be effective and not be cut off from the rest of Islamic society. No matter how hard he tries to make a corner of Lahore or Tehran or Cairo belong to the setting of Oxford or the Sorbonne, he will not succeed. The so-called Muslim intellectuals of the Westernized kind who complain that they are not understood and appreciated by Islamic society forget that it is they who have refused to appreciate and understand their own culture and society and are therefore rejected by their own community. This rejection is, in fact, a sign of life, an indication that Islamic culture still possesses vitality.

As far as philosophy is concerned, the countries where Muslim languages are used for university instruction are in a somewhat better position, especially Persia, where Islamic philosophy still continues as a living tradition and where it is not easy to say anything at all in the name of philosophy without being seriously challenged by the traditional intellectual elite. But of course even this part of the Muslim world has not been completely spared from condescending and apologetic studies of Islamic thought from the point of view of Western philosophy, though relatively speaking there is less Western philosophic influence there because of the two reasons alluded to above: the language barrier and a still-living tradition of Islamic philosophy. It would be interesting in this connection to compare the effect of the publication in Pakistan of Iqbal's two philosophical works in English, The Development of Metaphysics in Persia and The Reconstruction of Religious Thought in Islam, with the effect of their publication in Persia in their fairly recent translations into Persian.

Yet even in lands using Islamic languages books do appear in languages such as Persian, and particularly Arabic, on philosophy from a perspective totally alien to that of Islam and bearing such titles as Falsafatuna, Our Philosophy, as if philosophy as a vision of the Truth or quest after wisdom or sophia could ever be 'mine' or 'ours'. No Arab or Persian traditional philosopher ever used such an expression. For Muslims who have cultivated Islamic philosophy, philosophy has always been al-falsafah or al-hikmah, 'the philosophy', a vision of the truth transcending the individualistic order and derived from the Truth (al-Haqq) itself. The very appearance of such concepts and terms as 'our philosophy' or 'my thought' in Islamic languages itself reveals the degree of departure from the Islamic norm. It is against such errors that the weapon of the traditional doctrines contained in the vast treasury of Islamic thought must be used, and answers drawn from these sources be provided, before any further erosion of Islamic intellectual life takes place.

Existentialism and Tradition

Returning to the question of existentialism and traditional Islamic philosophy in Persia, it must be mentioned that because of the kind of traditional philosophy surviving there, based on the principiality of existence (asalat al-wujud), and itself called falsa/at al-wujud (which some have mistakenly translated as 'existentialism'), existentialism of the European kind has encountered strong resistance from traditional circles. Actually anyone who has studied traditional Islamic philosophy from Ibn Sina and Suhrawardi to the great expositor of the metaphysics of being, Sadr al-Din Shirazi (Mulla Sadra), will readily understand the profound chasm which separates the traditional Islamic 'philosophy of being' from modern existentialism, which, even in its apparently most profound aspects, can only reach, in a fragmentary fashion, some of the rudimentary teachings contained in their fullness in traditional metaphysics. Henry Corbin, the only Western scholar who has expounded to any extent this later phase of Islamic philosophy in the West, has shown the divergence of views between Islamic philosophy and existentialism and the correctives which the former provides for the latter, in the long French introduction to his edition and translation of Sadr al-Din Shirazi's Kitab al-masha'ir (rendered into French as Le Livre des penetrations metaphysiques). It is incidentally interesting to note that it was through Corbin's translation of Heidegger's Sein und Zeit that Sartre was first attracted to existentialism, while Corbin himself turned completely away from this form of thought to the ocean of the 'Orient of Light' of Suhrawardi and the luminous philosophy of being of Sadr al-Din Shirazi.

One last but urgent and basic problem must be mentioned, and that is the ecological crisis, which was brought into being by modern civilization but which is now a challenge to the very life of men everywhere, including, of course, Muslims in the Islamic world. Anyone who is aware of the situation of the modern world knows that the most immediate problem, at least of a material order, which faces the world is the ecological crisis, the destruction of the equilibrium between man and his natural environment. Islam and its sciences have a particularly urgent and timely message which, as mentioned above, can help to solve, to the extent possible, this major challenge to the world as a whole. However, this message unfortunately receives the least attention from Modernised Muslims themselves.

We know that Muslims avidly cultivated the sciences of nature, such as astronomy, physics and medicine, and made great contributions to them without losing their equilibrium and their harmony with nature. Their sciences of nature were always cultivated within the matrix of a 'philosophy of nature' which was in harmony with the total structure of the Universe as seen from the Islamic perspective. There lies in the background of Islamic science a true philosophy of nature which, if brought to light and presented in contemporary language, can be substituted for the present false natural philosophy. For it is this latter philosophy which, combined with a lack of true metaphysical understanding of first principles, is largely responsible for the present crisis in man's relation with nature.

Unfortunately, the Islamic scientific heritage has only too rarely been studied by Muslims themselves, and when such a study has been made, it has usually been based again on a sense of inferiority which has impelled the authors to try to prove that Muslims preceded the West in scientific discoveries and therefore are not behind the West in their cultural attainment. Rarely is this precious Muslim scientific heritage seen as an alternative path, a science of the natural order which could and did avoid the catastrophic impact which modern science and its applications through technology have created for men. Muslims with vision should be only too happy that it was not they who brought about the seventeenth-century scientific revolution whose logical outcome we see today. Muslim scholars and thinkers must be trained to revitalize the philosophy of nature contained in the Islamic sciences and to study these sciences themselves.

The end thus proposed is very different from the goal of so many Modernised Muslims who pride themselves upon Islam having paved the way for the Renaissance. They reason that since the Renaissance was a great event in history and since Islamic culture helped create the Renaissance, therefore Islamic culture must be of value. This is an absurd way of reasoning, which completely ignores the fact that what the modern world suffers from today is precisely the result of steps taken by the West, mostly during the Renaissance, when Western man rebelled to a large extent against his God-given religion. Muslims should be grateful that they did not rebel against Heaven and had no share in that anti-spiritual humanism which has now resulted in an infra-human world. What Islam in fact did was to prevent the individualistic rebellion against Heaven, the manifestation of the Promethean and Titanesque spirit which is so clearly shown in much of Renaissance art and which stands diametrically opposed to the spirit of Islam, which is based on submission to God. It is true that Islamic science and culture were a factor in the rise of the Renaissance in the West, but Islamic elements were employed only after they were divorced from their Islamic character and torn away from the total order in which alone they possess their full meaning and significance.

Muslims should revivify the study of the Islamic sciences, first in order to demonstrate to young Muslims, so many of whom have the tendency to stop praying upon learning the first formulae of algebra, the fact that for many centuries Muslims cultivated the sciences, including most of the mathematics taught in secondary schools today, and yet remained devout Muslims; and second, to bring out the underlying harmony of the Islamic sciences with Islamic philosophy, theology and metaphysics, a harmony that is closely related to the philosophy of nature alluded to above. The great masterpieces of Islamic science, such as the works of Ibn Sina, al-Biruni, Khayyam and Nasir al-Din Tusi, can all be employed with both ends in view.

To conclude, it must be asserted categorically once again that to preserve Islam and Islamic civilization, a conscious and intellectual defence must be made of the Islamic tradition. Moreover, a thorough intellectual criticism must be made of the modern world and its shortcomings. Muslims cannot hope to follow the same path as the West without reaching the same impasse or an even worse one, because of the rapidity of the tempo of change today. The Muslim intelligentsia must face all the challenges mentioned here, and many others, with confidence in themselves. They must cease to live in the state of a psychological and cultural sense of inferiority. They must close ranks among themselves and also join forces with the other great traditions of Asia, not only to cease to be on the defensive but also to take the offensive and provide from their God-given treasury of wisdom the medicine which alone can cure the modern world of its most dangerous malady and save it from its present day plight, provided of course that the patient is willing to undergo the necessary cure. But even if we take the most pessimistic point of view concerning the present day situation and believe that nothing can be saved, the assertion of the truth itself is the most valuable of all acts, and its effect goes far beyond what can usually be envisaged. The truth must therefore be asserted and the intellectual defence of Islam made on every front on which it is challenged. The result is in God's Hands. As the Quran asserts, 'Truth hath come and falsehood hath vanished away. Lo! falsehood is ever bound to vanish.' XVII; 81, Pickthall translation.

Wa'lldhu (flam).

10

Reality Crushed

In our time, numerous judicial problems have indeed been created and in order to solve them it is essential that scholars of Islamic jurisprudence and those having insight in these matters make collective efforts through regular discussions, debates and research. There are many such problems facing the Muslim world which require that the scholars of Islam and experts of modern science hold joint discussions to solve them in the light of established principles of Islam. The importance and necessity of this splendid job is being felt in various circles of Islamic scholars and some efforts are also being made at some places but due to lack of resources these efforts have not so far been materialised into an organised collective forum.

Personal Prejudice

This is not a matter of obstinacy or anybody's personal prejudice rather it concerns a problem on which depends the survival of Islamic thought and Islamic way of life. If it is not solved with solemnity and balanced thinking, the community will never be able to achieve the goal of unity. Hence the exigency of time demands that all concerned should think and ponder over this problem with a cool temperament disregarding sentimental pressures.

In our view the main cause of failure of this institution is that the people-in-authority could not differentiate between "Research" and "Distortion". They have taken the two words as analogous and thus found superfluous solutions to the problems not conforming to the ideology of Islam at all.

It was obligatory for the Islamic researchers of our time to acquire and explore the guideline of Islam provided about the problems being faced with the mankind in twentieth century. How can it be put into practice? How the practical difficulties in this way can be removed? It was their duty to have surveyed the Western civilization with a view of research and criticism rather than counterfeiting them. They should have discarded the things that clashed with the laws of Islam, and should have suggested alternate ways which conformed to Islamic laws and at the same time fulfilled the legitimate needs of time.

But the line of action of researches of the Institute of Islamic Research is quite in contradiction to this. On the one hand they pre-supposed that the thirteen hundred years old laws of Islam have now become worne out and outdated, and it is not possible to implement and comply with them unless some fundamental changes are made in them (They call these changes as "New interpretations"). And on the other hand it has rooted deep into their minds that ideological and practical expositions of Western civilization are all blessings and benedictions, and unless Muslims accept them in toto their survival in the present time is impossible.

The entire intellectual structure of Modernism has been constructed on the above two hypotheses As a result, the style of their working had been that any ideology or style of working from the West is first taken as granted to be cent per cent right and there is no way out for us in the present time than to accept it and adopt it. Their 'Research' is then wholly directed towards proving it to be in conformity with Islam, by reshaping and distorting Islamic teachings and even by changing the established commandments of Islam. They do not hesitate in denying the prophetic traditions, or write down a new dictionary to give new meanings to the verses of the Quran.

No Novelty in Approach

This is the very style for which the word "Distortion" should be used in place of 'Research". Our submission is that, if you believe that Islam is the natural religion, if you have faith that its principles and injunctions are not the product of any human brain but that of the All-knower Allah who is fully aware of all the needs of mankind for all times to come, if you are confident that the Islam proclaimed by Muhammad (PBUH) contains satisfactory solutions to all the problems and difficulties that may arise till the Last Day, then you must admit that the solution to the problems of twentieth century also lies in the same principles which were brought by the Holy Prophet Muhammad (PBUH) 1400 years ago. This is, however, subject to the condition that you sincerely try to get rid of the inferiority complex which has made West as the standard of righteousness in your eyes. Once you get the courage to lift up the veil of deception of the West from your mind you will have the chance to understand the problems with full confidence. It is then that you will discover new ways of survival in the present time fulfilling all the needs and demands of time on the one hand and save you from the unholy ways of the West. If you follow this course you will be able to acquire the wealth of peace and tranquillity that has never been imagined by the West.

We may be excused if you find our tone unmannerly but if you have any claim to realism, be realistic in analysing your approach. While seeking the solution to your problems you have the fear of being called conservative or superstitious or uncivilized by the West. This complex does not allow you to give a serious thought to the true Islamic virtues. You are always anxious to give Islamic sanction to all those things that have a label of liberalism on them. May be that this kind of action brings you some good name in the Western circles, but this is never going to solve your problems nor will it give you the status of a living and free nation. It is not sensible.

We may seem to exaggerate about your mode of action but an honest and realistic self-analysis will testify to the truth of our claim.

You have observed that the West has based its entire banking system on "Interest". This is the system which is regarded as one of the prominent virtues of modern civilization. So, you started investing all your energy to make the interest permissible in trading system. You never bothered to ask yourself if the interest was really inevitable for the Banking system and why cannot this be run on the Principles of 'Mudaribah' provided by Islam and why the Islamic Principle of 'Mudaribah' cannot be adopted in Banking? At the cost of the opposition of the Muslim Ummah you have compound interests but you never cared to find out the principles of interest-free banking which assures us more equitable distribution of wealth.

The "Insurance" is regarded as a symbol of civilization in the West. You accepted it as it was and tried to give it Islamic sanction by making fabricated interpretations in the Quran and Sunnah. But you never knew that there was an easier and fairer way of making some minor changes in the prevailing insurance system and thus bring them in conformity with the established principles of Islam, making it more useful institution'

Family Planning

The Western countries have recently launched great campaigns to preach "Family Planning". You also followed them in propagating it. For this purpose you consumed your energies to misinterpret the laws of Islam in favour of family planning. But you never thought how China is surviving with its 700,000,000 population? According to Chu-en-lai every new child brings a message of prosperity. In the hue and cry of the Western world you looked at one mouth of a newly born child and felt uneasy to think from where to feed it? But you did not see the two hands of the child to work. The small country like Israel realised the importance of population and has been using all the means of increasing its population. The Westerner had said that population rise is dangerous far developing countries. You accepted this "sincere advice" and imposed birth control as a law, but you failed to see how Vietnam had humbled the big power like America and why the Western countries are scared of Çhina? Americans had declared that in the East they would give financial aid only to those countries who would adopt the birth control. You took it as a sympathetic gesture from them but you did not try to argue why Israel gets the lion's share in aid inspite of being against the birth control?

You heard that polygamy is considered to be a crime in Western countries. In order to free yourself from this blame you made the excuse that Islam had allowed it only in some emergency conditions and now it is no more permissible. For this purpose you left no stone unturned in pulling and dragging the meanings of the verses of Holy Quran But did you ever try to investigate why the Westerners never feel the need of more than one wife? Thanks to Modern Civilization and the open practice of un-registered polygamy in every hotel, every night club and every park, there is no need of getting oneself involved in regular family life. The Westerners had publicised that polygamists are cruel to their wives. You started pleading that the fundamental conception of Islam is to stop such a tyranny and hence polygamy is forbidden in Islam. But you shut your eyes from the naked reality that there are innumerable people who are extremely cruel to their single wife. In fact the number of such people is greater. Hence this argument requires that single marriage also should be banned.

You observed that the Westerners consider Hijab (woman's veil) as a vice, so you started fabricating the established injunctions of Islam. But you never cared to think that by unveiling their women what disaster the West has brought to their homes? Did you ever care to know what is the cause of unabated grief of the serious thinkers of the West on this issue?

You came to know that co-education is practised in Western countries. You started advocating for it as an insignia of civilization, but never bothered to think of the reasons behind the dreadful scene of American culture presented by Kinsey Reports before the world?' Did you ever think who is responsible for ever increasing unlawful sexual relations in the young generation. What is the cause of ever decreasing standard of education?

Deity Miracles

You have read that many of the Westerners deity miracles and told them as superstition. Very obediently you also followed the example and tried to reject the miracles described by the Quran in detail. As a result of this you converted the entire Qur'an into a poetic and metaphorical book. But you never thought that those who had initially denied the miracles had also called the existence of God as the worst form of superstition. They had even mocked at prophethood and divine revelations. Further, you never paid any attention to the fact how rapidly the most recent researches of scientific knowledge are making miracles mote acceptable to human intellect.

Keeping all these facts in view, for God's sake, please tell us if there is any exaggeration in our assessment that you pay no heed to finding an Islamic and intellectual solution to these problems. On the contrary you are always looking for the Western ideologies. Whatever you receive from them as permissible you spend all your energy to prove it in conformity with Islam, with no concern to what damage you are causing to the Qur'an and Sunnah. When you notice any signs of dislike for something on the faces of Westerners you exhaust all your powers to declare it unlawful and prohibited in Islam even at the cost of giving away explicit injunctions of the Qur'an and Sunnah.

Further, it is noteworthy that so far you have taken into consideration only those problems which have been raised by the Westerners. You paid no heed to the multitude of genuine problems of our own society, and no attempt was made to solve these problems. A clear example of this is: You promptly noticed the injustice which the polygamist do to their wives even though such incidences are rare in our society, while the brutalities done by the monogamists are so common that hardly any family is devoid of it. You will find innumerable women who have no co-wives yet they are leading a miserable life due to inequity of their husbands. The plight of such women does not stir your heart, you feel no sympathy for their helplessness and make no attempt to free them ftorn the cruel grip of their cruel husbands?

Your pen did not move for a single word against the evil customs of our society with reference to marriages, dowry, Mehr, living allowances, housing and inter family relations. You made no move against the defective, timeconsuming and outdated judiciary system, which has deprived society of justice. In matrimonial matters you could see only one thing, that is, polygamy which is practised hardly by 10% of people, and you consumed all your efforts in proving it as unlawful. The reason of your serious concern against polygamy is that it was initiated from the West and hence it sounded most important to you, while other problems being local, could not achieve your serious consideration.

Moreover, the problems that ever came to your attention, you tried to solve them by strange method. Inspite of investigating into the real causes of the problems you just took the easy way of finding temporary and easygoing solutions.

Ignorance from the Teachings

Due to ignorance from the teachings of Islam the common people have developed a practice of throwing three divorces to their wives on trivial matters. This practice is absolutely wrong and impermissible which is usually the cause of social disorder. It was essential that a wide publicity was made to educate people on gravity of this sin and its evil consequences. It was further necessary to decide if any legal punishment for such a sin can be imposed or not? Surprisingly, you brought out the solution to this problem that makes a mockery of the entire judicial system of Islam. Your solution was that "three" should be counted as one, thus giving free licence to men to give as many divorces as they could without being acknowledged as three. Is it not like a person being beaten by another, when the oppressed man calls you for help you tell him "Keep taking the punishment, we shall never accept that you had been beaten". Is this the way of freeing the oppressed from oppression?

You observed that sometimes an orphan grandson is left unprotected after the death of his paternal grandfather. Your solution to the problem is to cut a portion of legacy of his paternal uncles and give it to him. But you failed to conceive that if it be set into practice how would you solve the problem of orphan nephews? Why should they be deprived of a share in the heritage of their uncles? You also ignored the basic moral obligation that you cannot remove the distress of one person in the Robin Hood fashion. For removing the distress of such helpless persons Islamic Law provides adequate relief These methods are explained in

"Kitab-un-Nafqat", "Kitab-ul-Wasiyyah" and "Kitab-uz-Zakah". If the rules laid down in them are implemented properly they would be of great help to the distressed.

The above observations if given due consideration, with no prejudices in mind, provide with the only conclusion that the Institute of Islamic Research and its co-workers are basically wrong in my very mode of thinking. As a result of it they have not only been unable to do any service to the country and the nation but in fact created disruption, uneasiness, confusion and anxiety throughout the country. How we wish that the authorities of this extremely important institute give serious, sincere and selfless thought as to how harmful and dangerous for national unity is the way adopted by them?

We have not made these submissions for supporting any group, but it is a sincere and devoted effort to incite them on giving a serious and sincere consideration to our deliberations.

Problem of Explanation

Some years ago, a convention of Ulema (Religious scholars) was held in Islamabad under the auspices of Ministry of Religious Affairs, Pakistan. In the open session of this convention the (then) president of Pakistan, Gen. Zia-ul Haq, was also present. One of the topics of this convention was "How to start the process of Ijtehad (re-interpretation) in the country". The extempore speech of the Editor of AlBalagh given on this occasion has now been published in a booklet by transcribing it from tape-recorded speech which is reproduced below.

> I conceive that the recommendations submitted by the four committees of this convention in this short time are promising and encouraging. When this programme was being announced yesterday it was not expected that such solid recommendations could be prepared in such a short time. But, on the whole, the recommendations prepared by all the four committees are very commendable and encouraging. Every person had to be a member of one of these committees therefore a member of certain committee did not get a chance to

express his views before other committees. I, therefore, seek to express my views with regard to the problems that were discussed by the committees that did not have me as a member.

The committee dealt with the ways and means to enhance the speed of Islamization which is the real object of this convention has done a remarkable job. I fully endorse every word of the recommendations by this committee and also request that they should be given thorough consideration and be examined with all their intentions and spirits and immediate action should be taken.

Similarly the recommendations made by the Unity and Consonant committee are also very encouraging and in fact, if they can be put to practice they will play a very effective role in checking the epidemics of disunity and disruption.

Just now I want to draw your attention about the third committee which have been formed in connection with the process of "Ijtehad", and its recommendations have been presented by Moulana Muhammad Malik Kandhalvi and Allama Syed Muhammad Razi Mujtahid. Since this gathering is, more or less, a representative gathering of Ulema (Religious scholars), I think the decisions taken here will have a far reaching effect. Hence I wish to state that contradicting misunderstandings are present about "Ijtehad" in our society at present. As a result at times we notice an extreme degree of inactivity and at other times equal degree of overactivity in this field..

In my opinion, and this is not my individual or exclusive opinion but it is derived from the Qur'an, Hadith and verdicts of jurists of Islam that "Ijtehad" is like a double-edged sword. If it is properly understood, and used within its limitations of fulfilling the conditions laid down for it, this can be a source of great treasure of Islamic laws, and a matter of great pride for the nation. But, if it is allowed to be wrongly used by incapable persons it will result in creating false concepts and irreligious movements as we read in the books like Al-milal Wan-Nahl'. Those views and claims had their sway for sometime but now they exist only in the pages of ancient books.

The same ijtehad can be used to find practical ways for the Muslim Ummaha, and the same can lead to such ridiculous interpretations as were advanced in our country. The Qur'an said:

And as the thief, man or woman, cut off the hands of both.

This Qur'anic verse was interpreted that 'thief man and thief woman" means "capitalists"; and "cut off their hands" signify "Nationalise their industries". This interpretation has not been made by a person of ordinary literary status, but by a person of our country who is supposed to be a renowned intellectual.

Similarly, in this country it has been expounded through ijtehad that "interest" is not forbidden, and that intoxicants are also permissible. It is through the same type of Ijtehad that they tried every evil of Western civilization to make permissible; and it is through this that an endless chain of religious manipulations has been started.

It is in this context that I have called it a double-edged sword. If it is not used with necessary precautions and some one starts attempting it without having the required proficiency he would open the door to distorting the religion, and would lead to extreme degree of misleading conceptions.

Some people think that "ijtehad" allows taking a decision through personal opinion in religious matters. This must be fully understood that this practice has never been regarded as "ijtehad" in Islam. The one who considers it as "ijtehad"' has in fact fallen into great error. The door of "ijtehad" had been opened by the Holy Prophet (PBUH), and the Hadith reported by Ma az bin Jabal has made it clear. The Prophet asked Maaz "How will you decide on a thing not found in the Book of Allah?" He replied, "I will follow the Prophetic traditions (Sunnah). The Prophet then asked, 'what would you do if you find nothing in sunnah?" He replied, I will do "ijtehad" with my personal opinion." It is quite apparent from this Hadith that there is no room for "Ijtehad" in matters explicated by the Qur'an and the Sunnah. If some one attempts Ijtehad in such matters it will not be called "Ijtehad" but fabrication or distortion.

If "Ijtehad" could be permitted in matters where explicit injunctions from the Qur'an and Hadith are present, there was no need for the advent of Prophets and Messengers. The purpose of Wahy (Divine Revelation) was that right way be shown to people through Wahy in matters, where man cannot make correct decision through his intellect. Had it been an open field for everyone to do as he or she thinks proper there was no need to follow the Qur'an or Prophetic traditions. It would have been sufficient to say that people should lead their lives according to their personal likings, opinions and reasoning as the time and circumstances demand. This misunderstanding must be removed about the application of Ijtehad, and whatever resolutions are passed must fully observe this point.

Sometimes, however, "Ijtehad" is not taken as a freedom of opinion to prevail over the Qur'an and tradition, but whenever the process of "Ijtehad" is discussed an impression is given that the Qur'an and traditions have been revealed to us for the first time and no work has been done in the field of interpretation and explanation for all these fourteen hundred years and that the meanings deduced by us through personal reasoning shall be "Ijtehad" that must be implemented.

This concept is sometimes deliberately propagated while the fact is that we are not living in a vacuum but we are living in an era which has the background of fourteen centuries of loudable efforts in the field of Qur'anic learning by renowned companions of the Prophet, their followers, religious scholars, jurists of Islam and devoted personalities of the Omamah. They have spent their lives in devotion to the cause of exegesis of the Qur'an and interpretation of the Prophetic traditions, and the sacrifices they have made for this cause are beyond our imagination. They had to go through the troubles of starvation and rough clothing and poorest means of sustenance for this noble cause and left behind a huge collection of this work. Now, throwing all this collection in a dust-bin and start making fresh interpretations through the agency of "Ijtehad" unsupported by the Qur'an and the Sunnah it will be an act of shameful self deception. It will mean that all the collections of the jurists be ignored and totally a Fiqh of Islam be prepared.

A sensible solution, however, that answers to new problems may be sought in the light of existing rules and principles derived from the Qur'an and traditions. This is the right application of "ljtehad" in the right direction. Indeed countless problems may arise in every new period that are not defined by the Qur'an and the Prophetic traditions or no answer to these problems is provided by the available Fatawa(verdicts) of the jurists. Being within these limits and seeking the solutions to newer problems and understand the intentions of jurists and the intentions of the Shariah is called true "ljtehad" and this is the "ljtehad" whose doors have not been closed to anyone so far.

This is a sheer propaganda that the door of Ijtehad is closed. Nobody has ever closed it. This door has been opened by the Holy Prophet and shall remain open till the Last Day, and as long as this Ijtehad remains in capable hands nobody can close it. This is the type of Ijtehad that is needed in the present time. Countless problems have come up before us about which we find no explicit injunctions or there are practical difficulties in their implementations. The door of Ijtehad is open for solving these problems.

Here, I wish to point out that the topic of the committee has been phrased "How to start the process of Ijtehad in our country?" The sentence seems to claim that the process of Ijtehad has not been started out so far, and now it is being started Which was not in practice before. I wish to submit that this supposition is not correct. The required Ijtehad which the Muslim Ummah really needs is not a new thing. It was in practice before. If now an organized method is provided to it, it would be appreciable. But to think that the scholars of Islamic learning had not been doing this Ijtehad before is not correct. The true Ijtehad, that is needed, had been 'in process and shall continue to be in future.

What we said above was about the principles in this regard. The recommendation of the committee that has come before us is that a Board of the Ulema (The Religious scholars) be formed to carry out Ijtehad and present their opinions on new problems. In this connection, I may be allowed to point out an important Islamic practice. The history of fourteen hundred years of Islam reminds us that Islam did never form a supreme authoritative institution or clergy an institution whose opinion should be the last word depriving everyone of the right of criticism as is the case with Christianity. It is in Christianity that Pope is regarded as beyond all errors and infallible to everything.

The system in Islamic Ijtehad has been that no authoritative organisation with absolute powers was ever formed. The opinions of the Ulema carrying out Ijtehad are publicised and are open to free criticism by other Ulema and ultimately the decision about their being right or wrong is made only on the basis of the collective consensus of the Ummah to accept an Ijtehad or reject it. Hence, if the intention of creating a Board of Ijtehad is that its interpretations are imposed on the Muslims as the last word, and other Ulema are not allowed to express their opinion against it, then in my opinion this is not a right objective.

Another thing to be noted is that establishing an institution exclusively for Ijtehad at this time may have some practical problems and may call for some financial implications as well. Hence I propose that we have already got an institution by the name of "Council for Islamic Ideology" and another institution by the name of "Institute of Islamic Research", this responsibility may be entrusted to them. As has been proposed by the committee, a comprehensive list of the problems which need Ijtehad be prepared and handed over to these institutions. However, the officials of these institutions should not limit these considerations to themselves but they should invite other Ulema and scholars of the country to express their opinion before a decision is announced by the Council for Islamic Ideology. It will reduce the financial burden on the one hand,and on the other the duplication of work will be eliminated. Otherwise the new Board for Ijtehad in the presence of the Council of Islamic Ideology may give birth to new problems. If a difference arises between the two institutions a third committee or institution will be needed to remove it. Hence it will be better if the Council of Islamic Ideology or Institute of Islamic Research are entrusted the work of preparing a list of such problems and then call for the renowned, qualified jurists and devoted scholars of Islam for a joint session, and take guidance from them and then arrive at a unanimous conclusion.

It has been reported with authentic sources in the tradition of Majm 'a-al-Zawaid by Hadhrat Ali bin Abi Talib that the Prophet (PBUH) was asked "We may be faced with problems after you in which there may be neither a command nor prohibition from you. What should we do in a situation like this?" In quite a few words the Prophet provided us with the right way. He said, "Consult the jurists (Legal experts) and the devotees cognisant with religion, and do not impose individual opinion as if it was the collective view of the Ummah". He thus advised to call for people having two qualifications, that is, they are jurists and devoted to the cause of Islam, consult them and then reach a conclusion.

If the Council of Islamic Ideology and Institute of Islamic Research keep these principles in view and consult the Ulema when needed, then publish their opinion allowing open freedom of criticism to other Ulema. Anyone having opposing views be allowed to express himself. In this way the process of ljtehad can continue in the same manner as it had been continuing over the last fourteen hundred years. In case we adopt self-conceived means and methods we cannot hope to make the desired progress.

In the end I wish to submit that any such institution if formed under the supervision of the State it is essential to take into consideration the fact that governments keep changing and rulers replaced. Hence it should be formed on the principles which keep them practicable under all circumstances. Thus the selection of the workers should be made on the basis of knowledge and devotion rather than on political grounds. If this factor is effectively incorporated in the basic terms of reference of such institutions, the process of ljtehad will, by the Grace of Allah, be a source of blessing to us, and we shall be able to guard against the dangers which could be created by the wrong use of Ijtehad in our society.

With these reservation I endorse the recommendations of the committee."

11

Modern Man in Distress

"Come you lost atoms to your Centre draw, And be the Eternal Mirror that you saw:

Rays that have wander'd into Darkness wide Return, and back into your Sun subside.

(Farid al-Din Attar, Mantiq al-tayr trans. E. Fitzgerald, Boston, 1899, p. 187)

My Guru spake to me but one precept. He said unto me, 'From without enter thou the inmost part!' That to me became a rule and a precept.

(Lalla, the Female Saint of Kashmir, Lalla Vakyani, trans. by Grierson and Barrett, London, 1920, p. 107, para 94)

Although the present work deals primarily with Islam and the Muslims, it is also concerned directly with the modern world—whose impact upon the Islamic world during the past century has brought havoc and confusion beyond comparison with anything that Islamic history has witnessed since its origin—and with the message of Islam and its significance for the contemporary West. Hence it is most appropriate to begin with the study of the situation of modern Western man, and by implication that of his imitators on other continents, a study which has become especially imperative and urgent as a result of the rapid deterioration of both modern society and the natural environment during the past few decades.

Inventions and Manipulations

The confrontation of man's own inventions and manipulations, in the form cf technology, with human culture, as well as the violent effect of the application of man's acquired knowledge of nature to the destruction of the natural environment, have in fact reached such proportions that many people in the modern world, especially in the West, are at last beginning to question the validity of the conception of man held in the Occident since the rise of modern civilization. But, despite this recent awareness, in order to discuss such a vast problem in a meaningful and constructive way, one must begin by clearing the ground of the obstacles which usually prevent the profoundest questions involved from being discussed. Modern man has burned his hands in the fire which he himself kindled when he allowed himself to forget who he is. Having sold his soul in the manner of Faustus to gain dominion over the natural environment, he has created a situation in which the very control of the environment is turning into its strangulation, bringing in its wake not only ecocide but also, ultimately, suicide.

The danger is now evident enough not to need repetition. Whereas only two decades ago everyone spoke of man's unlimited possibility for development understood in a physical and materialistic sense, today one speaks of 'limits to growth'—a phrase well-known in the West today—or even of an imminent cataclasm. But the concepts and factors according to which the crisis is analyzed, the solutions sought after and even the colours with which the image of an impending doom are depicted are usually all in terms of the very elements that have brought the crisis of modern man into being. The world is still seen as devoid of a spiritual horizon, not because there is no such horizon present, but because he who views the contemporary landscape is most often the man who lives at the rim of the wheel of existence and therefore views all things from the periphery. He remains indifferent to the spokes and completely oblivious of the axis or the Centre, which nevertheless remains ever accessible to him through them.

Problem of the Devastation

The problem of the devastation brought upon the environment by technology, the ecological crisis and the like, all issue from the malady of amnesia or forgetfulness from which modern man suffers. Modern man has simply forgotten who he is. Living on the periphery of his own existence he has been able to gain a qualitatively superficial but quantitatively staggering knowledge of the world. He has projected the externalized and superficial image of himself upon the world. And then, having come to know the world in such externalized terms, he has sought to reconstruct an image of himself based upon this external knowledge. There has been a series of "falls' by means of which man has oscillated in a descending scale between an ever more externalized image of himself and of the world surrounding him, moving ever further from the Centre both of himself and of his cosmic environment. The inner history of the so-called development of modern Western man from his historic background as traditional man—who represents at once his ancestor in time and his centre in space—is a gradual alienation from the Centre and the axis through the spokes of the wheel of existence to the rim, where modern man resides. But just as the existence of the rim presupposes spokes which connect it to the axis of the wheel, so does the very fact of human existence imply the presence of the Centre and the axis and hence an inevitable connection of men of all ages with Man in his primordial and eternal reality as he has been, is, and will continue to be, above all outward changes and transformations.

So-called Liberalism

Nowhere is the tendency of modern man to seek the solution of many problems without considering the factors that have caused these problems in the first place more evident than in the field of the humanities in general and the sciences dealing specifically with man, which are supposed to provide an insight into human nature, in particular. Modern man, having rebelled against Heaven, has created a science based not on the light of the Intellect—as we see in the traditional Islamic sciences—but on the powers of human reason to sift the data of the senses. But the success of this science was so great in its own domain that soon all the other sciences began to ape it, leading to the crass positivism of the past century which caused philosophy as perennially understood to become confused with logical analysis, mental acrobatics or even mere information theory, and the classical fields of the humanities to become converted to quantified social sciences which make even the intuitions of literature about the nature of man inaccessible to many students and seekers today. A number of scientists are in fact among those most critical of the pseudo-humanities being taught in many Western universities in an atmosphere of a psychological and mental sense of inferiority vis-a-vis the sciences of nature and mathematics, a 'humanities' which tries desperately to become 'scientific', only to degenerate into a state of superficiality, not to say triviality. The decadence of the humanities in modern times is caused by man's loss of the direct knowledge of himself and also of the Self that he has always had, and by reliance upon an externalized, indirect knowledge of himself which he seeks to gain from the outside, a literally 'superficial' knowledge that is drawn from the rim and is devoid of an awareness of interiority, of the axis of the wheel and of the spokes which stand always before man and connect him like a ray of light to the supernatural sun.

It is with a consideration of this background that certain questions created by the confrontation between the traditional concept of man and the 'scientific' one must be analyzed and answered. The first of these questions, that often arise in people's minds is 'What is the relation of piecemeal scientific evidence about human behaviour to what has been called traditionally "human nature"?' In order to answer this question it is essential to remember that the reality of the human state cannot be exhausted by any of its outward projections. A particular human action or behaviour always reflects a state of being, and its study can lead to a certain kind of knowledge of the state of being of the agent provided there is already an awareness of the whole. Fragmented knowledge of human behaviour is related to human nature in the same way that waves are related to the sea. There is certainly a relationship between them that is both causal and substantial.

But unless one has had a vision of the sea in its vastness and limitless horizons—the sea which reflect the Infinite and its inimitable peace and calm—one cannot gain an essential knowledge of it through the study of its waves. Fragmented knowledge can be related to the whole only when there is already an intellectual vision of the whole.

The careful 'scientific' study of fragmented human behaviour is incapable of revealing the profounder aspect of human nature precisely because of a prior limitation that so many branches of the modern behaviouristic sciences of man—veritable pseudo-sciences, if there ever were any—have placed on the meaning of the human state itself. There has never been as little knowledge of man, of the anthropos, in different human cultures as one finds among most modern anthropologists today. Even the medicine men of Africa (not to speak of the Muslim sages) have had a deeper insight into human nature than the modern behaviourists and their flock, because the former have been concerned with the essential and the latter with the accidental. Now, accidents do possess a reality, but they have a meaning only in relation to the substance which supports them ontologically. Otherwise one could collect accidents and external facts indefinitely without ever reaching the substance, or what is essential. The classical error of modern civilization, to mistake the quantitative accumulation of information for qualitative penetration into the inner meaning of things, applies here as elsewhere. The study of fragmented behaviour without a vision of the human nature which is the cause of this behaviour cannot itself lead to a knowledge of human nature. It can go around the rim of the wheel indefinitely without ever entering upon the spoke to approach the proximity of the axis and the Centre. But if the vision is already present, the gaining of knowledge of external human behaviour can always be an occasion for recollection and a return to the cause by means of the external effect.

Four Basic Qualities

In Islamic metaphysics, four basic qualities are attributed to Ultimate Reality, based directly on the Quranic verse, 'He is the

First and the Last, the Outward and the Inward' (LVII; 3). This attribution, besides other levels of meaning, also has a meaning that is directly pertinent to the present argument. God, the Ultimate Reality, is both the Inward (al-Batin) and the Outward (al-Zahir), the Centre and the Circumference. The religious man sees God as the Inward; the profane man who has become completely oblivious to the world of the Spirit sees only the Outward, but precisely because of his ignorance of the Centre he does not realize that even the outward is a manifestation of the Centre or of the Divine. Hence his fragmented knowledge remains incapable of encompassing the whole of the rim or circumference and therefore, by anticipation, the Centre. A segment of the rim remains nothing more than a figure without a point of reference or Centre, but the whole rim cannot but reflect the Centre. Finally, the sage sees God as both the Inward and the Outward. He is able to relate the fragmented external knowledge to the Centre and see in the rim a reflection of the Centre. But this he is able to do only because of his a prior awareness of the Centre. Before being able to see the external world—be it the physical world about us or the outer crust of the human psyche—as a manifestation of the Inward, one must already have become attached to the Inward through faith and knowledge. Applying this principle, the sage could thus relate fragmented knowledge to the deeper layers of human nature; but for one who has yet to become aware of the Inward dimension within himself and the Universe about him, fragmented knowledge cannot but remain fragmentary, especially if it is based upon observation of the behaviour of a human collectivity, most of whose members themselves live only on the outermost layers of human existence and rarely reflect in their behaviour the deeper dimension of their own being.

This last point leads to an observation that complements the discussion of principles already stated. Western man lives for the most part in a world in which he encounters few people who live on the higher planes of consciousness or in the deeper layers of their being. He is therefore, for the most part, aware of only certain types of human behaviour, as can be readily seen in the writings of most Western social scientists, especially when they make studies of such traditions as Islam. Fragmented knowledge of human behaviour, even if based solely on external observation, could aid modern man to become at least indirectly aware of other dimensions of human nature, provided a study is made of the behaviour of traditional man—of the man who lives in a world with a Centre. The behaviour of traditional men of different societies, especially at the highest level of the saints and sages—be they from the Chinese, the Islamic, the North American Indian or any other traditional background—in the face of great trials, before death, in presence of the beauty of virgin nature and sacred art, or in the throes of love both human and divine, can certainly provide indications of aspects of human nature for the modern observer. Such behaviour can reveal a constancy and permanence within human nature that is truly astonishing and can also be instrumental in depicting the grandeur of man, which has been largely forgotten in a world where he has become a prisoner to the pettiness of his own trivial creations and inventions. Seen in this light, a fragmented knowledge of human behaviour can aid in gaining a knowledge of certain aspects of human nature. But in any case a total knowledge of this nature cannot be achieved except through a knowledge of the Centre or axis, which also 'contains' the spokes and the rim. A famous saying of the Prophet of Islam states, 'He who knows himself knows his Lord'. But precisely because 'himself implies the Self which resides at the Centre of man's being, from another point of view this statement can also be reversed. Man can know himself completely only in the light of God, for the relative cannot be known save with respect to the Absolute.

The second query which is often posed today and to which we must address ourselves concerns the relationship of scientific 'objectivity' and its findings to the criteria of the universal and unchanging implied by the phrase 'human nature' as used traditionally. To answer this query, it is necessary before all rise to define once again what is meant by scientific objectivity, especially when it concerns the study of man. It has become commonplace, at least for specialists in the philosophy of science, to attribute objectivity to modern venture almost as if the one implied the other. No doubt modern science possesses a limited form of objectivity in its study of the physical world, but even in this domain its objectivity is encompassed by the collective subjectivity of a particular humanity at a certain moment of its historical existence when the symbolist spirit has become atrophied and the gift of seeing the world of the Spirit through and beyond the physical world has been almost completely lost. Certainly what the traditional Muslim sees 'objectively' is not the same as the vision of the world seen by modern men today 'objectively but without the dimension of Transcendence. Even in the physical world, all that cannot be caught in the net of modern science (to quote the well-known image of Sir Arthur Eddington) is collectively neglected, and its non-existence 'objectively' avowed. It is as if an audience of deaf people at a concert testified together that they did not hear any music and considered the unanimity of their opinion as a proof of its objectivity.

Physical World

Now if, in the domain of the physical world itself, the concept of the so-called 'objectivity' of modern science must be employed with great prudence and the qualitative and symbolic aspects of nature not neglected because they lie outside the 'objectively' defined world view of modern science, so much more does this 'objectivity' need to be reconsidered in the field of the study of man. The aping of the methods of the physical sciences in the study of man has enabled Western scientists to gather a great deal of information about men of all ages and climes, but little about man himself, for the simple reason that the philosophical background of modern science, ultimately Cartesian, is incapable of providing the necessary background for the study of man. Already in the seventeenth century the body-mind dualism of Descartes perverted in the European mind the image of the much more profound tripartite division of the being of man—corpus, anima and spiritus—expounded so fully in the Hermetic tradition and repeated so often in works of Islamic philosophy. To this error a worse illusion was added in the nineteenth century which prevented even the collecting of facts about men of different ages from becoming a way of reaching at least some form of knowledge of man himself.

This illusion is that of evolution as it is usually understood today. Evolution is no more than a scientific hypothesis that has been parading itself for the past century as a scientific fact; despite the lack of the least proof of its having taken place; in the biological plane, it is usually taught in schools as proven. The present discussion does not allow our entering into debate about biological evolution, although writings by biologists and geologists against it, especially works written in recent years, are far from few in number.' But as far as the study of man is concerned, it is precisely the intrusion of the idea of evolution into anthropology that has made the potentially positive relation of scientifically accumulated facts to an understanding of the universal and unchanging aspect of human nature well-nigh impossible. Western scientists and scholars, in the fields of anthropology, the social sciences, and even the humanities are trained almost completely to study only change. Any alteration, no matter how trivial, is more often than not considered as a significant change, while the immutable is almost unconsciously identified with the unimportant or the dead. It is as if man were trained to study only the movement of clouds and to remain completely oblivious of the sky, with its immutable and infinite expanses, which provides the framework for the observations of the cloud movements. No wonder that so much of the study of man provided by modern disciplines is really no more than a study of triviality, producing most often petty results and failing at almost every step to predict anything of significance in the social order. Many a simple traditional folk tale reveals more about man than thick tomes with pages of statistics on what are usually described as 'vital changes'. In fact the only vital change that is occuring today the ever greater alienation of man from his own permanent nature and a facptfulness of this nature, a forgetfulness which cannot but be transitory but is bound at the same time to have catastrophic effects upon that type of man who has chosen it. But this is precisely the one change which 'objective' scientific methods are incapable of studying.

Concept of Human Nature

Yet, in principle, there is no necessary contradiction between scientific facts accumulated objectively and the concept of human nature with its permanent and universal implications. Were the impediments of that mental deformation of evolutionary thinking, which is neither objective nor scientific, to be removed, the accumulation of facts about man would display in a blindly evident fashion the extra-spatial and extra-temporal character of man, if not beyond history—for this would lie beyond the reach of facts—at least in periods of history and in various regions of the world. Such an exercise would depict human nature as something constant and permanent (that nature which the Holy Quran refers as al-fitrah), from which at certain moments of history and among certain peoples there have been deviations and departures dut have soon been corrected by tragedies or catastrophes leading to a re-establishment of the norm. Sacred books, such as the Quran, contain besides other levels of meaning, a history of the human soul which emphasizes in a majestic fashion this conception of human nature. That is why the goal that is placed before man in all sacred books is to know and to return to the norm, to man's permanent and original nature, to the fitrah. As the Tao-Te Ching (XIX) states, 'Realize thy Simple Self. Embrace thy Original Nature'. For the goal of man cannot but be the knowledge of himself, of who he is.

He who knows others is wise;

He who knows himself is enlightened.

: Tao-Te Ching, XXXIII

Or, to quote a mediaeval Western contemplative,

If the mind would fain ascend to the height of Science,

let its first and principal study be to know itself.

: Richard of St Victor

In the light of the understanding which both revelation and intellectual vision have provided over the ages concerning the nature of man, the answer to the often posed question 'Can scientific knowledge capture something essential about man? can only be the following: We cannot gain an essential knowledge of man through any method that is based on an externalization of man's inner being and the placing of this externalized man, of the man who stands at the rim of the wheel of existence, as the subject that knows. If 'essential' has any meaning at all it must be related to the essence, to the Centre or axis which generates at once the spokes and the rim. Only the higher can comprehend the lower, for 'to comprehend' means literally 'to encompass', and only that which stands on a higher level of existence can encompass that which lies below it. Man is composed of body, psyche and intellect, the last being at once above man and at the centre of his being. The essence of man, that which is essential to human nature, can be understood only by the intellect, through the 'eye of the heart' ('ayn al-qalb in Arabic or chishm-i dil in Persian) as traditionally understood, the intellect which is at once at the centre of man's being and encompasses all the other levels of his existence. Once the eye of the heart becomes closed and the faculty of intellection, in its original sense, atrophied, it is not possible to gain an essential knowledge of man. That reflection of the intellect upon the plane of the psyche and the mind which is called reason can never reach the essence of man, nor for that matter the essence of anything else, no matter how much it concerns itself with experiment and observation or how far it carries out its proper functions of division and analysis, the legitimate and rightful function of ratio. It can gain peripheral knowledge of accidents, of effects, of external behaviour, but not of the essence. Reason, once divorced from the guiding light of the intellect, can at best confirm the existence of the *noumena*, of the reality of the essences of things, as we see in the philosophy of Kant, who, having limited intellect to reason, accepted the reality of *noumena* but denied the possibility of ever knowing them in themselves. But reason alone cannot know the essence itself. The knowledge that is essential is one that is ultimately based on the identity of the knower and the known, on the known being consumed by the fire of knowledge itself.

Man is at a particular vantage point to know one thing in essence, and that is himself, were he only to overcome the illusion of taking (to use Vedantic terms) the externalized and objectivized image of himself for his real Self, the Self which cannot be externalized because of its very nature. Scientific knowledge, like any other form of knowledge which is based by definition on the distinction between a subject that knows and an object that is known, must of necessity remain content with a knowledge that is peripheral and not essential.

In Search of Truth

One is naturally led to ask what is the relationship of particular scientific research in the modern sense to the quest for other kinds of knowledge about mankind in general. A relation of a legitimate and meaningful kind can exist— as seen in the Islamic sciences—provided the correct proportion and relation between ways of knowing is kept in mind. And that is possible only if a knowledge that transcends science, as currently understood, is accepted. The rim can serve as a point of access to the axis and the Centre only if it is taken for what it really is, namely the rim. Once the fact that the rim is the periphery is forgotten, the Centre also ceases to possess meaning and becomes inaccessible. Were a true metaphysics, a sdentia sacra, to become once again a living reality in the West, knowledge gained of man through scientific research could be integrated into a pattern which would also embrace other forms of knowledge ranging from the purely metaphysical to those derived from traditional schools of psychology and cosmology.

But in the field of the sciences of man, as in that of the sciences of nature, the great impediment is precisely the monolithic and monopolistic character which modern Western science has displayed since the seventeenth century. Putting aside the great deal of pseudo-science and simply erroneous theories prevalent in the modern sciences of man such as anthropology and psychology, the elements that are based on careful observation of human behaviour or the human psyche under different circumstances could be related, without any logical contradictions, to what traditional schools of psychology, such as those found in Sufism, or Yoga, or Zen, have also discovered about the human psyche, and especially about certain aspects of it totally unknown to most of our contemporaries. But to relate these elements to traditional schools is possible only if the doctrine of man in his totality, as expounded in traditional metaphysics—the 'Universal Man' (*al-insan al-kamil*) of Islamic esotericism is accepted, for as already stated only the greater can embrace the lesser. To claim to know the human psyche without the aid of the Spirit (Or the Intellect) and to claim a finality for this knowledge as 'truly scientific', independent of any other form of knowledge, cannot but result in the very impasse which in fact the modern world faces today. It can only end in a truncated and incomplete, not to say outright erroneous, 'science of man', which is asked to play a role for which it has no competence. Such a science is often more dangerous than ignorance pure and simple, is dangerous than simple ignorance except an ignorance which has pretentious to being knowledge and wisdom. Scientific research into the nature of man can possess a constructive relation-: Universal and perennial ways of knowing man only if it realizes its DOS and does not seek to transgress them. It can be legitimate only to overcome the 'totalitarian rationalism' inherent in modern man though not accepted by many scientists—and to assent to it really is, namely a limited and particular way of knowing things through the observation of their external aspects, their phenomena, based upon this empirical contact with things; a way that t anocxbic if taken for what it is, because things do also possess and the external and the exteriorized question concerning the worth of scientific research as a or essential knowledge about man—research which is being aped everywhere in the world today—must then be that it is worthless if considered as a source. How can a knowledge which negates the universal order in the matephysical sense and denies the possibility of essential knowledge serve as the sourse of a knowledge that is essential and universal? Scientific research can become a source of essential knowledge only under the condition that 'scientific' is understood in the traditional sense as al-'ilm, as a knowledge that issues from and leads to the principial order.

There is, however, one way in which scientific research can aid in gaining an awareness of something essential about the present predicament of modern man, if not of man's eternal nature. This is to make use of the experimental method employed by science to study modern scientific and industrial civilization itself. In science, whenever an experiment does not succeed, it is discontinued, no matter how much effort has been put into it, and an attempt is made to learn from the errors which were responsible for its lack of success.

Renaissance as an Experiment

Modern civilization as it has developed in the West since the Renaissance is an experiment that has failed—failed in such an abysmal fashion as to cast doubt upon the very possibility of any future for man to seek other ways. It would be most unscientific today to consider this civilization, with all the presumptions about the nature of man and the Universe which lie at its basis, as anything other than a failed experiment. And in fact scientific research, if not atrophied by that totalitarian reign of rationalism and empiricism alluded to above, should be the easiest way of enabling contemporary man to realize that modern civilization has failed precisely because the premises upon which it has been based were false, because this civilization has been based on a concept of man which excludes what is most essential to the human state.

Paradoxically enough, the awareness of the shortcomings of modern civilization has dawned upon the general Western public—and not upon a small intellectual elite of the kind that warned of the crisis facing the modern world as far back as half a century ago—not because of a sudden realization of man's forgotten nature but because of the rapid decay of the natural environment. It is a symptom of the mentality of modern man that the deep spiritual crisis which has been causing the very roots of his soul gradually to wither away had to come to his attention through a crisis within the physical environment.

Environmental and Ecological Crisis

During the past few years, so much has been written about the environmental and ecological crisis that there is no need here to emphasize the dimensions of the problems involved. The famous study that has emanated from M.I.T., Limits in Growth, has sought to apply the very methods of modern science to a study of the effects of the application of this science in the future. The Author of that work, as well as many others seriously concerned with the ecological crisis, have proposed a change in man's concept of growth, a return to non-material pursuits, a satisfaction with fewer material objects and many other well-meaning suggestions for change. But very few have realized that the pollution of the environment is no more than the after-effect of a pollution of the human soul which came into being the moment Western man decided to play the role of the Divinity upon the surface of the earth and chose to exclude the transcendent dimension from his life.

Two Tragedies

In this late hour of human history, we observe two tragedies, one in the West and the other in the East. In the Occident, where the crisis of modern civilization—a crisis which is after all the product of the West—is most fully felt, since it is related usually to the environmental crisis, solutions are proposed which contain the very factors that led to the crisis in the first place. Men are asked to discipline their passions, to be rational humanists, to be considerate to their neighbours, both human and non-human. But few realize that these injunctions are impossible to carry out as long as there is no spiritual power to curb the infernal and passionate tendencies of the human soul. It is the very humanist conception of man that has dragged him to the infra-human. It is as a result of an ignorance of what man is, of the possibilities of die depths of darkness as well as the heights of illumination that he carries within himself, that such facile solutions are proposed. For millennia religions have taught men to avoid evil and to cultivate virtue. Modern man sought to destroy first the power of religion over his soul and then to question even the meaning of evil and sin. Now many propose a solution to the environmental crisis a return to traditional virtues, although usually they do not describe the virtues in such terms because for the most part such people remain secular and propose that the life of men should continue to be divorced from the sacred.

Psychological Unbalance

It might be said that the environmental crisis, as well as the psychological unbalance of so many men and women in the West, the ugliness of the urban environment and the like are the results of the attempt of man to live by bread alone, to 'kill all the gods' and announce his independence of Heaven. But man cannot escape the effect of his actions, which are themselves the limit of his present state of being. His only hope is to cease to be the rebellious creature he has become, to make peace with both Heaven and earth and to submit himself to the Divine. This itself would be tantamount to ceasing to be modern as this term is usually understood, to a death and a rebirth. That is why this dimension of the problem is rarely considered in general discussions of the environmental crisis. The missing dimension of the ecological debate is the role and nature of man himself and the spiritual transformation he must undergo if he is to solve the crisis he himself has precipitated.

The second tragedy, occurring in the East in general and the Islamic world in particular, is that this world is for the most part repeating the very errors which have led to the failure in the West of urban-industrial society and the modern civilization that has produced it. The attitude of the East towards the West should be to view it as a case study to learn from rather than as a model to emulate blindly. Of course the politico-economic and military pressures from the industrialized world upon the non-Western world are so great as to make many decisions impossible and many choices well-nigh excluded. But there is no excuse for committing certain acts whose negative results are obvious, or for having no better reason for undertaking this or that project than the fact that it has been carried out in the West. The earth cannot support additional mistakes of the kind committed by Western civilization. It is therefore most unfortunate that no present-day power on earth has a perspective wide enough to keep the well-being of the whole earth and its inhabitants in mind.

Of these two tragedies, certainly the first overshadows the second, for it is action carried out in the Modernised, industrialized world that affects more directly the rest of the globe. For example, were the ecological crisis really to be taken seriously by any of the major industrial powers in their economic and technological policies rather than just in verbal statements, it would have an immeasurable influence upon those who of necessity emulate these powers in such fields. How different would the future of man be if the West were to remember again who man is, before the East forgets the knowledge it has preserved over the ages about man's real nature!

Confusion and Disorder

What contemporary man needs, amidst this morass of confusion and disorder of the mental and physical world which surrounds him, is first and foremost a message that comes from the Centre and defines the rim vis-a-vis the Centre. This message is still available in a living form in the Eastern traditions such as Islam and can be resuscitated within the Western world. But wherever this message be found, whether in the East or the West, if it issues from the Centre which is neither of the East nor of the West it is always a call for man who lives on the periphery and the rim of the wheel of existence to follow the spokes to the axis or Centre which is the Origin at once of himself and of all things. It is a call for man to realize who he is and to become aware of that spark of eternity which he contains within himself.

> There is in every man an incorruptible star, a substance called upon to become crystallized in Immortality; it is eternally prefigured in the luminous proximity of the Self. Man disengages this star from its temporal entanglements in truth, in prayer and in virtue, and in them alone.He who has crystallized this star within himself is at peace with both himself and the world. Only in seeking to transcend the world and to become a star in the spiritual firmament is man able to live in harmony with the world and to solve the problems that terrestrial existence by its very nature imposes upon him during this fleeting journey in the temporal which comprises his life on earth.

12

Spiritualism, the Last Resort

The need to recover a vision of the Centre becomes ever more urgent for western man as the illusory world he has created around himself in order to forget the loss of the transcendent dimension in his life begins to reveal ever more fully its true character. In such a situation, the response cannot, of course, come from anywhere but sacred tradition in all its authentic forms. But in as much as we are concerned here with Islam, the last of these traditions to manifest itself on the scene of human history, it is to this tradition that we shall confine ourselves, although much of what we have to say would apply to other traditions as well. Moreover, since in viewing a mountain from far away it is first of all the peak that is seen and then sought after, it is Sufism, the peak as well as the spiritual essence and esoteric dimension of Islam, which attracts most of those who feel the need to recover the Centre by submitting themselves to the message from the Centre in its Islamic form. The amazing increase of interest in the West in recent years in the study of Sufism, much of which is unfortunately diverted by counterfeit presentations of Sufi teachings, is a result of both the growing spiritual need felt by many men today and the particular characteristics which Sufism possesses as the esoteric dimension of the Islamic tradition. A perspicacious application of the comparative method, taking into account the structure of the Islamic and the Occidental traditions, would reveal that nearly every aspect of the Islamic tradition, from the procedures of law at Shari'ite courts to the description of Divine Beauty in poetry, can be of immense benefit in solving the problems of modern man. But it would also show that it is most of all the purely metaphysical and *gnostic* teachings of Islam, contained primarily in Sufism, which can provide the answers to the most pressing intellectual needs of men today, and that it is the spiritual presence contained within Sufism which can quench more readily the thirst of aspirants in search of God.

Sacred Tradition

Today the need to benefit from the teachings of sacred tradition lead naturally, because of the anomalous situation of the modern world where the usual channels of transmission no longer exist, to the heart or to the mos-universal aspect of various sacred traditions, to the Bhagavad-Gita and the Tao-Te Ching, rather than to their more outward expressions. Islam is no exception to this general tendency, and as more Westerners seek outside the confines of their own civilization for ways of escaping from the labyrinth within which they have become imprisoned, and turn in the direction of Islam, the interest in Sufism and in its amazingly rich message grows, a message which on the doctrinal level contains so wide a range, from the simple aphorisms of Abu Madyan to the vast metaphysical compendia of Ibn 'Arab!, from the gnostic prayers of Abu'l-Hasan al-Shadhili to-the ocean of mystical poetry of Rumi.

Before turning specifically to Sufism, it is necessary to make a few general remarks about the meaning of sacred tradition and its relation to the present spiritual and intellectual needs of Western man. In order to understand sacred tradition and to discuss the truth in its metaphysical sense, there must be (besides interest and the sense of need) the aid of Heaven and the presence of a discerning intelligence. It is, therefore, necessary first of all to turn an eye to the meaning of "sacred tradition', of which Islam is an eminent example, and also to the real nature of man's present-day spiritual needs. So much confusion has been cast upon these subjects as a result of the recent 'pseudo-spiritual' explosion in the West that there is no way of understanding what kind of contribution Sufism can make to the task of saving man from his current plight without clearing the ground of prevalent errors and misconceptions.

Today many people speak of tradition in ways very different from the usage we employ here and throughout our writings. It is therefore necessary to clarify the meaning of this key term once again. Those who are acquainted with the majestic works of the traditional authors in the West such as F. Schuon, R. Guenon and A. K. Coomaraswamy already have an understanding of the meaning of this term. It is the definition of tradition contained in the writings of these authors to which we adhere fully in all of our works. Therefore, by 'tradition' we do not mean habit or custom or the automatic transmission of ideas and motifs from one generation to another, but rather a set of principles which have descended from Heaven and which are identified at their origin with a particular manifestation of the Divine, along with the application and deployment of these principles at different moments of time and in different conditions for a particular humanity. Tradition is therefore already sacred in itself and the term 'sacred tradition' is, in a sense, a pleonasm which we have used only for the sake of emphasis. Moreover, tradition is both immutable and a living continuity, containing within itself the science of Ultimate Reality and the means for the actualization and realization of this knowledge at different moments of time and space. To quote Schuon, 'Tradition is not a childish and outmoded mythology but a science that is terribly real. Tradition is ultimately a sacred science, a scientia sacra, rooted in the nature of Reality, and itself the only integral means of access to this Reality, which at once surrounds man and shines at the innermost centre of his being. It is the call from the Centre which alone can allow man to return from the rim to the Centre.

As far as Sufism is concerned, strictly speaking it should not be classified along with other integral traditions such as Hinduism and Buddhism, because Sufism is itself a part of Islam and not an independent tradition. Islam can be spoken of as a tradition in the same way as one speaks of Christianity or Buddhism, whereas Sufism must be understood as a dimension of the Islamic tradition. This rather obvious point needs to be laboured because often today in certain circles Sufism is taken out of its Islamic context with particular motives in mind and then discussed along with other Oriental or Occidental traditions.

Spiritual Requirements

Sufism is actually like the flower of the tree of Islam, or in another sense the sap of that tree. Or it can be called the jewel in the crown of the Islamic tradition. But whatever image is used, there remains the undeniable fact that, taken out of the context of Islam, Sufism cannot be fully understood, and its methods, of course, can never be practised efficaciously, to say the least. Nor can one do justice to the wholeness of the Islamic tradition and its immensely rich spiritual possibilities by putting aside its inner dimension. In speaking about Sufism, therefore, in reality we shall be speaking about the Islamic tradition itself in its most inward and universal aspect.

As for the question of the present needs of Western man which the message of sacred tradition in genera) and Sufism in particular can fulfil, it is essential to analyze fully its content and meaning, considering the cloud of illusion which surrounds modern man and makes the clear discernment of his environment and 'living space', both external and internal, well-nigh impossible. As already mentioned in the first chapter, there has been so much talk during the past century about change, becoming and evolution that the permanent and abiding inner nature of man has been nearly forgotten, along with the most profound needs of this inner man. In fact the pseudo-dogma of evolution, as generally understood, which continues to dominate the horizon of much of modern anthropology and philosophy in the teeth of rapidly accumulating evidence concerning the essentially unchanged nature of man during the many millennia that have passed since his entering upon the stage of terrestrial history, has made it impossible for those who adhere to it to understand who man is. Moreover, the permanent nature of man having been forgotten, the needs of man are reduced to the sphere of accidental changes which affect only the outer crust of man's being. When people speak of human needs today, most often they mean the man who is confined to the rim and cut off from the Centre, the man who is only accidentally human and essentially animal, the man who no longer fulfils his primordial mandate as God's vice-regent (khalifah) upon the earth.

In reality, the needs of man, as far as the total nature of man is concerned, remain forever the same, precisely because of man's unchanging nature. "Man is what he is, or he is nothing." The situation of man in the universal hierarchy of being, his standing between the two unknowns which comprise his state before terrestrial life and his state after death, his need for a 'shelter' in the vast stretches of cosmic existence and his deep need for certainty (yaqin in the vocabulary of Sufism) remain unchanged. This latter element, the need to gain certainty, is in fact so fundamental that the Sufis have described the stages of gaining spiritual perfection as so many steps in the attainment of certainty.

Oriental Metaphysics

The very fact that in the West there is so much interest today in Oriental metaphysics and spirituality, the fact that so many people in Europe and even more in America search avidly for books of instruction or poetry and music associated with Sufism, is itself indirect proof of the fact that there is a pro-founder nature in man which does not 'evolve', a nature whose needs remain unchanged. This more permanent nature may be temporarily eclipsed but it cannot be permanently obliterated. The rationalistic philosophers of the eighteenth and nineteenth centuries never dreamt that a century or two after them so many people in the Western world would again become interested in religion, in metaphysics and cosmology, and even in the occult sciences, which in their unadulterated form are applications of the traditional cosmolog-ical sciences. These men would be surprised to discover that, a century or two after them, the works of Taoist sages or the Rishis of India or Sufi masters would be read more avidly than their own writings. The rationalistic philosophers of the past two centuries along with their anti-rationalist but still profane opponents regarded only the outer crust or rim of man's being, and they saw in its condensation and consolidation, its gradual separation from the world of the Spirit or the Centre, a progress and an evolution which they thought would be a continuous process. They did not realize that the crust would break of its own accord as a result of the advancement of the very process of its solidification, and that the needs of the inner man would manifest themselves once again on the scale we see before us today.

It was once asked of the Prophet of Islam what existed before Adam. He answered, 'Adam'. The question was repeated. He again answered, 'Adam', and added that if he were to answer this question to the end of time he would repeat, 'Adam'. The profound meaning of this hadith is that man in his essential reality has not undergone evolution and that there is no 'before man' in the sense of a temporal predecessor or a state from which man developed 'in time'. A million years ago men already buried their dead and believed in the Invisible World. Over ten thousand years ago, man not only produced masterpieces of art but even described the motion of the heavens in a most remarkable manner in myths and stories which reveal a power of abstraction that could match any of the feats of men of later periods of history.

Progressive and Evolutionary Theories

It is this man—obliterated temporarily by the progressive and evolutionary theories of the past few centuries in the West—to whom tradition addresses itself and it is this inner man whom tradition seeks to liberate from the imprisonment of the ego and the suffocating influence of the purely externalized and forgetful aspect of man. Moreover, it is tradition alone which possesses the means for his liberation, and not the pseudo-religions so prevalent today, which, seeing the resurgence of the needs of the inner man, try to entice those with a less discerning eye by means of parodies of the teachings of the sacred traditions, to which they almost invariably add something of the evolutionary pseudo-philosophy to make sure that men do not discover who they really are. But that inner man continues to abide within all men and to make its demands upon man no matter how far he seeks to escape from his own Centre and no matter what means he uses to obliterate the traces of the inner man upon what he calls 'himself'.

Of course when all is said concerning the permanent needs of man—needs which in fact must be emphasized in the strongest terms possible because they have been so forgotten in the modern world—it must be remembered that these needs concern only one pole of man's being, namely the essential pole. As far as the other pole is concerned, the pole which involves man's temporality and the historico-cultural conditions that colour the outer crust of his being, it can be said that man's needs have changed. They have changed not in their essence but in their mode and external form. Even in traditional societies, all of which have been based on immutable transcendent principles, the form in which the spiritual needs of a Japanese have been fulfilled has not been the same as that of an Arab. So much more is this true in the modern world, where men live in a desacralized milieu divorced from principles, where the psyche is separated from the Spirit which is its own source of life, where the experience of time and space, not to speak of all kinds of human relations, have altered completely and where the sense of authority has gradually disappeared. In such conditions there naturally appear new modes through which even the deepest human needs must be fulfilled.

Process of the Consolidation

The very fact of the advancement of the process of the consolidation of the world has introduced cracks in the closed world of materialism which permit not only the dark forces from below to enter into this world but also light from above. This process implies at the same time a reawakening of man to his real needs, which leads naturally to a desperate attempt to find means of fulfilling these needs. But precisely because of the changed external circumstances, many modern men do not understand the conditions or are not willing to undergo the necessary sacrifices to become worthy of receiving the message of Heaven, which in its unadulterated form is contained only within the living orthodox and sacred traditions of the world. Also, many authorities from these traditions—not to speak of the pretenders who have recently flooded the Western scene—have become habituated to the traditional world from which they have issued and therefore are not aware of the differences existing between the psyche of Western man and that of men of traditional societies, nor of the different forms that Western man's spiritual needs take because of the particular world in which he has been nurtured.

In speaking of present needs, it is essential to keep in mind both these poles, namely the permanent nature of man's needs, which makes all the traditional teachings about man and his final end pertinent and in fact vital, and the changed form of man's needs due to the particular experiences of modern man, which necessitates the application of these teachings to existing conditions. It must be remembered that traditional authority and authenticity must be preserved, that Truth cannot evolve, that it is man who must make himself worthy of becoming the recipient of the message of Heaven, not vice versa, that Truth cannot be distorted to suit the passing whims and fashions of a particular period and that there is an objective reality that determines the value of man and his thoughts and actions and finally judges them and determines the mode of his existence in the world to come. At the same time, it has to be recalled that this sacred tradition must be applied to the particular problems of modern man with a consideration of the anomalous conditions in which he lives, without this process distorting or destroying the authenticity of the tradition. The modern world is witness to an array of men and organizations which attempt to cater to the spiritual needs of modern man, ranging from authentic masters and organizations from the East unaware of the particular nature of the audience they are addressing, to the rare few who have succeeded in applying traditional teachings to the particular conditions of modern man, to the vast number of pseudo-masters and dubious organizations, ranging from the innocuous to the veritably satanic. which remind one of the saying of Christ about false prophets arising at the end of time. To draw from the resources of sacred tradition to fulfil present needs is to remain totally within the matrix of sacred tradition and at the same time to apply its methods and teachings to a world in which men have needs that are at once perennial and yet conditioned by the particular experiences of modern man.

Mental Processes

An important condition which has coloured deeply the mental processes of modern man and today lies at the heart of the new religious movement in the West, albeit usually unconsciously, is Cartesian dualism and the reaction which has set in against materialism in the West within the context of this dualism. Cartesian dualism divided reality into the material and the mental positing a non-material substance which somehow engulfs all the levels of non-material existence and reduces them to a single reality. The excessive materialism of the past centuries has now led many people to reject the materialism itself. But just as in physics a reaction is opposed to an existing action, so also has this philosophical and religious reaction set in within the already existing framework of the classical Cartesian dualism. For a large number of people, the reaction against materialism means, almost unconsciously, attraction towards the other pole of Cartesian dualism, name the non-material, without there being any discrimination within the non-material domain between the Spirit and the psyche, the ruh and the nafs Sufism. Hence, for many people who are unaware of this fundamental distinction, psychic phenomena have come to replace the spiritual and the religious.

Islam teaches that the rebellion against God takes place on the level of the psyche, not on that of the body. The flesh is only an instrument for the tendencies originating within the psyche. It is the psyche that must be trained and disciplined so as to become prepared for its wedding to the Spirit. Both the angelic and the demonic forces manifest themselves in this intermediate psychic plane, which is neither purely material nor purely spiritual. The paradisial and the infernal states refer to the macrocosmic counterparts of the various levels of this intermediate substance as it becomes moulded by angelic or demonic influences. This substance, moreover, within the microcosm, or man, stretches from the corporeal to the Divine Centre within the heart of man. Therefore, to identify all that is non-material with the religious or spiritual is sheer folly and a most dangerous error, which has come into being as a result of the optical illusion lingering from the delimitation of Reality into two domains by Cartesian dualism.

But it is an error that is very prevalent in the new religious movements in the West and especially in America today, an error which in certain cases can open the soul of man to the most infernal and dissipating influences, throwing the personality of those who fall prey to them into disequilibrium. To simply identify the non-material with the spiritual is to misunderstand the nature of Reality, the complexity of the human soul, the source and reality of evil and the spiritual work necessary to reach the Fountain of Life which alone can satisfy in a permanent and not an illusory and transient manner the spiritual needs of man.

This mistaking the psychic for the spiritual, so characteristic of our times, is reinforced by another powerful tendency issuing from man's need to break the boundaries of his limited world of experience. The Sufis have always taught that man is in quest of the Infinite and that even his endless effort toward the gaining of material possessions and his dissatisfaction with what he has is an echo of this thirst, which cannot be quenched by the finite. That is why the Sufis consider the station of satisfaction (rzrfa') to be an exalted spiritual condition attainable only by those who have reached the 'proximity' of the Infinite and have shed the bonds of finite existence. This need to seek the Infinite and overcome the limits of whatever is finite is clearly discernible the new religious ferment in the West today. Many modern men are tired of the finite psychic experiences of everyday life no matter how materially comfortable that life may be. Having no access to the authentic spiritual experience which in traditional societies provides the natural means of breaking the limits of finite existence, they turn to psychic experiences of all kinds which open for them new worlds and horizons, even if they be infernal. The treat concern with psychic phenomena, 'trips', extraordinary 'experiences', and the like, is deeply related to this inner urge to break the suffocating and limited world of everyday life in a civilization which has no purpose beyond moving with accelerated speed toward an illusory ideal state of material well-being that is always just round the corner.

This tendency, added to the one which unconsciously identifies the non-corporeal with the spiritual, has succeeded in bringing about a most dangerous confusion in the religious life of modern man in the West and particularly in America, where the need for a rediscovery of the world of the spirit is most keenly felt. From the Sufi point of view, which has always distinguished clearly between the psychic and the spiritual, so many of those who claim to speak in the name of the Spirit today are really speaking in the name of the psyche, and are taking advantage of the thirst of modern man for something beyond the range of experiences that modern industrial civilization has made possible for him. It is precisely this confusion which lies at the heart of the profound disorder one observes in the religious field in the West today, and which enables elements that are as far removed as possible from the sacred to absorb the energies of men of good intention and to dissipate rather than to integrate their psychic forces.

The sacred, as already stated, is related to the world of the Spirit and not of the psyche. It is whole and holy; it illuminates and integrates rather than causing men to wander aimlessly through the labyrinth that characterizes the psychic and mental worlds whenever these worlds are deprived of the light of the Spirit. The sacred, precisely because it comes from God, asks of us all that we are. To sacralize lite and to reach the sacred we must become ourselves sacred, like a sacred work of art. We must chisel the substance of our soul into an icon which will reveal us as we really are in the Divine Presence, as we were when we were created, the *imago Dei*; for as the Prophet of Islam has said, 'God created man upon His Own image.' In order for man to become this work of art, to become him-self again, he must surrender and dedicate himself fully to the commands of the Spirit, to the sacred. It is only the sacred that can enable man to remove the veil which hides his true nature from himself and makes him forget his own primordial, theomorphic nature (the fitrah mentioned in the Quran). And it is only the sacred, which comes from the Spirit and not the psyche, that can be the source of ethics, of aesthetics in its traditional sense, of metaphysical doctrine and of methods of realization. The psyche may appear fascinating or absorbing. But in itself it is always no more than amorphous, full of impressions that are transitory and partial. It is only the spiritual or the sacred which is permanent and total and which precisely because of its totality embraces the psychic and even the corporeal aspects of man and transforms and illuminates them.

The application of sacred tradition—whether it be Sufism or some other Way—to the actual needs of man cannot begin at a more critical point than this present juncture of human history, where it can provide the means of discerning between the spiritual and the psychic and, by extension, between those whose teachings are of a truly spiritual nature and those whose message is rooted only in the psychic and supported solely by psychic phenomena, related to experiences which without the protective matrix of sacred tradition can lead to the most infernal depths of cosmic existence and to states that are much more dangerous to the soul of man than various forms of crass materialism.

Turning to the Sufi tradition itself, it must be said that the understanding of it, as of many other traditions, is made difficult in the modern West because of the presence of another optical illusion which mistakes the mental understanding of metaphysics for the full realization of its truths. This illusion, which is the result of the separation between the mental activity of certain men and the rest of their being, and which is directly related to a lack of spiritual virtues, is a major hindrance in the application of the sacred teachings of various traditions to the present needs of Western men. There are those who possess intellectual intuition, itself a gift of Heaven, and who can understand the doctrines of Sufism or other forms of Oriental metaphysics, but who are not willing to live their lives in accordance with the teachings of the sacred tradition whose flower they are able to scent from far away. Such people mistake their vision of the mountain peak, theory in its original sense, for actually being on top of the mountain. They therefore tend to be little all the practical, moral and operative teachings of tradition as being below their level of concern. Most of all they mistake the emphasis upon the attainment of spiritual virtues (fada'il in Sufism) for sentimentality, and faith (iman) for 'common religion' belonging only to the exoteric level, forgetting the fact that the greatest saints and sages have spoken most of all of spiritual virtues and that one of the most widely used names for Sufism is 'Muhammadan poverty' (al-faqr al-muhammadi). Without this poverty or faqr, the cup of man's existence has no empty space into which the nectar of Divine Wisdom can be poured. Without it no spiritual attainment is possible, no matter how keen the intelligence may be.

Spiritual Realization

This prevalent error of identifying the theoretical understanding of metaphysics with spiritual realization is related to the anomalous situation of our times in which the purest metaphysical teachings of various traditions are easily available in translation for just a few shillings at every bookshop, works ranging from the Song of Solomon to the Tao-Te Ching. Obviously, such has never been the case in a normal situation. In a traditional society, most of those drawn to the metaphysical and gnostic aspects of their tradition are attracted through gradual instruction which prepares them for the reception of gnostic doctrines only after long training. Moreover, their knowledge of tradition is through personal contact. They live the exoteric form of the tradition—which is absolutely necessary and indispensable—in their everyday lives, and they contact esotericism most often by encountering a master or his disciples, or by visiting the tomb of a saint, or by having a dream which incites them to seek a particular master or go to a particular place. Even when their contact with esotericism is through reading, it is most often through literature and parables which gradually arouse their interest in the Way. For every thousand people in the Islamic world who read the poetry of Hafiz or Rumi; only one or two read the purely doctrinal treatises of Sufism.

Today in the West there is a truly anomalous situation in which the contact of most men with tradition must of necessity begin from the top and through the channel of the written word or books, which play a special role in an age when the usual channels of oral transmission have become blocked in so many parts of the world. As a matter of fact, the very availability of the highest metaphysical teachings of not one but most of the sacred traditions today— not to speak of the remarkable expositions of the authentic traditional writers in the West—is a result of the Divine Mercy, which has made possible this compensation during an age of spiritual eclipse, inasmuch as one irregularity deserves another. But the danger present in this situation is precisely the mistaking of the mental understanding of some sacred text for the living of a tradition, which involves not only the mind but the whole of man's being.

With this reserve in mind, it must nevertheless be added that even on the plane of the mind the presence of expositions of traditional doctrines, whether they be of a metaphysical or a cosmological order, can fulfil one of the deepest needs of modern man, who can be characterized as a being who thinks too much and often wrongly, and who is over-cerebral. Even a mental understanding of traditional doctrines can therefore be like a blanket of snow which brings with it peace and calm and quiets the agitation of the sceptical and questioning mind. It can bestow upon man an intellectual certitude which corresponds to what in traditional Sufi terminology is called 'the science of certainty' ('ilm al-yaqin) and therefore make the person who has attained such a degree of knowledge aware of the fact that the ultimate aim of knowledge is not to collect an ever-increasing number of facts and to chart areas beyond the present 'frontiers' of knowledge, but to reach the Centre within and to gain a vision of or even become the knowledge which has always been and will always be. This calming of the agitated mind by providing answers to questions posed by reason, answers which are the fruit of revelation, illumination or intellection, then provides the necessary background for the actual illumination of the mind and, in fact, of the whole being of him whose reason has been nourished by traditional knowledge rather than left to its own machinations.

Importance of Doctrinal Works

Considering the importance of doctrinal works in this process of calming the mind and preparing the person of a contemplative bent for true intellectualism, it is unfortunate that, as far as Islamic metaphysics is concerned, few of its riches in this domain have been translated into English in comparison with what one finds from Hindu, Buddhist and Taoist sources. A few of thf greatest masterpieces of Islamic metaphysics, such as the Fusus al-hikam of Ibn 'Arabi and al-Insan al-kamil of al-Jili are now known and partially translated, but a vast treasury of works by both Sufis and Islamic theosophers such as Suhrawardi, Ibn Turkah al-Isfahani, Mir Damad and Mulla Sadra, who have composed major doctrinal and metaphysical treatises, remain almost completely inaccessible to a Westerner without a mastery of Arabic or Persian. In this way, the application of the teachings of Islam in its esoteric and metaphysical aspects to the present-day needs of Western man is handicapped by a lack of well-translated material which would make the vast treasures of this tradition accessible to those capable of reaping their fruit. Also, the true appreciation of all that the Islamic tradition can offer to contemporary man has become difficult, since in the case of other traditions their most universal teachings are relatively well-known, but in the case of Islam most studies in Western languages have been devoted to its legalistic and formal aspects, while its most universal aspects have not received the attention they deserve.

Some who wish to follow a tradition today are in fact deceived by this situation into thinking that Islam is concerned only with law, Divine justice and punishment, rigour, etc., while it is possible to follow other traditions by simply reading their gnostic treatises or even by taking some particular initiatic practice out of context and practising ic, without having to be burdened with moral considerations or questions of Divine justice and punishment. Actually, this is a most unfortunate "modern delusion arising from the fact that, as a result of a reaction against an unintelligible moralism within certain forms of modern Christianity, many people today belittle the importance of morality, and as a result of the rebellion of modern man against Heaven and of the loss of the meaning of authority, the importance of the fear of God in religious life has been well-nigh forgotten by most Western men today. The prophetic utterance, 'Fear of God is the beginning of Wisdom' (ra's al-hikmah makhafat Allah), which echoes the well-known Pauline dictum, holds true not only for Islam or Christianity but for all traditions. In Islam there is a Divine Law (Shari'ah) which concerns man's actions and which all Muslims, Sufis or non-Sufis, must follow. There is also emphasis upon the fear of God, and an eschatology which is related to God's judgment of human action on earth. But then these elements are also present, in other forms, in Hinduism and other Oriental traditions. Hinduism has not only produced the Gita and the Vedanta but also elaborate treatises on pralaya, the Last Judgment, and on karma and the serious consequences of human action on earth for man's posthumous states. It would be the worst illusion to imagine that one can practice, let us say. Yoga and forget all about morality or the consequences of human acts in the eyes of God simply because one has moved from one tradition to another. In every integral tradition one can find the fear, the love and the knowledge of God in one form or another. As Al-Ghazzali has said, he who fears the Creator runs towards Him and loves Him, and he who loves Him knows Him.

The historic manifestations of Sufism reveal the phases of fear (makhafah), love (mahabbah) and knowledge (ma'rifah), and the cycle repeats itself within the soul of every man who is able to attain spiritual realization. If one can complain from one point of view that the gnostic and metaphysical works of Islam have not been translated widely enough, one can be thankful from another point of view that the integral teachings of Islam, including the Shari'ah, are there to test the seriousness of those who would aspire to reach its inner chamber, by requiring them to become first of all aware of the justice and majesty of God. Such an awareness creates in man an awe and fear that is absolutely positive and that melts away from the substance of the soul all that is alien to its primordial nature.

Protecting Criterion

In fact, it is in order to evade this test and this protecting criterion that recently pretenders have appeared in the West who wish to divorce Sufism from Islam and present it as if it had nothing to do with the teachings of Islam and its Shari'ah, which provides the Divine matrix for human action and protects the man who follows it from the wrath of God. This effort is no more than sheer delusion. In all authentic manifestations of Sufism, the fear of God, described so majestically in the Quran and incorporated in the attitudes promulgated by the Shari'ah, prepares the ground for the love of God, and the love of God in turn leads to gnosis, the knowledge of God, which cannot sink its roots into the being of man unless the soil of this being has been prepared for such a Divine plant by the fear of God and His love, a love which in Islamic spirituality always accompanies knowledge.

So far, most of what has been said concerns all traditions, but it is now appropriate to ask what is unique about Sufism itself as it concerns the present needs of man. There is an Arabic saying which states that 'the doctrine of Unity is unique' (al-tawhid wahid). This means that at the highest level there is only one truth, in which all traditions are unified. But as the Divine Truth descends from the one peak downwards towards men, it takes on the characteristics which distinguish one tradition from another.

Sufism, being the inner dimension of Islam, shares, in its formal aspect, in the particular features of this tradition. Since Islam is based on Unity (al-tawhid), all of its manifestations reflect Unity in one way or another; this is especially true of Sufism, in which the principles of the revelation are most directly reflected. The presence of the principle of Unity in Sufism means, among other things, that its methods and practices unify what in other traditions are usually separate and distinct. To use the terminology of Hinduism—which is a miracle on the religious plane because of the different spiritual forms that have existed within it—the way of karma Yoga, bhakti Yoga and jnani Yoga are combined in Sufism into a single way, one might say into an 'integral Yoga'. It is especially important to note that whereas in Hinduism the jnani and bhakti types are quite distinct, Sufi spirituality is essentially a jnani one which, however, is never divorced from the bhaktic element. Some Sufis may emphasize one aspect more than another. Some, like Ibn 'Arabi, Ibn 'Ata'allah al-Iskandari and Shabistari, may speak more of gnosis (ma'rifah) and some like 'Attar and Hafi? more of love. But in no instance does one find in Sufism a path of knowledge completely separated from love or a path of love without the element of gnosis, like the kind of love mysticism found in Christianity and also in medieval Hinduism. Moreover, this combination of knowledge and love in Sufism is always based on the support of the Shari'ah, or, in a sense, on a way of work or action.

Also because of the unitary nature of the Islamic revelation, the contemplative and active ways have never been totally separated either outwardly or inwardly in Sufism. There is no outward monasticism in Islam, and the most intense contemplative life in Islam is carried out within the matrix of life within society. The Sufi has died to the world inwardly while outwardly he still participates in the life of society and bears the responsibilities of the station of life in which destiny has placed him. In fact he performs the most perfect action, because his acts emanate from an integrated will and an illuminated intelligence. Rather than being in any way contradictory, the contemplative and active lives complement each other in all Islamic spirituality, as we shall have occasion to discuss more fully in the next chapter, and the methods and techniques of the contemplative life are such that they can be performed in whatever outward circumstances a person may find himself in and in whichever form of active life he may have to participate.

This unitive character of Sufism, both in its own methods and in its relation to man's outward life in society, offers obvious advantages for men living in the modern world, where inner withdrawal is usually more of a possibility than is outward separation from the world. Also the unitive nature of Sufism is a powerful remedy for the disintegrated life from which so many people in the modern world suffer. The total integration of the personality achieved in Sufi training is the goal sought by much of psychotherapy and psychoanalysis, which, however, can never achieve this goal, for their methods as practised today are cut off from the grace of the Spirit which alone can integrate the psyche and, as a result, they usually lead to its disintegration rather than to its integration. God has placed religion in the world to enable man to overcome his complexes, in addition to performing numerous other functions for him. Any caricature and parody of religion and especially of initiatic techniques cannot but result in a caricature and parody of the effect religion has had over the ages in removing man's complexes and integrating his personality.

The pertinent question that will undoubtedly be asked is: granted that Sufism does contain these characteristics, what are the possibilities of practising it? Of course one cannot gauge the mercy of Heaven, for the 'spirit bloweth where it listeth', but as far as the traditional teachings of Sufism are concerned, it is always emphasized that there is no practice of Sufism possible except through a master who is referred to traditionally as *shaykh*, *murshid* or pir. The only exception is that of special individuals (*afrad*) who are disciples of the ever-living but hidden prophet Khadir and who are in any case chosen for the Way by Heaven. Therefore this possibility is not an option for man to choose. As far as the aspirant is concerned, the only way open to him is to find an authentic master. The question of the practical possibility of living according to the disciplines of Sufism, therefore, comes down essentially to the possibility of finding an authentic master who can instruct the disciple as to how and what he should practise. As far as the Western world and especially America are concerned, it is necessary to mention the danger of false masters, of those who pretend to be guides without possessing the necessary qualifications, which are given by God alone. Even in classical times, when the danger of 'false prophets' mentioned by Christ was much less than in these late hours of human history, authentic masters took care to warn against the perils of submitting oneself to an unqualified 'master'. In his incomparable Mathnawi, Jalal al-Din Rumi says:

'Since there is many a devil who hath the face of Adam, it is not well to give your hand to every hand.

'The vile man will steal the language of dervishes, that he may thereby chant a spell over (fascinate and deceive) one who is simple,

'The work of (holy) men is (as) light and heat, the work of vile men is trickery and shamelessness.

'They make a woollen garb for the purpose of begging. They give the title of Ahmad (Muhammad) to Bu Musaylim . . .

'The wine of God, its seal (last result) is pure musk, (but) as for (the other) wine, its seal is stench and torment.

There is a mystery in the way man chooses a master and a spiritual path, which is alluded to by Rumi himself and which cannot be solved by rational analysis alone. The problem is this: how can a candidate for initiation who does not as yet possess spiritual vision distinguish a true master from a false one when there must already be a true master to actualize the possibilities within the disciple and to enable him to distinguish the wheat from the chaff? Herein lies that mysterious relationship between the Spirit and its earthly embodiments which escapes being understood discursively. Man believes that he chooses the Way but in reality he is chosen by the Way. What man can do is to pray to find a true master and have reliance upon God while searching. He can, moreover, apply the universal criteria of authenticity and orthodoxy at a time when there are many more pretenders than when Rumi wrote about them, at a time to which Christ referred in his initiatic saying, 'Many are called but few are chosen.'

Way of Protecting

The Truth has a way of protecting itself from profanation, but the soul of man can be destroyed if moulded in the hands of someone who does not possess the right qualifications and who is no more than a pretender. Better to remain an agnostic or a materialist than to become a follower of some pseudo-spiritual movement which cannot but do harm to what is most precious within man. The Sufis compare man to an egg that must be placed under a hen for a specific period in order to hatch. If, however, it is placed underneath a hen which leaves the egg early or does not take the necessary care of it, then the egg will never hatch and cannot even be eaten. It will become useless and can only be thrown away. This parable depicts the danger of placing oneself in the hands of a pretender, in the care of those who brush aside centuries of tradition for a supposedly higher and more 'evolved' form of spirituality, or who want to crash the gates of Heaven by means of Sufism without the grace and aid of the Prophet of Islam, whose spiritual presence (barakah) alone can enable the initiate to rise upon the ladder of perfection extending to Heaven. We live in dangerous times when the possibilities of error are many, but also by compensation the paths towards God are opened before men in ways never dreamt of before. It remains for each individual to practise discernment and to distinguish between the true and the false, between the way of God and the way of Satan, who is traditionally known as the 'ape of God'.

Despite all the false masters and forms of pseudo-spirituality, there are still authentic Sufi masters, and the possibility of practising Sufism in the West is certainly present. But we believe that such a possibility will concern only a few of the vast number of people interested in Sufism today. Most likely in the near future Sufism will exercise its influence in the West not on one but on three different levels. First of all, there is the possibility of practising Sufism in an active way. Such a path is naturally meant for the few. It demands of man complete surrender to the discipline of the Way. To practise it one must follow the famous saying of the Prophet, 'Die before you die.' One must die to oneself and be reborn spiritually here and now. One must devote oneself to meditation and invocation, to inner purification, to the examining of one's conscience and many other practices prevalent among those who actually walk upon the Path (salikun). There are already some who practise Sufism seriously in the West, and, besides the pseudo-Sufi movements of little import, certain branches of Sufism have already sunk their roots in the West and have established authentic branches there. This group is surely bound to grow, although it cannot embrace all of those who are attracted to Sufism in the West today.

Mysticism in Effect

The second level on which Sufism is likely to influence the West is by presenting Islam in a more appealing form to many who would find in Islamic practices what they are seeking today in the name of Sufism. Because of a long historical background of conflict with the West, Islam has, until quite recently, been treated in the Occident in the most adverse manner possible. Many who would find exactly what they are looking for in the daily prayers and the fasting of Islam, in its integration of the secular into the sacred, in its dissemination of the sacerdotal function among all men, in its arts and sciences and many other features, are driven away from it because of the way in which it is usually presented to them. Sufism could help to explain Islam by elucidating its most universal and hence, in a sense, most comprehensible aspect, and therefore making it more approachable to outsiders. Usually when people want to study Hinduism they begin with the Bhagavad-Gita and not the Law of Manu, whereas in the case of Islam, as already stated, the legalistic aspects are usually taught first and the most universal teachings, if touched upon at all, follow afterwards in a disjointed manner. As it becomes more fully realized that Sufism is an integral part of Islam and the flower of this tree of revelation, the possibility of the practice of Islam for many who are now attracted to Sufism but who cannot undertake the difficult disciplines of the Path itself will become more evident.

There is no question here of proselytizing, as far as we are concerned, but the fact remains that many in the West are seeking Oriental religious forms to practise and follow in their everyday lives, but put Islam aside because they do not identify it with its spiritual aspect, of which Sufism is the essence. Once this identification is clearly made, Sufism may play a role in the West similar to the role it played in India, Indonesia and West Africa in spreading Islam itself. Of course in the West its method and the extent of its activity will certainly be different from what we find in the above instances, but its function will be similar. It will open a possibility within Islam for many earnest Western seekers attracted to Sufism today, and it can also make available to them that intermediate region between esotericism and exotericism which is known to those who have studied the structure of Islam carefully.

Finally, there is a third level upon which Sufism can play an important role in the West, that is, as an aid to recollection and reawakening. Because Sufism is a living tradition with a vast treasury of metaphysical and cosmological doctrines, a sacred psychology and psychotherapy hardly ever studied in the West, a doctrine of sacred art and traditional sciences, it can bring back to life many aspects of the Western tradition forgotten today. Until recently, the usual historical works in Western languages on Islam relegated Sufism, along with other aspects of Islamic intellectuality, back to the thirteenth century, and described it as if it had died out long ago. Now, as more people in the West discover that it is a living tradition, contact with its riches can certainly play the role of re-awakening Western man to many of his own forgotten treasures. The trends of the past two decades have not been hopeful, but the possibility is nevertheless present.

Moreover, Sufism possesses teachings concerning the nature of man and the world about him which contain keys to the solutions of the most acute problems of the modern world, such as the ecological crisis. Its teachings, if conveyed in contemporary language, could aid in solving many present-day problems which have come into being in the first place because of the forgetting of first principles. Its very presence could create, through a kind of 'sympathetic vibration', the revival of a more authentic intellectual activity and the revivification of precious aspects of the Western tradition which were covered by the dust created by the storm which shook the West during the period that has paradoxically come to be known as the Renaissance.

If, however, Sufism is to provide for some of the present-day needs of the West, it must be able to preserve its own integrity and purity. It must be able to resist the powerful forces of deviation, distortion and dilution visible everywhere today. It must serve the world about it like a crystal which gathers the light and disseminates it to its surroundings. At the same time it must be able to address the world around it in a language which that world understands. Sufism cannot leave unanswered the appeal of those who call upon it. Nor can it in any way compromise its principles in order to become more fashionable or more widely heard, to become a fad which would disappear from the scene with the same rapidity with which it had become popular.

Fads and Fancies

In order to present Sufism in a serious manner above and beyond transient fads and fancies, it is therefore necessary to remain strictly traditional and orthodox from the point of view of the Sufi tradition and at the same time intelligible to Western man with the particular mental habits he has acquired and the reactions towards things he has developed within himself. Also, in order really to accept and practise the teachings of Sufism, it is necessary for the modern aspirant to realize that, in fact, he is drowning, that sacred tradition is a rope thrown towards him by the Divine Mercy, and that with its aid alone can he save himself. In the present situation, those who are rooted in the Sufi tradition and who can also expound it in a manner that is comprehensible to modern men and that addresses their real needs bear a great responsibility upon their shoulders. It is for them to preserve the purity and integrity of the message, yet to be able to transmit it to men conditioned by the factors that characterize the modern world. But in performing this task, such men fulfil their highest duty and accomplish the most worthy act of charity, for there is no higher form of charity than the expression of the Truth, which alone can provide for man's deepest and most abiding needs.

13

Awakening in the West

Having dealt with the present state of Islam in the Islamic world, it is now necessary to turn to more specific problems caused by the advent of modernism within the mind of those Muslims of various Islamic lands who, while Modernised, still concern themselves with Islam and its history. In contrast to traditional Islamic scholarship, where in all branches of the sciences terms are clearly defined and always used with a specific meaning in mind, there has appeared during the past century among a large number of Modernised Muslims dealing with their own tradition a tendency toward ambiguity and the careless use of many important terms, a tendency which reflects a confused state of mind to say the least. Words and expressions have been used by many of them in such a way as to betray the state of cultural shock and often the sense of inferiority vis-a-vis the West from which they suffer. Their writings reveal most of all a slavery of the mind to the norms and judgments of Western civilization. Moreover, these norms are usually hidden under the veil of an 'Islam' of which there often remains little more than a name and certain emotional attachments, an Islam which has become devoid of the intellectual and spiritual truth which stands at the heart of the Islamic revelation. In the present analysis, it is our aim to discuss three widely used expressions, namely 'decadence', 'deviation' and 'renaissance', which are employed often in reference to Islamic history and to the present-day Islamic world, and which reflect in a profound fashion the attitude of a certain type of Modernised Muslim toward the whole of Islam as a religion and as an historical reality.

Decaying State

Let us begin with the term 'decadence', which appears very often in the writings of modern Muslim scholars, who continually refer to the condition of the Islamic world before the advent of modernism as one that could aptly be described as 'decadent'. This value judgment immediately raises the following question: "decadence with respect to what, or in respect to which norm?' There must be a norm by which something is measured and in relation to which it is judged to have decayed. Here, while some take the early centuries of Islam as a norm, most often it is the value-system adopted consciously or unconsciously from the modern West that provides, in a hidden and subtle manner, the norm and criterion for determining the state of decadence. This can be best illustrated by the question of science understood in its current Western sense. Many Modernised Muslims, like so many other Orientals, equate science with civilization and judge the value of any human society and its culture by whether or not it has produced science, disregarding completely the lessons of the history of science itself. Islamic civilization is then considered to have begun to decay when it ceased to produce outstanding scientists as the West understands the function of the scientist today. And even the date of this cessation of activity is taken by most Muslim writers from Western sources, where, until very recently, interest in all aspects of Islamic intellectual life has for the most part been limited to the period when Islam influenced the West. As a result, everything in Islam from philosophy to mathematics suddenly 'decays' mysteriously somewhere ardund the seventh/thirteenth century, exactly when the intellectual contact between Islam and the West came, for all practical purposes, to an end. Modern Muslim authors who hold this opinion do not even bother to do any research of their own or even to delve into the more recent and less-known research of those Western scholars who have shown how important Islamic astronomy was in the ninth fifteenth century or how actively Islamic medicine was pursued in Persia and India until the eighteenth century.

Western Criteria

The result of this concept of decadence, which is based upon the modern Western criteria for 'civilization' in its worldly aspect rather than on the traditional Islamic perspective which looks upon the Medina community as the most perfect Islamic society—a society according to which all other Islamic 'societies' are judged—has been to atrophy the minds of young Muslims and make them lose confidence in themselves and in their own culture. Rather than depicting the decadence which did take place in the Islamic world as a gradual and normal process of 'aging' and of becoming ever farther removed in time from the celestial origin of the revelation, and without, moreover, emphasizing the very recent nature of this decadence, such authors present the fantastic and abhorrent theory that the Islamic world began to decay in the seventh/thirteenth century. They remain completely oblivious of the fact that if this had been the case it would have been impossible for Islam to continue to nurture a vast civilization and remain a living force to this day. They brush aside such masterpieces of art as the Shah Mosque of Isfahan, the Blue Mosque of Istanbul, or the Taj Mahal, or the literary masterpieces of a Jami or a Sa'ib Tabrizi, or the metaphysical and theological syntheses of a Mulla Sadra or a Shaykh Ahmad Sirhindi, not to speak of the ever-living spiritual tradition of Islam contained within Sufism, which has continued to produce great saints to this day. Surely, had decadence, as envisaged by those Modernised Muslim writers who have adopted completely Western norms of judgment, taken hold of the Islamic world at the early date so often posited by this group, there would have been no Islamic civilization left for such a group to 'revive' during the present century. Islamic civilization would have died out long ago and become only a subject of archaeological interest, as in fact so many orientalists would like to consider it.

Departure from Reality

As for the term 'deviation', it is in fact rarely used by modernists, and is seen only in the writings of the more orthodox Muslim writers who are still aware of the presence of a spiritual and religious norm by which to judge any human society including their own, for to speak of 'tradition' in the widest sense of the word al-din is also to speak of the possibility of deviation. In fact, in the place where this term should be used, namely in reference to modern Western civilization, which is itself a major deviation and anomaly, not to say 'monstrosity' to use the words of R. Guenon, the group of modern writers with whom we are concerned shy away from utilizing it, again precisely because they lack an objective norm with which to judge the temporal flux determining the specific conditions of time and space of any particular 'world', a norm which must of necessity transcend this flux. This is all the more startling since traditional Islamic sources provide all the material that is necessary to discover such a norm and to formulate such a critique in a language comprehensible to contemporary man.

When we come to the word 'renaissance', we find a profusion of the wildest uses of this term in nearly every context, ranging from art and literature to politics. The modernists never tire of speaking of nearly every form of activity in the Islamic world as a renaissance, whose Arabic translation, al-nahdah, has become such a prevalent word in contemporary Arabic literature. There is something insidious about the carefree use of this word, for it recalls the Renaissance in the West when the re-birth of certain elements of Graeco-Roman paganism, deadly from the spiritual point of view—not the positive elements of this ancient tradition which had already been integrated into Christianity by the Church Fathers, especially St Augustine—dealt a staggering blow to Christian civilization and prevented it from reaching its natural period of flowering as a Christian civilization. One cannot but recall in connection with the Renaissance the coming to life once again in the West of the Promethean and Titanesque spirit which stands at the very antipode of Islam. What many Muslims today often take as renaissance is usually precisely the re-birth in one form or another of the very forces that Islam came to supplant, forces which are identified in the traditional Muslim imagery with the age of ignorance wjahiliyyah. That is not to say that a form of 'renaissance' in a particular domain is impossible, for the appearance of a great saint can cause a 'renaissance' of spirituality in a particular region of the Islamic world. A great master of Islamic art can revive a particular artistic form, or a powerful intellectual figure can cause the revival of some aspects of Islamic intellectual life, provided he is himself genuinely rooted in the Islamic intellectual tradition. But most of what is paraded as 'renaissance' today is nothing of the kind. How often has a directly anti-Islamic form of thought been hailed as the 'renaissance' of Islamic thought, or an activity directly opposed to the teachings of the Shari'ah as an Islamic social renaissance! Intellectual honesty would require us at least to avoid using the epithet 'Islamic', even if the term 'renaissance' must, for some reason, be employed. Here again, it is the lack of vision of the objective Islamic norms which causes many people entranced by the errors of the modern world to identify simply any change and activity in the Islamic world with an Islamic renaissance, in the same way that in the secular world of the West and its dependencies in other continents any change is equated with 'progress' and 'development', even if this change is in every way a debasement and diminution of the quality of human life.

Vision of the Objective

In all these cases, the common error results from the loss of vision of the objective, transcendent and immutable Islamic principles which alone can enable one to judge from an Islamic point of view whether a particular form or activity or period of human society is decadent, deviated or resurgent with the characteristics of a true renaissance. Without the Absolute the relative can never be fully understood, and without the immutable one cannot gauge the direction of flow of that which changes. But because of a 'metaphysical myopia' combined with a blind submission to the follies of the modern West, which has lost its vision of the Immutable, the group of Modernised Muslims under discussion possess neither the intellectual vision to perceive the immutable essences of things, their malakut in Quranic terminology, nor the binding faith to remain steadfast to the norm established by the prophetic tradition (Sunnah and Hadith). Since the first of these ways of reaching the immutable principles of things is of an intellectual and spiritual order, it is brushed aside by the modernists of the type in question without too much popular opposition, and their energy is then concentrated on the subversion of normal faith in the immutable structure of traditional Islam, an undertaking which, because of its clearly religious colour, is bound to arouse greater opposition among believing Muslims. But in both cases the ultimate motive is the same. It is to remove the only objective Islamic criteria according to which one could judge present day Islamic society and in fact the modern world in general.

The desire to remove these objective and God-given criteria becomes, therefore, concentrated in the attempt to weaken, in the eyes of faithful Muslims, the trans-historical significance of the prophetic Sunnah and Hadith by subjecting them to the so-called method of 'historical criticism', according to which the absence of the record of something is usually equated with the non-existence of the thing itself. The Holy Prophet provides for Muslims, both individually and collectively, the perfect norm for their private and collective lives, the usvsatwi hasanah of the Holy Quran. As long as bis Sunnah is respected and kept intact, there remains within the Islamic community a divinely appointed norm by which to judge human behaviour and, along with the Holy Book itself, the means to provide the basis for the collective life of human society as well as for the inner religious life of its members. The attack against the integrity of the Hadith literature has as one of its major objectives, whether realized consciously or not, to remove the divinely ordained criterion for judging Muslims and therefore to leave the door open for men to follow the line of least resistance before modernism and to surrender to their passions or to the transient fashions of the day, however demonic they may be. All of this is done, moreover, in the name of an 'Islamic renaissance' and by criticizing as reactionary or decadent any group which refuses to imitate blindly the cheapest products of Western civilization. The ambiguous and often wishy-washy judgments of many of the modernists with respect to Islam, past and present, is inseparable from the attempt to blur the clear example and norm for human life provided by the Quran and the Sunnah. And, conversely, many orthodox Muslims who have sought to defend the integrity of Islam have found it necessary to emphasize over and over again the significance of the prophetic norm as contained in the Hadith and Sunnah, without which even the message of the Holy Quran would become, in many parts, incomprehensible to men.

It may now be asked, 'Once this criticism has been made of the prevalent use of such terms as renaissance, decadence and deviation, what can these terms really signify if we accept the full authority of the Quran and the Sunnah, as well as the gradual unfolding of the tradition in stages to our own day?' To this question one can give a precise answer, which, however, because of the difference in premisses and point of departure, will be very different from that given by the modernist group in question.

Impact of Renaissance

Renaissance in the Islamic sense can only mean a rebirth, or literally renaissance, of Islamic principles and norms, and not just a rebirth of no matter what. Every sign of life is not a sign of spiritual life, and every activity that occurs among Muslim peoples is not necessarily an Islamic activity, especially during this age of the eclipse of so many aspects of the Truth. A renaissance in its Islamic sense would correspond to tajdid, or renewal, which in its traditional context is identified with the function of a renewer or mujaddid. Islamic history has been witness to many renaissances in the true sense of the word in the form of the activity of a mujaddid in one part or another of the Islamic world. But always such a mujaddid has been the embodiment par excellence of the principles of Islam, which he has sought to re-instate and apply to a particular situation. He thus differs profoundly from the 'reformer' in the modern sense, who is usually a 'deformer' because he is willing to sacrifice an aspect of the Islamic tradition for this or that contingent factor, most often made to appear irresistible by being called 'an inescapable and unavoidable condition of the times'. One wonders what would have happened to Islam during and after the Mongol invasion if such 'reformers' had appeared and had tried to make Islam conform to what were then surely the most irresistible 'conditions of the time', those connected with the victorious Mongols and their ways of life. A true Islamic renaissance is, then, not just the birth or re-birth of anything that happens to be fashionable at a particular moment of human history but the re-application of principles of a truly Islamic nature.

And here the primary condition for a genuine Islamic renaissance becomes clear. This condition in our day resides in independence from the influence of the West and from all that characterizes the modern West. A Muslim far away from the influences of modernism can possibly experience spiritual renewal while remaining oblivious to what is going on in the modern world. But a Muslim intellectual or religious leader who wishes to renew the intellectual and religious life of the Islamic world, now under such heavy pressure from the West and from modernism in general, cannot hope to bring about an Islamic renaissance on either the intellectual or the social level except through a profound criticism of modernism and of the modern world itself. To speak of an Islamic renaissance and at the same time to accept without any discrimination all that the modern world stands for is a pure chimera and the wildest of dreams, a dream which in the end cannot but turn into a nightmare. Today, truly Islamic activity, especially on the intellectual plane, cannot take place without a profoundly critical attitude towards the modern world, combined with a deep understanding of this world. Nor is the practice of giving opinion, or ijtihad, possible in the field of Islamic law for a mind that has been transformed by the tenets of modernism. If, despite all the talk about an Islamic renaissance among Muslim modernists during the past century, no such thing has taken place—certainly not issuing from their quarter—it is precisely because they lack this absolutely necessary critical view and at the same time a profound knowledge of the modern world and the means to assess its transient values in the light of the eternal principles of Islam. It is certainly time for those who want to speak in the name of the Muslim intelligentsia and who wish to bring about a renaissance of Islam to stop speaking from a position of inferiority vis-a-vis the West and begin to apply the sword of metaphysical discrimination, contained in its purest form in the shahadah, to the modern world itself.

Decadence and Deviation

Within such a perspective, the meaning of decadence and deviation also becomes clear. Decadence is always a falling off from a perfect norm, but following a course that is still related to that norm, while deviation is a complete departure from that norm itself. Moreover, there are two forms of decadence, one passive and the other active: one which the civilizations of the East have undergone during the past few centuries, and the other which has been followed by the modern West during the same period and which, because of the active and dynamic quality of the West, became properly speaking a deviation. Many Orientals—Muslims as well as others—have mistaken this activity for true life precisely because they have seen it in contrast to the relative lack of dynamism and activity within the traditional Oriental world. Today, strangely enough, before the startled eyes of many Modernised Easterners, this deviation of the West is turning into decadence of a form that is easily recognizable, even to them. It can, in fact, be said that the curve of Site of modern Western civilization, beginning with the termination of its spiritual normalcy during the Middle Ages, has gone from 'renaissance' to deviation to decadence, this last phase becoming ever more evident during the last two decades. As for that interpretation of Islam of the group of modernists just mentioned, the curve can be described as going from decay to 'renaissance' to deviation—a deviation which will surely be followed by another phase of decadence, but of a type different from that which the modernists sought to remedy to begin with. Fortunately, however, the totality of the Islamic tradition remains above this process.

Eternal and Immutable Principles

There is only one way to escape the insidious chain of deviation leading to decadence. It is to remain faithful to the eternal and immutable principles of Islam, which stand above all becoming, and then to apply these principles to whatever situation Muslims are faced with, to whichever 'world' presents itself to them. To take any transient spatio-temporal set of conditions or 'world' as the criterion of the validity of Islamic principles and teachings is to reverse the natural order of things. It is to put the cart before the horse; it is to make the contingent the criterion of judgment for the eternal. Its result can only be an unfolding similar to the fatal course pursued by the West, the end of which is the impasse which modern civilization now faces and which threatens the very existence of man on earth.

The Muslim 'intelligentsia' cannot do anything better than to benefit from the lessons that can be drawn from a deeper study of the stages in the history of the modern West which have brought it to its present crisis. If they wish to speak for Islam and to renew its life they must remember the extremely heavy responsibility they bear. It must be recalled that a true death is better than a false life, and that if one wishes to renew the life of the Islamic community it must be the renewal of a life whose roots are sunk deeply in the Divine. There is no way to avoid both decadence and deviation and to achieve a true renaissance but to re-apply the principles and truths contained in the Islamic revelation, which have always been valid and will always continue to be so. And in order to be able to apply these principles to the outside world it is first of all necessary to apply them to oneself. Man must become spiritually revivified before being able to revive the world about him. The greatest lesson that all true reformers today can learn from the numerous failures of even well-intentioned reformers in the modern world is that the real reform of the world begins with the reform of oneself. He who conquers himself conquers the world, and he in whom a renewal of the principles of Islam in their full amplitude has taken place has already taken the most fundamental step toward the 'renaissance' of Islam itself, for only he who has become resurrected in the Truth can resurrect and revive the world about him, whatever the extent of that 'world' might be according to the will of Heaven.

14

Islam and Modern Age

What is modernity ? This is the first question, which comes to one's mind. In fact, search for "Modernity" by itself is a commendable desire and a natural urge of humankind. If this urge was not there, man would not have reached from stone-age to atomic era, could not have gained access to aeroplanes and spacecrafts from camels and bullock carts nor would have progressed to electric bulbs and search lights from wax candles and earthen lamps. All these material advancements and scientific achievements which have put nooses on the planets and conducted their buckets to the bottom of sea, are in fact an importunate effect of man's inherent trait that he is a "modernist" and avaricious of "better to best" achievements.

Hence Islam, being a natural religion, is not opposed to modernism as far as it implies to be modern in simple sense of the word. Very often it has been appreciated and given due encouragement. Particularly the use of latest and newer methods in industry and craft and war technologies is proved from prophetic traditions. On the occasion of battle of Ahz ab when the tribes of Arabia joined together and raided Madinah, a renowned companion Salman Farsi suggested a new technique for its defence which was never practised in Arabia before. He suggested digging of a trench around the city. This was hailed by the Prophet PBUH and lie himself took part in digging the trench (Albidayah wan-Nih'ayah 4:95).

Two New Weapons

On the advice of Salman Farsi the Prophet used two new weapons in the battle of Ta'if which, according to some narration were constructed by Salman himself. One of them was catapult which served as cannon of the time; the second was "Dababah" the Tank of the time (Al- wan-Nih'ayahy 4:95). Not only this, but Ibn-e- has reported that the Prophet PBUH had sent two of his companions, namely'Urwah Ibn Masud and Ghitan Ibn Salmah to the city of Jarash in Syria to learn the techniques of manufacturing Dababas, Manjaniq (catapult) and Dhabur. Jarash was the famous industrial town of Syria and Dhabur was a weapon similar to Dababa which was used by Romans in their wars. These two companions could not take part in the battle of Hunayn and Ta'if because they were in Syria learning this technology (Tabqat-e-lbn- vol. 2, p. 221, Tarikh Tabri p. 353 vol. 2., Al- wan-Nilfayah p.345 vol 4).

lbn-e-Jarir has reported that the Prophet (PBUH) had asked the people of Madinah to promote agriculture by increased cultivation and use of camel skulls in their fields for increased production Kinzul-(Ammal p. 199 vol: 2).

According to one narration the Prophet advised people to promote their business by increasing trade in clothes because a cloth-merchant always wishes that the people remain prosperous and free from worries (Kanz-ul Ammal p. 199, vol. 2).

Also lie persuaded many people to go to Omman and Egypt for trade Kanz-ul-(Ammal p. 197, vol. 2)

To get the benefits of agriculture and minerals he said:

> Seek your living in the hidden wealth of the Earth (Kanz-ul 'Ammal p. 197, vol. 2).

The people of Arabia were ignorant of naval fleet, but the Prophet (PBUH) had joyously predicted that some of his people will travel through the sea for Jehad in the way of Allah as if they are kings on a throne (Sahih Bukhari, Kitab-ul-Jeh ad). He described several virtues of the first naval fleet of the Muslims. Consequently Hadhrat Mu'awiyah (RA) prepared the first naval fleet during the caliphate of Hadhrat Usman Ghani (RA). This enabled the access of Muslims to Cyprus, Rhodes, Crates and Scicily and then the entire Mediterranean Sea came under their command.

Hadhrat Amr bin Aas (RA) in tile year 8 used the method of "Blackout" during the war of zat-us-salasil against Lakhm and Juzam and ordered his troops that there should be no lights nor any fire kindled for three nights in the battlefield. When the troops reached Madinah and the Prophet (PBUH) came to know of it he inquired the reasons for this action. Ámr bill 'Aas replied O Messenger of Allah, my troops were less in number than the enemy troops, hence I ordered to keep all lights off at night lest the enemy may boost its morale by finding the low count of our troops". The Prophet was pleased with this tactics and! Offered his thanks to Almighty Allah (Jam'a-ul-Fawa'id p. 27, vol.2).

These were the few examples of the Prophetic era which have been casually mentioned. The aim of this description was to emphasize that Islam has not objected to any modern advancement just because it is recent and modern. Rather it has encouraged modernity for rightful purposes and within rightful limits.

However, in its own sphere it remains a reality that whereas modernity has elevated man's material status to great heights, given him newer inventions and provided him with better means of comfort and ease in life, it has, at the same time, caused man to suffer from many depravities and led him to many disastrous ends. It is due to the same modernity that human history is full of Pharaohs and Shiddads who were not contented with any limit of power and authority. Their lust for authority took them to the extent of claiming deification to them. The same modernity gave birth to Hitler and Mussolini whose ever increasing urge for expanding territorial boundaries demanded a new piece of land every day. It is the same modernity that has engulfed the whole world in the tornado of nudity and obscenity, and has provided an excuse for fornication, and more so it has led, under thunder claps to the passage of a bill in the British House of Commons to legalise homosexuality. It is in the shadow of the same modernity that Western women are openly displaying banners on the streets demanding legalisation of abortion. And it is the same modernity which is providing argument for justifying marriage with true sisters, daughters and other blood relations.

It proves that "Modernity" is a double-edged sword which can be used for the benefit of mankind and to cut its own throat. Hence any new thing is neither acceptable just for being new nor rehatable just because it is new. That Much is clear and obvious. But the most important question is, "what is the criterion to decide which invention is useful and acceptable and which is harmful and not acceptable.

Logic and Reasoning

One way to determine this standard is to follow the dictates of reason alone. Hence, in secular societies this decision rests with logic and reasoning. But the difficulty in it is that those people who robbed humanity of all the attributes of morality and character in the name of 'Modernity' and put it on the road to barbarism and brutality were all men of reason and philosophy, and there was none of them who had not made pure intellect as their guide. 'Me reason is that once free of the divine guidance of Wahy 'inteflect' becomes like a beloved of every Tom, Dick and Harry, so that each of different kinds of contradictory elements considers it to be its exclusive property while in fact it belongs to none of them'. In such an "Intellect" one can find glamorous justifications for every evil concept and filthiest of action. For example, the names of Hiroshima and Nagasaki cause the humanity sweat with shame, but the scholarly and world-farne book "Encyclopedia Britannica" has mentioned the disasters caused by Atom Bomb in these cities after the introductory sentence as follows:

> "Former Prime Minister Winston Churchill estimated that by shortening the wár, the Atomic Bomb had saved the lives of 10,000,00 US soldiers and 250,000 British soldiers". (Britannica vol.2. p. 647, 1950).

Several examples of similar rational interpretations can be presented. With due apologies to modesty I would like to present another example in the light of which correct position of pure intellect would become clear. In the history of Islam than has passed a sect known as Bati- A renowned leader of this sect Udayd-ullah al- has written:

> "What can be more surprising that a person having claim to wisdom acts so stupidly that lie has with him beautiful sister or daughter. His wife is not so pretty, lie marries her daughter or sister to a stranger If these ignorant ones had any trace of wisdom they would have known that they themselves had a greater right on their sisters and daughters than a stranger. The main reason of this stupidity is that their Master has forbidden good things on them."

No matter how you react to this disgusting and repulsive statement, it is an obvious example of what havoc is caused to human reason when it is not guided by divine guidance. What argument is there with reason to reject As hideous suggestion of marrying with real daughter and sister? Hence we see that the dream of bayd-ulla Qirwani is coming true centuries afterwards, and voices are being raised in some Western countries to legalise marriages with real sisters.

In short carried by the wave of Modernity, if the decision for good and bad is left on reason alone the result will be that no value of life will remain intact. Besides, man will be lost in the labyrinth of contradictory opinions and concepts from which no way out could be traced. The intellectual level of every person is different from the other. The reason is that independent of divine guidance of Wahy is regarded by man as free but in fact it becomes the slave of his beastly Passions and sensual desires. This is the worst form of servility. In the Qur'anic phraseology it is termed as passion, and it is about this that the Qur'an declared:

> If Truth becomes subjected to their passions great tumult will occur between the earth and skies and the creations therein

A group of philosophers has been mentioned in the discussions of Legal Theory. Their coticept of morality is called the Cognivist Theory. The farnous legal expert Dr. Friedman has summerised this view in his book "Legal Theory" in these words:

> "Reason is and ought only to be the slave of the passions and can never pretend to any other office than to serve and obey them (p.36).

The end result to be derived from this view, in the words of Dr. Friedman, is:

> "Every thing else but also words like 'good' 'bad' I ought' 'worthy' are purely emotive, and there cannot be such thing as ethical or moral science (pp.36,37).

However bad or wrong this view may be to form the basis of moral conceptions, it provides a true and realistic interpretation of secular reasoning. Factually, there can be no other outcome of submission to secular reason that no such thing as "Morality" should exist in the world, and nothing but passions should govern the words and deeds of man. In fact secular reasoning and 'morality' can never go together because a gage is arrived in the pursuit of 'modernity' when a man's conscience regards an action as bad yet he feels bound to adopt it because 'modernity' and secular reasoning offer no argument to reject it. The western thinkers of today are helplessly facing the same predicament. A large number of British thinkers do not like the legalisation of homosexuality adopted by the Parliament a few years ago but they were obliged to accept it because in the doctrine of purely intellectual "modernity" there remains no option but to legalise every evil that has prevailed in the society. How admonishing are words of Wolfender Committee which was appointed to consider this issue:

> "Unless a deliberate attempt is made by society acting through the agency of the law to equate this fear of crime with that of sin, there Must remain a realm of private morality and immorality which in brief and crude terms is not the law's business."
>
> (The Legal Theory).

In fact, once reason alone is made a judge to decide what is good and bad man will be deprived of every standard that may be used as a basis to stop a new practice harmful to society. Reason has to be made to follow divine standard of good and bad.

General Trend of Modernity

The law-makers are extremely worried that in the presence of general trend of modernity what method can be adopted through which at least some exalted human values might be preserved. An American judge Carduzo has written that the most important legal need of today is that a philosophy of law should be organised which could create a harmony between the contradictory and antagonistic demands of stationary and revolutionary values. But the fact is that this job cannot be done through reason and philosophy. The entire disruption has started because the function of Wahy (Divine Revelations) has been imposed on the intellect of man and in this way a burden has been placed on its shoulders which it cannot bear.

It is only on the basis of some valid arguments that a law can be called perpetual and free of changes, but the human intellect is incapable of producing any such argument. Today some people may regard a law as unalterable on the basis of their reasons but tomorrow others may realise that it is not fit to be a perpetual law and they would declare it alterable. The only solution to the problern is that instead of making his self to be a slave of his passions he should submit it to the Being who created him and the entire universe. Since that Being is fully aware of all the changes that would occur, no body else can determine which principles of law are unalterable.

The famous author of jurisprudence, George Paton, has written:

> "What interests should the real legal system protect? This is a question of values in which legal philosophy plays its part .... But however Much we desire the help of philosophy, it is difficult to obtain. No agreed scale of values has ever been reached indeed It is only in religion that we can find a basis, and the truth of religion Must be accepted by faith or invitation and not purely on the result of logical argument. (Portion: Jurisprudences p.121).

In short secular intellect has totally failed to define the good and bad. Hence there is no solution to the problem except that the man should seek guidance from God and follow the revealed doctrines. There is no other way of salvation for humanity. The Qur'an said:

"is lie who has a clear proof from his Lord like those to whom their evil deeds are made alluring and they follow their caprices?" (Muhammad: 14)

Hence the only solution to the problem is that every new trend or custom and convention should be judged, not on its apparent shine and glitter but on the basis of standards laid down by Allah, the Lord of the Universe ? Once one finds any injunctions of Allah and His Messenger concerning it, then it Must be followed without the least hesitation. The Qur'an says:

> "And it is not for a believing man or a believing woman, when Allah and His Messenger have decreed a matter to have choice in their matter" (Q: 3335)

Another verse of the Holy Qur'an speaks:

> "But no, by your Lord, They will not believe until they make you (O Prophet) the judge of what is in dispute between them, then find no vexation in their hearts over what you decide and submit with full submission" (Q:4:65)

Whatever injunctions Allah has revealed in His Book or through His Messenger (PBUH) pertain to such matters that if they are let to be decided by reason they have led to aberrance; and since Allah is well aware of all the past and future happenings only His commands can be obeyed in every time. Hence it is stated:

> "Allah makes clear (His commandments) to you, lest you go astray. And Allah is knower of every thins." (Q: 4:176)

This makes another thing about "Modernity" very clear that the need for divine revelations (Wahy) and commandments of Allah was felt because it was difficult to achieve true guidance in this matter through intellect alone. It is, therefore, essential that the divine injunctions be followed exactly as they are. It is a wrong practice that any prevalent custom of time be first taken as correct on the basis of self-reasoning, and then attempts be made to fit the Qur'an and Traditions to it by making distant interpretations. Such a method cannot be called submission to the will of Allah. Rather it amounts to alteration and amendments for which no man is authorised, because that would annul the very purpose of sending divine guidance. True submission means that the commandments of Allahshould never be allowed to be altered or modified even if the entire mankind collectively so desire. Allah says:

> "And perfect are the words of your Lord in truthfulness and justice; there is none who can change His words; and He is the Hearer, the knower. And if you (O Prophet) obey most of those on earth they would lead you astray from Allah's way, They follow nothing but surmise, and they do but guess. Surely your Lord knows best who astrays from His way. And He knows best who are rightly guided." (Q: 6:115-117)

> (And when Our clear revelations are recited to them) those who hope not for the meeting with Us say, "Bring a Qur'an other than this or after it. Say (0 Prophet) "It is not for me to alter it of my own accord, I follow nothing, except what is revealed to me (Q: 10: 15).

This kind of true obedience may bring opposition of the people and one may face difficulties but those who stand this test of the time, are rightly guided in this world and the Hereafter. Allah says:

> "And those whos strive in Our way, We shall certainly guide them in Our ways. Indeed Allah is with the good doers." (Q: 29:69)

It is not the way of a true Muslim that he accepts what he finds to fulfil his material desires and rejects what calls for some material loss or puts him through some trials. This attitude, in Quranic terms, leads one to lose both in this world and in the Hereafter.

> "And among mankind is he who worships Allah upon the very edge-so that if good befalls him he is contented with it, but if a trial befalls him he turns round on his face. He loses this world and the Hereafter. That is indeed a manifest loss." (Q: 2111)

The only way to judge between desirable and undesirable modernism is to examine it in the light of Quranic injunctions. If it is not in opposition to Allah's Commandments it may be accepted otherwise it Must be rejected without misinterpreting and distorting it even though it may be against the common trend of time. Reproaches and mockery coming from the people should not be allowed to change his firm belief. A true Muslim has a clear answer to such negative remarks provided by the Qur'an:

> "Allah mocks at them and lets them loose in their impertinence in which they keep wandering."

Affairs of Life

This attitude is meant for such affairs of life as have been ordained to be Obligatory, Incumbent, Traditional, Desirable or Forbidden and Detestable. Hence these injunctions are unalterable in every period. However, for things that fall under the category of being "permissible" man has been authorised to adopt or to abandon them according to the needs and demands of time. In fact, there are very few matters which Islamic Law has explicitly defined as Obligatory, Incumbent, Traditional, Desirable, Forbidden and Detestable, and are unalterable. On the contrary, most of the affairs of life fall under the category of "permissible" and decisions about their adoption or rejection can be made according to requirements.

We can see that the field of activity with regard to modernism as provided by Islam is very vast in which one can live a modern life without deviating from the way of Allah in the least. In them the man may apply his intellectual abilities and may achieve enormous heights of knowledge and discoveries as well as Science and Technology, and make them more and more useful for mankind.

Greatest Challenge

The greatest challenge for the Islamic world today is to recognise these limits of 'Modernity", without interfering the confined limits of unalterable injunctions of Islam. Unfortunately the present attitude of Islamic world is in clear contrast to it. Our scholars have been markedly slow in the spheres which demanded their active efforts, while they are actively busy modernizing the unalterable Commandments of Allah with the consequence that Muslims are deprived of the amenities and comforts that modern time has provided to humanity and the evils of modernism are at liberty to prevail in our society with no check from our side. May Almighty Allah give us the ability and courage to fulfil our obligations to modern times while safeguarding our ideological heritage.

15

Islam's Contemporary Role

Today, the Islamic World occupies a very significant place on the map of the world. It has been the cradle of people who have played an important and determining role in history. In it lie treasures of unlimited wealth and powers. It has petrol which is the life stream of industrial and military powers. It is a link between Europe and the Far East and is the pulsating heart of the entire Muslim world, to which this world turns, with ever-lasting affection and devotion, for its religious and spiritual needs. Its significance is also heightened by the possibility of its becoming a theatre of a third World War. It has hands that are strong and minds that are sharp and bodies that can endutre the hardships of war. It has big markets and some land of great fertility. It has Egypt, through which runs the Nile, and which, with its fertile soil and its long tradition of civilization and culture, occupies a special position in the world. In the Arab World lies Palestine which, with its neighbouring lands is distinguished for its natural beauty, delightful weather and its strategic importance. It contains Iraq which is famous for its valour, courage and for its great reservoirs of petrol.

It has in it the Arabian peninsula which is unique in being the religious and spiritual nerve-centre of the MuslimWorld, where the annual assemblage of the people of the entire World for Hajj has no parallel anywhere. It has wells that produce almost the. greatest quantity of oil in the world.

These are some of the factors that have made the Muslim World the focus of attention of the Western powers, the centre of their aspirations for supremacy, and the battleground of their struggle for leadership. All this, in turn, has resulted in creating a strong sentiment in these countries for Arab nationalism.

World of Difference

There is a world of difference between the point of view with which aEuropean looks at the Islamic World and that with which a Muslim looks at it. Even the way a nationalist Arab regards it is quite different from the way a Muslim from another part of the world does. To the Muslims in general, the Arab World is the cradle of Islam, a refuge for humanity, a tower of light and the very source of Muslim leadership. A Muslim believes that Muhammad, the Prophet of Islam, (Peace be on him!) is the soul of the Arab World, the cornerstone of its prestige and the title to its glory. Without Muhammad this land, inspite of its riches and wealth of resources, will be no more than a picture without colour or a body without spirit. It is Muhammad alone who brought the Arab World into being. This world, before he came, was a world of divided people and warring tribes over which hovered clouds of ignorance and darkness. Its potentialities lay untapped and its real virtues undiscovered.

The Arabs, at that time, could not, even in their wildest dream, think of waging a successful war against such imperial powers of the day as Rome and Persia. The very thought was impossible for them to conceive. Syria, which subsequently became an important part of the Arab World, was still a Roman colony and at the mercy of a ruthless and cruel dictatorship. It did not even understand the concept of justice or know the meaning of freedom. Iraq was the victim of the tyranny of the Sassanide rulers of Persia. New levies and ever-increasing heavy taxation had almost broken the back of the people. The Romans held Egypt and treated it like a milch animal from which is to be squeezed out the last drop of milk but which is badly looked after and poorly fed. Along with political domination, it was also subjected to religious persecution.

Then came a breath of fresh air. Muhammad, (Peace be on him!) appeared. He arrived at a time when the Arab World was on the verge of destruction and the pulse of its life was at a very low ebb. It was he who gave it a new life, a new sense of direction, knowledge, wisdom and enlightment and taught it self-discipline and self-reliance. By his coming the Arab race was completely transformed. It was now the ambassador of Islam, a messenger of peace and security, a source of comfort and grace to the people and the torch-bearer of culture and civilization.

Today we speak of Syria, Iraq and Egypt with pride. Had there been no Prophet of Islam with his message, there would be no Syria, no Iraq, no Egypt, in fact, no Arab World. Not only that, the world could not have reached the high level of culture and refinement it did, nor could knowledge, art and science achieve such high standards.

If today anyone of the countries wishes to turn its face from Islam to the West, cast nostalgic eyes at its pre-Islamic state or emulate the West in its ordering of life, its laws, its forms and systems of government and does not accept the Holy Prophet as its preceptor, guide and leader, it should give up the blessings he brought and revert to its previous state. It will then go back to an age in which Roman and Persian imperialism held absolute sway, persecution and tyranny reigned supreme and in which people were steeped in ignorance and darkness and the Arabs stagnated in a life of obscurity.

The Islamic World with its glorious history and its great achievements in refinement and culture, in knowledge and scholarship, in arts and science is the product of the advent of Muhammad (Peace be on him!) and the message he brought.

Islamic World and the Holy Prophet

Faith in Islam is the only unifying force of the Islamic World and the Holy Prophet its only leader and guide. It was this faith which enabled the Arabs to face successfully all opposition and conquer all difficulties in their march forward to secure a fair deal for humanity. It is still the real source of all its strength and is available even today. It still remains the most effective weapon with which the Islamic World can hold on its own against its foes, preserve its existence and forge ahead and recover the prestige and power it had once. If the Arab World has to fight any of its foes, it can not very well do so on the support it gets from England or the alms it receives from America or even the money it gets by selling its oil to Western powers. It can only fight with the help of that faith, spiritual strength and fervour with which it had fought Rome and Persia simultaneously and inflicted on both of them a crushing defeat. It cannot fight with a heart that is in love with life and fears death, a hand that has been enfeebled by a life of ease and luxury and a mind that has been riddled by doubt and scepticism and in which high ideals and mean urges, noble thoughts and base instincts keep up a constant struggle. It has to be remembered that no one can fight the battles of life on borrowed heart with a faith that is weak and a mind that is torn with doubt.

The most important duty of Muslim leadership and of the Arab League is to inspire the hearts of its soldier, farmer and its common man with faith, rekindle in them the zeal for righteous. strife and struggle in the path of God, breed in them contempt for material wealth, its pomp and show and train them to face death with a smile. They should be taught to give once again their best to life so that it is blessed again as it was blessed by the sweat and toil and sacrifice of their fore-fathers.

Neglecting Habits and Practices

It is unfortunate that the Arabs today seem to be neglecting habits and practices that kept their martial characteristics alive and active. Take, for instance, horsemanship for which the Arabs were famous all over the world. Horsemanship is now almost a forgotten art and is fast disappearing from the daily life of the Arabs. If horsemanship is allowed to disappear completely from Arab life, it will be a national loss and will greatly impair their manly spirit which used to be the most distinguishing trait in the Arab character, The horse is being superseded by the automobile and there is a real danger of the Arab horse, the pride of the world, becoming extinct. The Arabs have practically given up all those manly activities like horsemanship, archery and wrestling that keep up the martial spirit and have instead adopted games and sports which have but little value. It is encumbent on Arab educators to revive the martial spirit in their people, rekindle in them love for the hard life and train them to face difficulties and hardships with courage and fortitude. 'Umar, the Leader of the Faithful wrote thus to the Arab Governors appointed to non Arab countries :

> "Keep aloof from a life of ease and avoid expensive and ornate style of dress: keep up your habit of working in the sun for sunshine is the bath of the Arabs. Remain accustomed to simple dress, hardship and labour and be steadfast and patient; retain the habit of leaping on horse-back with alacrity and keep up the practice of archery and marksmanship. The Holy Prophet, has said, O Ye Arabs, keep up practising archery because your great ancestor (Ismail) was a great marksman" and again : "Remember (the power which the Qur'an emphasises) is marksmanship."

It is an essential part of the duties of Arab educators to fight against everything that saps the spirit of manliness and breeds effeminacy or incompetence, ban all indecent journalism and obscene literature that corrupts youth by propagating hypocracy, shamelessness, and the pursuit of sensuous pleasures. They should not let such charlatans enter the camp of the Holy Prophet which corrupt the morals of Muslim youth and who, for a handful of silver, paint in glowing colours sin and libertinism, indecency and immorality.

Sense of Honour and Discipline

History bears witness to the fact that whenever a race begins to lose its manliness, sense of honour and discipline, and its women fight against their very nature, give way to license in the name of freedom, and ape man in the name of equality, become indifferent to domestic virtues and seek to avoid the responsibilities of motherhood, then such a community is doomed. Hardly any trace is ever left of its greatness. Such was the fate of the Greeks, the Romans and the Persians and towards such a fate seems to be heading Europe and the world at large today.

Owing to various influences the Arabs have, unfortunately, acquired habits of spending extravagantly on the non-essentials of life and on pomp and show. And side by side of this extravagance, there exist poverty and wretchedness, want and hunger. When a person looks at the big cities of the Arab World he is filled with shame and his distress verges on tears by the appalling disparity among classes which he finds there. He sees, on the one hand, a man who spends lavishly on the luxuries of life and, on the other, a destitute who cannot afford to have even one meal a day or a piece of cloth to cover his naked body. When Arab men of wealth sail by in their powerful limousines, a host of hungry children clad in rags runs by, begging for coppers.

As long as lofty mansions stand by the side of hovels and hunger and want exist side by side with opulence, doors on communism and other forces of disruption can never be closed. No propaganda, however loud and persuasive, and no power however -strong and pervasive can do it. Unless the Islamic system with all its virtues is established in these lands, the immutable retributive laws of God will usher in, as a reaction. A system that will be ruthless and cruel.

It is imperative for the Arab states, as it is for the rest of the Muslim World, to acquire self-sufficiency in all their financial, commercial, industrial and educational needs. These countries possess, all the necessary prerequisites of such a self-sufficiency. The people of these lands should, to begin with, use only what they produce with their own efforts out of their own resources.' These states should learn to do without Europe in all spheres of life. They should not look to Europe for food, cloth, arms and machines. And they should certainly not depend on the crumbs from Europe's table.

Current Scenerio

The situation today is that, if for some unforeseen reason, the Arab World is obliged to take up arms against a European power, it cannot fight it because it is indebted to that power and depends a great deal on its help. This dependence has gone to such a length that even the fountain pen with which an Arab state signs an agreement with a European power, is made in West. If and when the Arab World has to fight, it fights with arms and ammunition manufactured in West. The great tragedy of the Arab World today is that it can not utilise, without outside help, its great reservoirs of wealth, energy and power. Instead of coursing in its own veins, its life blood is transfused into the veins of others. It is the army officers of Western powers that train its armies, and the American and European experts and agents that look after the other departments of its life.

If the Arab World has to come to its own, as it must, then it should be the master in its own home, It should be able to look after its own needs and requirements, have complete control over its economy and over the training of its soldiers and technicians. It should certainly train its own people to shoulder responsibilities and discharge them efficiently with integrity and loyalty.

As has been said earlier, the Prophet of Islam, (Peace be upon him!) came with his message at a time when mankind had reached almost the last stage of misery and wretchedness.

Humanity and its Deprivations

To relieve humanity of its deprivations was beyond those who were, at that time, the over-lords of life. They had neither the vision nor the normal courage nor even the desire to undertake such a task. Luxurious living had sapped their energies and greed and avarice had undermined their courage. They had become incapable of giving up even an iota of their comforts for any noble cause. They could not face hardships and had no stomach left for trials and tribulations inherent in such a struggle. They could not look beyond their immediate interests, could have no thought for others and were not willing to give up anything for the collective good of mankind.

Mankind stood in sore need of those who were cast in a different mould. It needed men who held life cheap and who could risk their wealth and prosperity, even their lives for its sake.

Mankind cried out for those who cared neither for loss nor gain and who would not hesitate to sacrifice the high hopes and aspirations entertained of them by their own people and about whom these people would say what the people of Sileh said about him "O' Saleh, we had such high hopes of thee."

Salvation of Humanity

The salvation of humanity is not achieved by force of arms. It depends on the moral courage and the spirit of self-sacrifice of a handful of people who, by worldly standards, are often considered to be lacking in good fortune. It is they, who courting dangers and trials, release millions of people from their miseries and lead them from despair to hope and from wretchedness to grace. They are the people who consider it a cheap bargain if, by the sacrifice of a few many are able to achieve dignity and prosperity and if, by some loss of prosperity and wealth, the doors of material and spiritual well-being are opened on many.

Romans and the Persians

The Prophet of Islam, (Peace be on him!) was ordained at a time, when the Romans and the Persians who shared power in the world, had become effete and had neither the moral courage to risk the comforts of their life nor the stamina to face the trials and hardships of the struggle for humanity at large. They could not give up even a small portion of the luxuries with which they had surrounded themselves. Such people were scarce among them who, by controlling their physical appetites and instincts, greed and avarice, liberate themselves from the bondage of luxurious living and lead a more purposive life dedicated to high and noble ideals. For such a cause. a different people were chosen by divine dispensation. The Arabs were chosen to the companions and followers of the Holy Prophet of Islam and his great mission to ennoble life. These people were filled with the spirit of dedication and renunciation and prepared themselves to sacrifice all that they possessed in meeting the great trials that faced them in fulfilling the mission. The artificialities of sophisticated culture and luxurious living could not lure, nor worldly pomp and show, charm them. They were rich because they knew contentment; they were wise because they understood the higher values of life. The Prophet of Islam, (Peace be on him!) himself faced, in full measure, trials and hardships, privations and dangers in carrying out completely his great mission. He set his face against all worldly desires and ambitions, and everything that, stood in the way of his mission. Worldly success with all its allurements could cast no spell on him nor could any power on earth make him deviate from his path. The choicest gifts of life like political power and supremacy, wealth and luxury which could ensnare the heart of any man, were un-hesitatingly spurned by him when offered to him, while he was still a young man, by the Quraish. Again when, on the insistence of the Quraish, his own uncle tried to dissuade him from his mission, he said "O My uncle, I swear by God that if the Quraish put the sun in my right hand and the moon in my left, I will not give up my mission till it prevails or I perish in my efforts."

This striving for truth at all costs, this supreme indifference towards worldly ease and comfort and this deliberate choice of a life of dedication, hardship and trial set an inspiring example to his followers and to those who had a noble mission to discharge and a high destiny to fulfil. In the discharge of his mission, the Holy Prophet of Islam (Peace be on him!) denied ease and comfort and goal living not only to himself but to all those who were near to him like his wives, children, relatives and friends. Those who were close to him alwiys received less and much was taken from them. They were the first in the struggle and last to reap its benefits.

Whenever he prohibited anything, he prohibited it first for his own people. Whenever there was any opportunity for material gain, others were considered first and his own people last. They were often deprived of the good things of life when and if they came the way of the Muslims in general. When he prohibited usury, he begun with his own uncle Abbás bin Abdul Mutallib, whose business of money lending was the first to be wound up and the interest that had accrued annulled. He acted in the same manner when he stood up to mitigate the evils of blood feuds and absolved those who had killed his own kinsman, Rubia bin Haris bin Abdul Mutallib, of his blood. When zakat i.e. the poor tax (which is a real blessing and will abide till the end of the world) was promulgated, he forbade for ever his own farnily and his descendants from accepting any portion of it however poor they may be.

When after the conquest of Mecca, his cousin Ali Ibne Abi Tilib, (MayGod be pleased with him!) claimed, on behalfof Banu Hashim, the custody of the key of the Ka'ba. He met with a stem refusal. The Holy Prophet sent for Othmiin bin TalhA and putting the key before him said "Othmin ! This key is yours, take it. This is the day of recompense for obligations and pledges fulfilled. This key will remain with you for ever. Nobody can take it from you unless he takes it unjustly with a cruel hand ". He preached austerity and simplicity of life to his wives and told them, in clear terms, that if they were willing to share with him a life of hardships they could stay with him. If, on the other hand, they preferred a life of ease and comfort, they were free to leave him. He told them of what God has said "O Prophet, say to your wives: " If you desire the comforts of life then come, I will give you some worldly goods and send you away with good grace. If, however, you prefer God, his Prophet, and the life hereafter, then for those of you who do good deeds, God has prepared a great reward." The world knows what their choice was. When his own daughter. Fatima (RA) approached the Holy Prophet, with her hands blistered by constant grinding of corn and asked for a slave from the common pool so that she may have a little respite from this onerous work, she was told that her claims could be considered only after the claims of other people had been met. Instead of a slave she was given a special form of prayer for the glorification and praise of God. This was how all his relatives were treated. The nearer the relation, the greater his responsibility. Such examples of selflessness inspired and sustained those who, by embracing Islam, had lost a great deal of their worldly possessions. Many of them were those who were used to a lit of ease and comfort and woe known for their rich and luxurious way of living. Many had lost even the very means of earning a livelihood.

Destiny of Mankind

Events that were to shape the destiny of mankind seemed to wait for these people to decide whether they were willing or not to sacrifice themselves for the ultimate good of man. The decision was given in no uncertain terms. The Arabs decided to face the struggle and triumphed. They stood trials and lazed privations with a fortitude that is rare in the history of man. And more was demanded of them. When the Ansars in Medina, who, in serving Islam, had completely neglected their farms and orchards, their main source of subsistence, asked for a little time to look after them, they were pulled up and were in the words of the Qur'an, told "Spend in the path of God and do not destroy yourself with your own hands."

Such were the lessons of self-restraint and discipline which the Prophet, (Peace be on him) taught not merely by word of mouth but by precept to those who were to carry the message and discharge its great responsibilities. Such was also the training of those Arabs and others who subsequently accepted the mission and who had their full share of the difficulties and privations in the struggle for its propagation. They are admonished by God thus:

> "If you hold your parents and children, your brothers and sisters, your wives and families, the wealth you have acquired and the trade you fear to lose, dearer than God and His Apostle, then wait God sends His dispensation. God never leads to victory those who obey not (his behest)
>
> "At another place it is said: " It is not for the people of Medin and the Arabs of the neighbourhood to refuse to follow God's Apostle or to prefer their own lives to him."

Such were the people on whose resolve and courage, renunciation and sacrifice were to be built the prosperity and happiness of mankind. And they were tested again and again. They are told:

"But surely we will test you with something of fear and hunger, some loss of goods, or lives, of the fruit(of your toil). "Again they are told: " Will they be left alone 117 inerely saying we believe and not be tested"

If the Arabs had hesitated to accept this leadership and feared to shoulder its great responsibilities, the darkness and ignorance of contemporary life could not have diminished nor the period of its misery and wretchedness shortened:

"If you do not do this, there would be tumult and aggression on earth and great mischief, thereof."

The world stood at the cross-roads in the 6th century A. D. Two alternatives were open to it. One was for a band of dedicated and divinely inspired people to go forward, risk prosperity and wealth, kith and kin and all that is dear to man's heart, deny all pleasures of life and offer even their heads for the collective good of mankind. The other was to let things be and continue a life of narrow self-interest, of self-indulgence, of preferring personal gain to the general well-being of human beings. In that event the world lulled by ignorance and apathy would have remained immersed in the quagmire of misery and darkness.

God, however, willed well for humanity and gave the Arabs the resolve and the courage to take up the first alternative. The fate of humanity was decided and man began to march forward under the leadership of the Arabs. The Prophet (Peace be on him!) breathed into the Arabs the spirit of faith and renunciation, and taught them to believe wholeheartedly in the life to come, and the great rewards it offered to those who believe and do righteous deeds. Buoyed by hopes of this reward and inspired by the spirit of service, these Arabs turned their eyes away from the comforts of life, renounced all that man's heart covets and sacrificed themselves in order to help humanity achieve happiness and dignity. They toiled with faith and sincerity and did not hesitate even to give up their lives. God, therefore, blessed them with the best of rewards: "Verily God loves those who do righteous deeds."

The world today has reached a state very similar to that in which it found itself in the 6th century A. D. A time has, surely, come when the Muslims (who are the followers of the Holy Prophet) should come forward and offer once again their lives in order to change the fate of humanity. To release it from its present miseries and save it from impending disasters, they should risk once again their ease and comfort, wealth and possessions even their future prospects. Then would life be transformed once again and Man walk in dignity towards the goal of his high destiny. The other alternative is that the Arabs remain engrossed in petty aims of personal gain, of preferment for offices and posts, salaries and income and securing better and still better means of personal comfort and ease. In that case the world would remain in the slough in which it has been floundering for sometime now.

Enslaved by Thoughts of Selfishness

If the Muslim youth, enslaved by thoughts of selfish ends, remains tied down to the comforts and distractions of big cities, if the pivot around which revolves his life is but the stomach and material comfort, if all efforts and energies are directed towards his own personal well-being and wordly success, then the resurgence of humanity will remain a mere dream never to be realised. The youth of the pre-Islamic period had equally big stakes in life and equally high intelligence, but, in pursuing the path of its choice, it sacrificed its physical comforts and even its future. The poet Umraul Qais was able to say:

> "Were I trying for an ordinary life, a little would be enough. But, I aspire for a greatness that lasts and is worthy of a man like me."

Once is needed the courage of Muslim Youth who could, with its sacrifice, build a bridge so that life could cross ovcr to its essential nobility and happiness. Life, like soil, needs fertilizers. That, which can fertilize life so that it gives of its best, is the renunciation of the Muslim Youth of its personal ambitions in order to bring Islam to its full fruition and fill God's earth with peace and plenty. Today a forsaken humanity demands the courage and resolve of those who can for its sake, give up ease and comfort, opportunities of worldly gain and concern for individual success and prosperity.

If the Muslims in general and the Arabs in particular, decide to take up the challenge and if, by the sacrifice of the few, humanity is brought back from the path of ruin to the path that leads to salvation, then it will be a cheap bargain indeed, the pins of which will far outweigh the sacrifices that are made.

" O heart, it is all gain in the bargain of love. Its only loss of life, and it is not such a loss after all."

Because of its characteristics, its situation, and its political importance, the Arab World has the right and the necessary competence to shoulder the responsibilities of the mission of Islam. It can easily take up the leadership of the entire Muslim World, strengthen itself to look at Europe in the face, and, by the grace of God and the strength of its faith, acquire supremacy over it, and lead the world once again from darkness to light, from wretchedness to grace, from destruction and ruin to peace and prosperity. In the words of the Muslim messenger to the court of Xerxes, "It could once again lead men from the worship of Man to the worship of God, from the narrowing trivialities of life to the expanse of faith, from the injustices of creeds to the justice and equality of Islam".

The whole world is looking towards the Muslims as its saviour and the Muslim World to the Arabs for guidance and leadership. Can the Muslim World fulfil the expectations of the world? Can the Arab World rise to the occasion? For long a bruised and maimed humanity has been crying, in the words of Iqbal, for succour, still believing that the hands that built the Ka'ba can build humanity again:

"Thou art the custodian, the trustee of the Eternal Order.

Thou art the right and the left flank of the Lord of the Universe:

Oh! thou creature of dust, thou art the Time and thou art the Earth.

Drink the wine of conviction and get away from the tavern of uncertainty.

Wake up! wake up! from thy deep slumber, From thy deep slumber, awake, from thy deep slumber, awake, awake.

From thy deep slumber, from thy deep slumber awake.

I cry mercy from the wantonness of Europe.

I cry mercy from the Sheerins and Purvazes of Europe.

The world has become dissolute by the exploitation of Europe.

O! thou builder of the Ka'ba, arise and build a new world again.

16

World of Islam

For nearly all of its fourteen centuries of history Islam has filled the whole of the 'living space' of that part of the cosmos called the Islamic world, leaving no vacuum to be filled by elements which could properly be called un-Islamic. The earthly manifestation of Islam was practically synonymous with the Islamic world, and everything in the Islamic world from the method of ploughing fields to composing poetry was inseparable from the spirit and form of Islam. It is only now, when, as a result of the encroachment of modernism, the homogeneity created by the Shari'ah on one level and Islamic art on the other has been partially destroyed, that it is possible to speak of Islam in the Islamic world as distinct from other elements of a completely non-Islamic and even anti-Islamic nature which have crept into this world to destroy in part its marvellous unity and homogeneity. It is true that in the traditional world of Islam there were also occasional forms of decadence in both art and thought of the type characteristic of the European Renaissance, but they were so peripheral and so much on the fringe and were, moreover, overwhelmed so rapidly by the spiritual presence of the tradition that they cannot in any way be compared in dimension with the spread of modernism in the Islamic world today. No matter how much effort certain Orientalists spend in seeking to resuscitate the rationalistic tendencies of an Ibn al-Rawandi or Muhammad ibn Zakariyya' al-Razi, or to display in art exhibitions certain naturalistic vases, frescoes and paintings of Umayyad, Ottoman,

Mogul or Persian origin, they cannot hide the overwhelming evidence of the presence of the spiritual character of the Islamic tradition, a presence which obliterated all such transient phenomena in the Islamic world.

A Divided Community

The unity of the Islamic world, however, is now partially broken as never before, not only politically—which had occurred already during the Abbasid period—but even religiously and culturally, by the erosion caused by Westernisation, a process which as well as introducing a totally foreign element into the Islamic world also reflects directly an alien world which itself suffers from the most glaring forms of disunity and contradiction. Numerous works have been written in the West with various degrees of success on modern movements in the Islamic world, but few have considered the effect of the inner contradictions and tensions of Western civilization itself upon the confusion caused in the Islamic world by present-day modernizing elements. It is enough to see the difference of perspective and approach existing today among philosophers, sociologists and educators of Muslim universities, reflecting the centres of learning in which they were trained in continental Europe or England or America, to realize how complicated the pattern of Westernisation—which of course has been synonymous with modernization until now— actually is.

Colonisation and Westernisation

In addition to the historical accidents of Colonisation and Westernisation, there is also another factor to consider which reflects the multifarious tendencies within Western civilization itself. Because the Islamic world has always been a unity, it has until now functioned as an organism in which each part has played a particular role. During the classical period of Islamic civilization, each part of the Islamic world was especially known for its mastery of a particular art or science, from sword-making to navigation, from astronomy to Kalam. On a more inward level, each of the Islamic peoples, such as the Arabs, Persians, Turks,

Berbers and Black Africans, emphasized a particular devotional aspect of Islam and even a particular interpretation of the Shari'ah, while the Shari'ite rites as well as the pure metaphysics of *Tasawwuf* and the techniques for its realization provided the thread of unity through this diversity.

The spread of modernism has had the effect not only of sowing the seed of confusion in the minds of those who are affected by it and therefore loosening the hold of Islam upon them, but also of separating different parts of the Islamic world from each other more than ever before. There is much talk of easy communication today, but as a matter of fact, intellectually and culturally, there is less communication between various parts of the Islamic world today not only than during the period of the classical caliphate but even than after the Mongol invasion, when Moroccans worked along with Syrian astronomers in Maraghah under the leadership of Nasir al-Din al-Tusi. The various parts of the Islamic world, which for centuries complemented each other and functioned organically and harmoniously, are now left to themselves to recreate a totality from something which was always part of a greater whole and was continuously enriched by other parts of the whole.

As a result, when one studies the situation of Islam and Islamic culture in the Islamic world today, one sees a certain element of this totality better preserved in one land and another element in another land. In one part of dar al-islam, certain parts of the Shari'ah are performed impeccably and certain other parts relatively negleted. In one place the juridical sciences are still studied and taught in their fullness, and in another the theological ones or certain other traditional sciences. Some of the Muslim peoples have preserved the formal aspects of the Shari'ah more strictly, and others place more emphasis upon their inner content and are less observant concerning the exactness of the outward forms. Likewise, in the domain of the sacred art of Islam, some have preserved the most beautiful Quranic psalmody, others calligraphy and yet others architecture. Some continue to preserve the traditional dress but are more Modernised in their minds and attitudes than others who have been forced to abandon their traditional dress but whose psyche and mind remain less affected by modernism.

Historical Factors

Many historical factors, ethnic characteristics, internal social and political elements and the like have created a pattern in which, overlying the deeper layer which unifies the Islamic peoples and displays the unity and totality of Islam, one can observe a differentiated patchwork of modern ways of thinking and acting throughout various Islamic countries, reflecting both the confusion of the Western world and the complicated processes through which this confusion reached the Islamic world. In the periods when Islamic civilization was at its height, when its homogeneity reflected the varities of Islam on all levels of human life, a perceptive Muslim could gain a vision of the totality of the Islamic order through contact with any of its great centres; but today, such an experience of Islam in its totality is not easy to come by, even for a Muslim acquainted with only a part of dar al-islam, not to speak of an outsider. For example, in the intellectual field, a person possessing the necessary intellectual and spiritual capabilities and living in Cairo or Damascus or Isfahan of the fourth eleventh century, or even of the eleventh/seventeenth century, would have been able to gain knowledge through traditional education of the hierarchy of the Islamic sciences extending from the supreme scientia sacra contained in Sufism to various traditional schools of philosophy and the natural sciences to theology and the various juridical sciences. Although not impossible today, the task of attaining such a knowledge is certainly much more difficult than before for a Muslim brought up in a traditional madrasah, not to speak of one whose Westernized education has cut him off from many of the essentials of his own intellectual heritage. In fact, the spread of modernism in the Islamic world was facilitated precisely by this diminution in the knowledge of Islam's totality on the part of many Muslims. Yet it is precisely this total knowledge, not limited to a single level but embracing the whole, that is necessary if an intelligentsia capable of answering all the challenges that the Western world poses for Islam is to be formed.

Recreation of Practical Thinking

Strangely enough, one of the results of the shock received by certain Muslims in their encounter with the Western world has been a re-awakening of interest in the totality of Islam. In these cases, a 'rediscovery' of Islam, and even a kind of renewal of some people's vision of their own faith, has taken place, in such a way that such persons could, in a sense, be called jadid al-islam, (having just become Muslim) with all the positive qualities connected traditionally with this term. The impact of modernism upon the Islamic world, combined with a certain amount of decadence which set in some domains of life and thought beginning in the twelfth/eighteenth century, destroyed the homogeneity of that world and veiled the totality of the tradition even from Muslims. To understand the nature of the impact of modernism upon the Islamic world, and to prepare to combat its evils, requires on the part of the Muslim intelligentsia a rediscovery of the vision of the whole of their tradition and a stepping outside the boundary of their national and local experience to view the encounter of Islam and modernism in other parts of the Islamic world. For them as well as for the student studying Islam from the outside, the study of the parts cannot but help them to gain a knowledge of the whole.

It must be added, however, that the emphasis laid upon the necessity of studying Islam in each part of the Islamic world today in its confrontation with various forms of modernism must not lead to negligence of the traditional and unchanging aspects of Islamic life so often forgotten in the studies made by Western students as well as by modernistic Muslims. We have had occasion to mention in our previous writings on Islam the danger of the type of method used by most modern students of Islam grounded in such pseudo-sciences as modern sociology and the like or paralyzed by the historicism which grew out of nineteenth-century European philosophy. But it is necessary to repeat here that for a mentality trained to measure and to consider as significant only that which changes, the only noteworthy phenomenon in any part of the Islamic world becomes that which is related to some kind of rebellion against the existing traditional order. If there are a dozen traditional commentaries written upon the Quran they are considered as mere repetitions, but if there is one which breaks with the traditional canons, it is immediately hailed as a significant departure and made known through articles in various European languages. One can hardly emphasize enough how diabolical this propaganda on behalf of perverted tendencies or trivial mental exercises has been and how on the one hand it has led the Western reader to the wrong conclusion about the contemporary state of Islam, and on the other hand it has misled the Muslim in whom the power of faith (imdn) has become weakened by the illusion that traditional Islam is something that belongs only to the past and that by identifying himself with modernistic theories and interpretations he is allying himself with forces that must of necessity prevail in the future.

Serious Encroachments

In reality nothing could be farther from the truth. Despite serious encroachments upon the body of Islam by modernism and by the confusion caused within the mind and soul of certain Muslims caught between the pull of their tradition and Western ideologies and values, Islam remains very much a living tradition on both the exoteric and the esoteric levels. Were this not so it would hardly be possible to speak of applying the teachings of Islam to the problems faced by modern man. If nothing had been left of Islam save some kind of sentimental or apologetic modern interpretation, one could hardly expect it to provide an antidote for the maladies caused by modernism itself. But authentic and traditional Islam continues to live. It is there to be studied and rediscovered in its totality by turning both to the oral and written sources of the tradition as it has been lived and transmitted since its revelation, and to its present-day manifestations in the souls and lives of the Muslim peoples in various parts of the Islamic world under the different historical, political and social conditions imposed upon the once unified dar al-islam during the most recent period of Islamic history. Being more acquainted with the Arab and the Persian worlds, it is to these parts of the Islamic world that we turn in seeking to understand something of the state of Islam in the Islamic world today and in its confrontation with modernism. These countries form only a part of the Islamic world, but they continue to be of great importance and centrality because of the fundamental role they have played as the heart of dar al-islam since the foundation of Islamic civilization.

17

Scene in Iran

The situation of Islam in the Arab World differs from its situation in the rest of the Islamic world in that the Arab Muslim, even if Modernised, does not see in his pre-Islamic past anything but the 'age of ignorance' (al-jahiliyyah), which he can hardly extol even in a modernistic and nationalistic milieu, and also in that the contemporary Arab Muslim cannot separate himself from his ethnic and linguistic attachment to the earthly vessel of the Quraniç revelation. In contrast to this situation, the non-Arab Muslims have a distinct pre-Islamic past completely different from the background within which Islam was revealed, and do not share the ethnic and linguistic bonds with the earthly embodiment of the Quranic revelation, at least not to the same extent as the Arabs.

Centuries Old Civilization

This distinction is particularly true of the Persians, who had a brilliant pre-Islamic civilization of great spiritual and artistic beauty, and played a major role in the very foundation of Islamic civilization. They and the Arabs (al-'ardb wa'l-'ajam in traditional Islamic sources) together founded Islamic civilization and have influenced nearly every phase of its subsequent history. In fact, although Islamic thought and culture succeeded in freeing itself from becoming only 'Arabic' or 'Persian' during the Umayyad and Abbasid periods, both of these peoples left their indelible mark upon its historical deployment and development. The

Persians, on the one hand, played a central role in building Islamic civilization and, on the other, were able to integrate within the universal perspective of Islam many elements of their pre-Islamic past, which thus became completely Islamicized. They therefore not only became thoroughly Islamic and have remained one of the most productive of Islamic peoples intellectually and artistically, but they were also able to preserve their own identity and remain distinctly Persian, creating a second cultural focus within the unity of Islamic civilization, which in its classical phase and almost up to modern times could be divided culturally into the Arabic and the Iranian zones. The situation of Islam in present-day Persia, and modernism's threat to the remarkable unity created between Persia's ancient past and Islam, cannot therefore be understood without reference to the historical background and an analysis of the forces and elements that were integrated to create the classical Islamic culture of Persia.

When we look at Persia today we see that it is one of the most overwhelmingly Muslim countries in the world. The life of the vast majority of Persians today is dominated and moulded completely by Islam, while, at the same time, the religious and cultural life of the country naturally reflects the long history of the Persian people. Because the Persians became thoroughly Islamicized and yet created a distinctly Persian Islamic culture related on a certain plane with their pre-Islamic past, to understand their present-day religious life—particularly in the form of Ithna 'Ashari or Twelve-Imam Shi'ism, which is dominant in Persia today—it is necessary to cast a brief glance at the religious history of the people who have lived on the Iranian plateau during the past three thousand years.

Major Religious Influences

Persia has been both a centre from which major religious influences have radiated and a cross-roads at which the religious traditions of the Mediterranean world and Asia have met, resulting often in new currents of religious life. Having originally belonged to the same ethnic and linguistic stock as the Aryan conquerors of

India, the early Iranians who settled on the plateau possessed a religion akin to that of the Vedas. From this early background there arose the reform of Zoroaster and the establishment of the specifically Iranian religion of Zoroastrianism. Although the dates of Zoroaster are still much debated, there is no doubt that in the fifth century BC his teachings became the official religion of the Persian empire. The sacred book of Zoroastrianism, the Avesta, is the most precious religious document of the early history of Persia as well as a basic source for the study of the Iranian languages. Zoroastrianism, with its firm belief in the angelic world, its accent upon the moral dimension of human existence, its emphasis upon the reality of the after-life and Last Judgment, and its stress upon the purity of the elements and the sacred character of human life, left an imprint both on the later religious life of Western Asia and on the general outlook of the Persians.

The positive qualities which this religion implanted in the souls of the Persians survived and became transmuted into the Islamic mould after Zoroastrianism itself had decayed and lost the spiritual struggle against the new forces of Islam. For example, the care that many devout Persians take in keeping their clothing, food and habitat clean in a ritual sense, sometimes even over-emphasizing this element of religion, is founded upon an old Zoroastrian teaching reinforced by the emphasis of Islam upon cleanliness. Whatever survived of Zoroastrianism in the Persian soul was, however, thoroughly Islamized and interpreted in the light of the unitary point of view of Islam.

From the matrix of Zoroastrianism, which is the stable and orthodox background of Iranian religions, there grew several religious movements which had world-wide repercussions and also shook the foundations of Zoroastrianism itself. With the fall of the Achaemenian Empire, Hellenistic influences spread throughout the domain of the Persian people. This cultural movement was combined with a religious one known as Mithraism (considered as a distinct religious movement and not general devotion to Mithra, which ante-dated Zoroastrianism itself) which itself contained important Hellenistic elements. The mystery cult of Mithra, which spread as far West as Germany and Scandinavia, was a synthesis of Zoroastrian, Hellenistic, Babylonian and Anatolian elements, as well as pre-Zoroastrian Persian religious practices. If, for the world at large, this religious movement meant the spread of Iranian religious elements, for Persia itself it implied perhaps more than anything else the establishment of a religious sanction for the syncretic cultural life through which the Persians were now passing as a result of the conquests of Alexander and the establishment of Seleucid rule.

Parthian Period

During the Parthian period, Zoroastrianism and the proper Persian cultural tradition began to reassert themselves until, with the advent of the Sassanids, the religion of Zoroaster became once again the official state religion, remaining in this position until the fall of the Sassanid empire. Nevertheless, its authority did not go unchallenged even on the religious plane. In the third century AD, a second world-sweeping Iranian mystery religion, Manichaeism, came into being. Its founder, Mani, first found favour with the Sassanid ruler but was finally put to death through the opposition of the Zoroastrian priesthood. His cult nevertheless spread from China to France and in Persia itself gained many adherents. At once a socially revolutionary and a religiously mystical movement, it marked a major protest against established religious institutions. Although some of its cosmogonic and cosmological teachings found a place in certain forms of Islamic philosophy, for Persians of the later period Manichaeism has appeared as a rebellion against religious authority. It has never enjoyed the same status as Zoroastrianism, from which it came into being and against which it revolted.

Sassanid Period

The Sassanid period was also witness to other religious movements such as Mazdakism, a 'religious communism' known today mostly through what its enemies, both Zoroastrian and Christian, wrote against it. This movement, which was soon crushed, was again a protest against the Zoroastrian social order and foretold the collapse of this order which occurred with the coming of Islam. Also at this time there developed within Zoroastrianism the philosophico-religious school known as Zurvanism, which indicates a blend of Iranian religious thought with certain Greek philosophical ideas. Finally, it must be remembered that through rivalry with the Byzantines the Sassanids encouraged Oriental Christian sects, especially the Nestorians, these sects were given a free hand to establish schools and missions throughout the Sassanid empire, with the result that notable Christian communities came into existence in Persia and became an important minority religious community in the Islamic period. The Jews also had had several centres in Persia from Achaemenian times, and continued to thrive under both Zoroastrian and Muslim rule. The tolerance toward minority religions shown by Cyrus the Great has been with few exceptions the rule in the religious history of Persia.

The major spiritual transformation in Persia came, strangely enough, not from one of the new members of the family of Iranian religions but from a religion of Abrahamic and Semitic background, namely Islam. Although the military defeat of the Sassanids before the Arab armies was a sudden and rapid process, the spiritual struggle between Islam and Zoroastrianism was a gradual one and did not really terminate until the fourth/tenth century. This fact itself indicates that the Persians accepted Islam, not through force, as is claimed by some modern historians, but because of an inner spiritual need. When the Persians regained their political independence from the caliphate there were still very sizeable Zoroastrian communities in Persia. But instead of showing any inclination to return to this tradition, the newly independent Persian rulers became themselves the champions of the spread of Islam, while insisting on the independence of the literary and cultural life of Persia. Most of the Muslim lands of Asia have, in fact, been Islamicized through the intermediary of the Persian form of Islam. And to this day, when a Persian thinks of the domain of 'Persian culture' he sees before him nearly the whole of the Eastern lands of Islam, from the Western borders of the Iranian plateau to Western China, with Iraq as an intermediary realm where the Persian, Arabic and, later, Turkish elements met.

Islamic History

During early Islamic history Persia was dominated by the Sunni form of Islam. In fact it was from Khurasan that the theological defence of Sunnism was made during the tenth and eleventh centuries, by such masters of theology as al-Juwayn! and al-Ghazzali, when many other lands of Islam were dominated by Shi'ism. Yet, certain centres in Persia such as Qum were from the beginning Shi'ite and the Persians in general had a particular reverence for the household of the Prophet of Islam from the earliest centuries of Islamic history. The figure of Salman al-Farisi, the Persian who in search of the ideal prophet journeyed all the way to Arabia to meet the Prophet and became so close to him as to be called 'one of the members of the household' (ahl-i bayt) of the Prophet, has the deepest significance for the religious consciousness of Islamic Persia. During the early centuries, therefore, Persia was at once a major centre of Sunni Islam, producing such scholars and theologians as al-Bukhari, al-Ghazzali and Fakhr al-Din al-Razi, and a land within which important centres of Shi'sm existed, where many of the greatest early Shi'ite theologians such as Ibn Babuyah and Kulayni were born and nurtured.

Before the Mongol invasion, a devastating material and social calamity for Persia, the forces of Isma'ilism were also strong in this land. Although the centre of their power was in the Yemen and later in Egypt, from the third ninth century onward, there were outstanding philosophers and theologians of this school in Persia, men like Abu Hatim al-Razi, I.lamid al-Din al-Kirmani and Nasir-i Khusraw, who have left us so many doctrinal works on Isma'ilism. Moreover, with the 'resurrection of Alamut', Isma'ilism gained major political power in Persia and continued to exert political pressure until the destruction of Alamut by Hulagu.

Establishment of the Safavids

Between the Mongol invasion and the establishment of the Safavids, Persia moved gradually toward Shi'ism through both social, political and purely religious factors marked by the activity of certain Sufi orders and several outstanding Shi'ite theologians.

Yet, at the time of the establishment of the Safavids and the recognition of Shi'ism as the official state religion, most of Persia was still Sunni. The change, however, was made relatively rapidly and soon the country became predominantly Shi'ite, although noticeable Sunni elements have survived to this day in such areas as Khurasan and Kurdistan.

Persia was also from the beginning of Islamic history one of the lands in which Sufism, the esoteric and mystical dimension of Islam, spread rapidly and expressed itself in the most striking literary and artistic forms. Some of the greatest early Sufis, like al-Bastami and al-Hallaj were Persian, and later the direct influence of Sufism transformed Persian poetry into one of the most universal forms of literature. Both through the direct presence of Sufi orders and through the effect of Sufism upon Persian literature, music, architecture and other forms of art as well as certain social organizations, the spirit of Sufism has left an indelible mark upon many facets of the life of the Persians. It must be remembered, however, that being esoteric in character, Sufism has always preserved its inner teachings for those who have been qualified to follow the Sufi path. It is only the external manifestations of Sufism that have a general cultural and social bearing and are so noticeable a strand in the fabric of Persian life and culture.

It is in the light of this background that we must study the role of Islam in present-day Persia. Because of this long period during which the Persians have become Islamicized in the deepest sense possible, the world view of the Persian today is determined more than anything else by the teachings of Islam. Like other Muslims, the Persian is born, lives and dies with the verses of the Holy Quran echoing in his ears. He sees the world about him in the light of the conception of the Divine and His creation as delineated in the Holy Quran. There is, in fact, in spite of the secularist tendencies of the past fifty years, still no conception of a way of life in which religion is only one element among many or of a world view in which the religious factor is only one dimension. The total world view is religious, and even the apparent negation of religion by certain people has itself a religious significance.

After the Advent of Islam

The universe in which the Persian lives, like that of all Muslims, is one created and sustained by Allah, the Omnipotent and Omniscient Creator, Who is at once the Origin and End of all things, the First and the Last. His will reigns supreme over both the world of nature and the lives of men and their societies. He has knowledge of all things and His majesty causes all that is beside Him to melt into nothingness. Yet he has given man free will to pursue his own life and to choose the 'right path' (al-sirdt al-mustaqim) of his own accord, without compulsion. The secret of man's life lies between these rwo·logically contradictory assertions, of the absolute Omnipotence 'of Allah and of man's free will and responsibility before Him as the Supreme Judge.

Every Muslim is aware throughout his life of the ultimate significance of his actions beyond this world of change and corruption. The Persian Muslim, like his other brethren in faith, may, because of his own weakness, sometimes live a life that is mundane and even directly against various Divine injunctions, but he never doubts for one moment the presence of the Divine Command (al-amr) and his responsibility to follow it. As already stated for Muslims in general, so also for Persians it can be said that there are some who do not heed the voice of the Divine, but there is practically no one who doubts the presence of 'His voice'. That is why after a life of debauchery a man may become suddenly devout, and even in the midst of the most profane life remains aware of the presence of the transcendent dimension of life.

Inasmuch as the will of God is manifested in Islam in the form of a concrete and all-embracing law, the SharPah, the Persian is always aware of the religious character of all facets of life. Since the Shari'ah covers all aspects of human life, to the vast majority of Persians all laws which they encounter and all acts which they perform during their daily lives possess a sacred character even if non-Shari'ite laws have been promulgated in certain domains. Most Persians feel that they are performing a religious duty when they work to make a living, even if the particular work they perform is not itself of a traditional religious nature. By contrast, the small Western-educated classes that have been affected by the Western distinction between the religious and the secular often do not attach this religious significance to their daily work. For them the Sharpah is identified with specific acts of worship which in fact they rarely perform. But they are a small minority. For most Persians, both the uneducated and the educated, the all-embracing nature of the Divine will which governs all facets of man's life through a sacred law is very much a reality and a permanent factor in their general world view.

The Divine will is also seen by Persian Muslims, as by other Muslims in general, in the world of nature, of which the phenomena, in conformity with the teachings of the Holy Quran, are considered as the 'signs of God'. There is no ultimate distinction between the Divine Law governing men and the laws governing nature, between religious and natural law as understood in the West. Nature is a complementary aspect of the religious reality that is revealed directly through revelation. It can therefore incite the deepest intellectual and contemplative response in the traditional Persian, who turns to it both as a source of enjoyment and as the background for the spiritual life. The very austerity of nature in Persia, the high mountains, the vast deserts, the green valleys hidden high in mountain ranges, evoke an awareness of the transcendent. The visible itself is but a veil for the invisible and the laws of the world of nature but a part of the universal law which of necessity governs all things.

The Persian is also keenly aware of the transient nature of things, a point so often emphasized in Islam. He lives with the reality of death and a realization of the instability of all that surrounds him. For him the angelic world, the hierarchy of spiritual beings that stands above the world of material forms, is a constant reality, one that is emphasized in both the ancient religions of Iran and in Islam. If this world is impermanent and transient, there stands beyond it the permanent and luminous world of angelic substances.

Transient Nature

The awareness of the transient nature of this world is combined with a great joy in life and its beauties which reflect the beauty of the higher orders of existence. Few people are given as much to the enjoyment of life's pleasures and beauties as the Persians, but this attitude is always compensated for by the realization that a moment once gone never returns and all that is physical and sensual has an ephemeral character about it. These two attitudes are often reflected even in the distinctly religious activity of chanting the Holy Quran, during which people weep and are carried beyond worldly cares, but which is frequently held in the most beautiful gardens where the best refreshments are served and the voice of the reciter possesses the finest musical quality. At their most spiritual level, these two attitudes are to be found in all Persian Sufi poetry: here one is constantly reminded that the Infinite reflects an aspect of Its beauty at each moment, but because of Its Infinity Its theophanies (tajalliydt) never repeat themselves.

There is also an element of tragedy which characterizes the Persian and which is seen fully in the ethos of Shi'ism. This is not the humanistic tragedy of the later Greeks, a rebellion of man against the gods, associated with the Promethean mentality so characteristic of the decadent period of Greek culture and post-mediaeval Europe, but is a spiritual quality based on man's submission to God and yet his separation from Him. The tragic and sad element (hussn), which does not at all negate the aspect of joy (farah) in life, is always of a religious character and a basis for contemplation. It is most directly reflected in classical Persian music, where the apparently sad quality is in reality a nostalgia for the Divine. It is a tragedy based on the realization that the human condition contains an apparent contradiction. Man is in desperate need to realize the Divine and to become aware of his own spiritual nature. Yet this realization is made well-nigh impossible by the distance that separates him from the Divine and by his need to await Divine assistance to accomplish this end.

Closely connected with this point of view is the concept of the intermediary and intercessor before God, and the expectation of a future saviour, both so important to Shi'ism; man is in need of an intermediary between himself and God. Even after the descent of a revelation, the role of the intermediary must continue. Therefore, after the Prophet of Islam there must be Imams who act as intermediaries between men of later generations, and God. There must also be a future saviour, the Mahdi, who will redeem the world from its state of corruption. From the Shi'ite point of view, he too is an Imam, in fact the twelfth Imam of Shi'ism, but an Imam who, although living and present, is in occultation (ghaybah) and will not reveal himself until a future moment known only to God. The very expectation of his appearance (intizar) is a religious virtue. The ideals of appealing to saints and Imams and of patiently awaiting one who will in the future eradicate injustice and corruption and therefore end the hardships of present-day life are constant elements of the Persian religious outlook.

Religious Institutions and Organizations

As far as religious institutions and organizations are concerned, the most important centre in the life of the Persians, as in that of other Muslims, is the mosque, whose size varies from the colossal Friday mosques of major cities to single rooms in small towns and villages. Its architecture also varies from ornate tiled mosques to mud structures whose walls are covered by whitewash. In all its forms, the mosque is the centre of both religious and social activity in the community. Its door being always open, it remains a calm sanctuary amid the turmoil of daily life, a place where people wander in to say their prayers as well as to consider a transaction or simply to relax with friends in the contemplative and peaceful atmosphere which the mosque creates. In the cities, in fact, the bigger mosques are nearly always situated in the bazaars and are an inseparable part of daily life.

The mosque is also used for congregational prayers, particularly those of Friday, as well as for special occasions of religious mourning or feasting or funerals. The Friday prayers, however, are less emphasized in Persia than in those Muslim lands where Sunni Islam predominates. This is because in the absence of the Mahdi the Friday prayers do not carry any political significance as they do in Sunni Islam, and their importance is not greatly emphasized by the *'ulama'*. Rather, the religious climate is such that the canonical prayers performed individually and often at home are considered as important as prayers at mosques, so that many who do not go regularly to mosques nevertheless do perform their prayers and other religious rites privately at home.

The role of the mosque differs both between the life of the country dweller and the city dweller, and between that of the traditional and the modern Persian. In the countryside, the imam of the mosque often acts as the teacher for elementary education, especially early religious education, and he is the arbitrator in most disputes. After daily prayers, people usually gather about him to pose questions about problems which would otherwise have to be taken to court. In the smaller cities, these customs are retained to a certain degree, but in larger cities both functions, elementary education and judging cases, are performed outside the mosque, although in the second case the arbitrator is himself usually a religious authority. The larger mosques in big cities also perform an educational service on a higher level, in that they are usually affiliated with a religious school or madrasah in which more advanced religious education is carried out.

As for the modern educated classes, particularly those who have been educated in the West, as a rule they do not go to mosques except on special occasions. Many of them do make pilgrimages or participate in the mourning of Muharram or funeral rites, all of which are usually connected with mosques, but they rarely attend their local mosques for daily prayers. Although there are notable exceptions, one can say that in this aspect of religious life they are sharply distinguished from the rest of Persian society.

Madrasah System

The madrasah system, which has its roots in the early centuries of Islamic history, is the means whereby the intellectual aspect of the religious tradition is kept alive. In these schools, which are endowed and usually connected with a major mosque, students who have undergone an early religious education continue their studies. They are fully supported by the madrasah, receiving accommodation on the premises as well as board and other expenses. There is no pressure on them to finish their studies in a certain period as in modern universities, nor are any specific degrees conferred upon them. Some stay in a madrasah for their whole life and, if competent, become teachers in their turn. The students mostly choose the field of the transmitted (naqlt) sciences, studying law, the principles of jurisprudence, Quranic exegesis, hadith, etc. Some, however, choose the intellectual ('aqli) sciences, and pursue logic, Islamic philosophy, theology, etc.

The largest madrasah system today, which is in Qum, has over six thousand students, and there are other major centres in Mashhad, Tehran, Isfahan and several other cities. Moreover, besides the official lessons taught in the madrasah, classes are often held in the homes of individual professors and masters, often in more advanced phases of study. These classes are particularly important in the field of traditional Islamic philosophy or theosophy (hikmafi) as well as in gnosis ('irfan). In these private circles, many who do not belong to the madrasahs also participate, including often some who have had a modern, rather than a purely traditional, education. One could even say that most of the teaching of the Islamic intellectual sciences in Persia today is performed outside formal institutions and in private circles.

Shi'ite Imams

Shrines, or tombs of the Shi'ite Imams, their descendants and Sufi saints, play a major role in the life of all classes of Persians. They consist usually of a mausoleum and a mosque, often with a madrasah and a library attached, and are supported by endowments and donations. Of those within Persia itself, the most important is that of the eighth Imam, 'All al-Rida, in Mashhad, which is visited by hundreds of thousands of people every month. It has a vast complex of mosques and courtyards around the central mausoleum, as well as dispensaries, hospitals, a major library, a museum, a madrasah, etc. Over a thousand people are fed at each meal free of charge and there is no time of the year when the shrine is not completely filled with throngs of the faithful from not only all corners of Persia itself but also the Arab World and the Indo-Pakistani sub-continent. Next to Mashhad, the holy city of Qum is the most important, inasmuch as it is the site of the tomb of Imam Rida's sister, Hadrat-i Ma'sumah, and the seat of the most influential Shi'ite mujtahids. It too, is frequented by many pilgrims throughout the year. The tombs of Hadrat-i 'Abd al-'Azim near Tehran in Rayy, Shah Chiragh in Shiraz and cih Ni'matallah Wall, the famous Sufi, near Kirman, are all shrine institutions of prime importance. Other shrines are located on tops of mountains in difficult locations, in awesome sites of nature connected with the traditional xoence of sacred geography. There is no city or town without a site of pilgrimage and a saint to whom the people turn in their moments of trial as well as in moments of thankfulness. All of these shrines play a fundamental role in daily religious life, inasmuch as people turn to these saints as intermediaries between them and God and ask through them what they wish to ask of God. There is hardly anyone in Persia, even the most modern, for whom the power of the grace or barakah of these shrines has ceased to exist.

The Sufi centres, called khanaqah in Persian, are also major focuses of religious life, although Sufism itself transcends the exoteric dimension of religion and is concerned with the esoteric teachings of Islam. The khanaqah is usually either the home of a living Sufi master or the tomb of a dead one which has become the centre of the order. In either case, it is a complex of buildings in which thefuqara', or dervishes, meet for their sessions of spiritual practice and where there are rooms for travelling dervishes as well as cells for those who make spiritual retreats (khalwah). On special religious holidays such as the birthdays of the Prophet and 'All as well as during days of mourning, the khanaqahs open their doors to all who come to participate in the ceremonies held there. Even at other times the khanaqah acts as a pole of spiritual attraction for the community itself, even if those outside its organization are not completely aware of all that is taught within its walls to members of the order'.

The major Sufi orders in Persia today are the Ni'matallahi, with many branches throughout the country; the Gunabad! (itself a branch of the Ni'matallahi) centred in Khurasan; the Dhahabi with its major centre in Shiraz; the Qadiri, powerful mostly in

Kurdistan and the Persian Gulf region; the Khaksar, popular especially among craftsmen; and the Naqshband!, having its centre in Kurdistan. These orders, many of which have close contacts with branches in other Muslim lands, continue to influence the general structure of society and cultural life, in particular literature, music and calligraphy. The very presence of a living gnostic path of spirituality also has its effect on intellectual pursuits, especially traditional Islamic philosophy, which for this very reason is not just a rational form of knowledge but a theosophy or hikmah, ultimately an aid to spiritual realization. But, of course, because of the nature of Sufism, the profoundest influence of its teachings remains confined within the circle of the spiritual elite.

The institution of religious endowment (waqf), which is one of the important Islamic institutions, is the means whereby the above-mentioned religious organizations as well as many others are in most cases supported. Usually cultivated lands, even pastures, wells, trees, etc., are given as endowment for a particular religious institution. A person is chosen to act as keeper and executor of the endowment, and under his direction the income is to be spent in accordance with the will of the founder. Today, a certain amount of organization has been given to this matter through the establishment of a department of waqf by the government. But the institution is far from being government-controlled, and in most cases it is still the person in charge of the endowment or his family who hold power in their hands.

Impact of Modern Civilization

In traditional Persian society, as in other similar societies, every social institution possessed religious and spiritual significance. In modern times, although, as a result of the encroachment of secularism, some of these institutions no longer have a direct religious colouring, others have a religious connection even if they are not, strictly speaking, religious organizations. Of these the guilds (asnaf) are of great importance. Existing in all the bigger cities, the guilds draw members of a particular occupation such as bakers, bricklayers or carpet-weavers into an organization which still preserves in many fields its original connection with Sufi orders and the chivalrous brotherhoods or futuwvsat. Most of the guilds have a particular reverence for 'All, the traditional patron saint of all Islamic guilds, and possess a strong feeling of fraternity'. Even labour organizations which resemble unions in the Western sense possess some of the characteristics of the guilds, and it is difficult in most cases to draw a line between the guild and the union.

In certain quarters, some social significance still pertains to the remnants of orders of chivalry centred around gymnasia called ssur-khdnah. Again closely connected with the name of 'All, these orders served traditionally to enhance the spirit of chivalry (jawan-mardi) and to build up moral and spiritual character'. In their centres, bodily exercises are performed to the beating of a drum and the chanting of religious and epic verses. Traditional Persian cities, like other Muslim cities, have had local strong men who have kept the peace and protected the morals (namus) of their quarters of the city. Such types have usually been connected in Persia with the zw-khanah and still perform this function in many cities, although they stand in rather stark contrast to some of the Westernized youth in the Modernised parts of Tehran who are devoid of the traditional virtues of chivalry inculcated by these orders.

Finally, mention must be made of certain recently founded organizations usually connected with bureaucratic professions and some which are affiliated to Sufi orders. There are also lodges of Freemasons which, in the Persian climate, have in a few cases gained a Muslim colouring, while some attempt has even been made to connect them to certain of the khanaqahs.' In a few cases, there has come into being a Persian version of an organization resembling these lodges but of a more directly religious character and attracting many from the modern educated classes. In all these cases, a religious element is present, though it varies from one organization, and even from one individual, to another.

Because of the all-embracing nature of the Sacred Law or Shari'ah, there is in reality no aspect of social life in Persia, as in the rest of the Muslim world, which is completely divorced from religious principles, even if modernism and older historical forces resuscitated as a result of the influence of modernism have removed certain aspects of social life from the direct jurisdiction of the Shari'ah. Those domains of social life in which the Shari'ah is still directly applied in Persia are personal law such as marriage, divorce, etc., as well as much of civil law. In this domain, even what was taken from European codes was taken with the approval of the 'ulama' and was integrated into the matrix of the Shari'ah through the practice of 'independent juridical opinion'. Moreover, those who practice law and administer it are nearly all either products of the madrasahs or the law schools and theological faculties where they have been exposed to Islamic jurisprudence (fiqh).

It is rather in the domain of economic life that non-Shari'ite practices are most often seen. In the field of taxation, non-Islamic systems have been used from Umayyad times in addition to the Islamic religious tax which, in Sufism, consists of zakat and khwns. Many wealthy men, especially merchants in bazaars, do, however, continue to pay the religious taxes in addition to those demanded by the government. The religious tax is, in fact, a major source of support for centres of Shi'ite learning in such cities as Qum.

Religious Spirit

The religious spirit manifests itself in economic life not so much in specific norms as in attitudes. The Islamic view of the permitted (halal) and forbidden (haram), the condemnation of usury, of amassing wealth in gold and silver, of usurping the right of orphans, and many other injunctions, even if not practised by all, penetrate subtly into economic life. Also, the more philosophical attitude of uncertainty about what tomorrow will bring, distrust of purely human causation, the feeling of the impermanence of things, all play their role in fields of economic life where specific religious norms may seem to be absent.

As for political life, since Shi'ism in contrast to Sunnism does not accept the religious legitimacy of the institution of the caliphate and believes monarchy to be the best form of government in the absence of the Mahdi, the Persian monarchy possesses a positive religious aspect. Ever since the establishment of Shi'ism as the official state religion by the Safavids, the monarch has been considered from the religious point of view as the legitimate ruler who should govern with the consent of the 'religious scholars' or 'ulama', and whose duty it is to uphold the SharVah and to promulgate Islam. This view is explicitly mentioned in the present Persian constitution. The connection of the monarchy with the religious structure of Shi'ism in Persia has been a persistent element of Persian history during the past four centuries, and gives a religious tone to political life even if parliamentary government is not itself an institution of Islamic origin.

Religious and Modern Secular Norms

The confrontation between religious and modern secular norms is best seen in the present educational system in Persia. There are, in fact, two systems of education, one the madrasahs which produce religious scholars, lawyers, imams of mosques, etc., and the other the modern educational system leading to university degrees in various fields. Here religion is taught as a subject among others in the elementary and secondary school curricula, but one does not find the pervasive religious character of all education that has always existed in traditional Islamic society. In the universities also, besides faculties of theology, subjects connected with religious philosophy, law etc., are taught in faculties of letters and law, but here again other subjects are left outside the religious sphere. There is a direct confrontation between religious and 'secular' disciplines of learning, a confrontation which did not exist in the traditional Islamic world view where every science, be it natural, mathematical or philosophical, possessed a traditional and sacred aspect and was never divorced from the total religious and intellectual life of Islam.

As far as philosophy is concerned, it is important to note that traditional Islamic philosophy is still very much alive in Persia. Secular European schools of philosophy are taught in universities but have had comparatively little effect upon the general intellectual life of the country. In fact the very presence of a living Islamic intellectual tradition has prevented facile and shallow modern interpretations of Islam in Persia such as are found in some other Muslim countries. Moreover, as mentioned before, even modern philosophical discussions, once translated into the Persian language, have had to take cognizance of the presence of the Islamic philosophical tradition.

In literature, architecture, the plastic arts, music, theatre, and other forms of artistic and cultural life, traditional forms which have a completely religious and spiritual basis subsist while modern forms have been introduced with varying degrees of 'success' among certain classes. In such cases as the theatre, where the traditional form consisted solely of passion plays, Western forms of theatre depicting problems of Western man have had little appeal to the vast majority of the population, their popularity remaining limited to the few, among Western-educated people located mostly in Tehran. A few attempts have also been made to use Persian and Islamic themes and motifs. In the other arts, the traditional forms have sometimes been used in new contemporary settings, occasionally with success, but often with a result that falls far short of genuine traditional art forms. But by and large, the traditional religious forms of artistic and cultural expression subsist and in certain cases dominate, while the Modernised minority in Persian society surrounds itself ever increasingly with various aspects of Western artistic expressions and forms.

Important Religious Practices

The most important religious practices of Persians, like those of all Muslims in general, are the rites of prayers, fasting, pilgrimage and sacrifice, which are all slightly coloured by the secondary aspects that these rites have acquired against the background of Persian culture. Their essential element is that of the universal norms of Islam itself. The daily prayers, which most Shi'ites usually perform three times a day by connecting with a short pause those of noon and afternoon as well as those of evening and night, punctuate the rhythm of daily life. It would not be an exaggeration to say that the conception of time and the flow of life itself are determined by these canonical prayers, which are considered as the pillar of Islam. In addition the very devout perform supererogatory prayers (nawafil) and there are special prayers connected with hope, fear, expectation etc.

Fasting as a religious rite is connected particularly with the holy month of Ramadan, although, again, many devout people fast on different occasions throughout the year, especially the beginning, the middle and the end of the lunar Islamic month. During Ramadan the rhythm of life changes and there is a perceptible transformation of the most external aspects of daily life. Many of the Modernised Persians do not fast, but on the whole the fast is observed throughout the country. During the holy month, days become calm and sombre and the evenings gay. Many more social calls are made to relatives during the evening, and at this time after the breaking of the fast religious and social life become completely intertwined.

The climax of the holy month comes during the nights of the 19th to the twenty first, the period during which the first Imam 'All was struck on the head while praying in the mosque at Kufa and died of the wounds two days later'. During these nights, all amusements and parties are halted and mourning is observed in both homes and mosques. The period culminates in the night of the zist, called the 'night of vigilance' (ihya'), during which mosques are thronged until the morning hours. People perform a hundred prostrations (rak'ah) of prayer and chant litanies and supplications (especially the famous Shi'ite prayer called Jawshan-i kabir) until the rising of the sun.

Persian Religious Life

Pilgrimage, as already pointed out, plays a major role in Persian religious life. The obligatory pilgrimage is, of course, that made to Mecca (hajj), by virtue of which man crowns the religious performances of his life. Since making this pilgrimage requires financial means and the ability to provide for one's family in advance, those who make the hajj (who are called haji in its Persian pronounciation) are identified with a certain wealth and economic well-being. The haji is respected bv all devout people, but, in the bazaar particularly, to be a haji also confers social and economic advantages. And since all hajis in the bazaar are not always beyond reproach in their dealings, some criticism of them can be sensed among the Modernised classes. For many years, in fact, making the hajj had become rarer in the modern educated segment of Persian society. But this has changed completely in the last decade, and now the annual hajj caravan includes people from every walk of life.

The other places of pilgrimage, especially Najaf, Karbala, Samarra, al-Kazimayn in Iraq, and Mashhad and Qum in Persia, are also of the greatest significance in daily religious life. These centres, as well as the smaller sites connected with different saints, bring the barakah of the centre of Islam and of the Prophet to the outer territories. These centres are all echoes of the supreme centre where Heaven and earth meet. There is hardly a Persian who does not make at least a few pilgrimages to a tomb of some saint with the continuous hope of being able to visit the more 'central' ones whenever possible. Although some pilgrimages involve special hardship, the centres being located on mountain-tops or places with a bad climate, most pilgrimages combine religious asceticism with the enjoyment of God's bounties and the beauties of art and nature. For a large segment of the population, such a pilgrimage is the most enjoyable experience of the year, although it is also a time of the most intense purification, a period of prayer and asking for forgiveness that leaves its mark upon the person long after the pilgrimage has come to an end.

The hajj terminates with the feast of sacrifice ('id-i adha or 'id-i qurban) commemorating the sacrifice of Abraham. During this day, not only in Mecca but throughout the Muslim world, sheep are sacrificed. Herds are marked with special colours and brought into the city before the occasion, and on the morning of the 'id the sacrifice is made, the meat being given to the poor and to neighbours. But besides this, sacrifice is made throughout the year. Firstly,all meat that is used for daily food is slaughtered ritually and sacrificed, and secondly, on almost any joyous occasion, such as the arrival of a traveller from a long journey, the birth of a child (particularly a son), the arrival of an honoured guest, and the building of a new house, sacrifices are made, usually of sheep but sometimes of other lawful animals, including, occasionally, camels'.

A religious practice that is particular to the Shi'ite world, ęspecially Persia, is the raudoh, which was developed in its present form during the Safavid period. The roudoh (a word derived from the title of the work Rawdat al-shuhadd', meaning the 'Garden of Martyrs') consists of sessions during which sermons are delivered combined with the chanting of verses of the Quran and religious poems, with special emphasis on the tragedy of Karbala. These sessions are held most of all during the two-month period of Muharram and Safar, revolving around the death of Husayn and its aftermath. Much religious and moral preaching to the public takes place on these occasions. The rawdah is held in mosques as well as in private homes. On the crucial dates of the ninth and tenth of Muharram on which the tragedy of Karbala itself occurred, there are even government-sponsored rawdah throughout the country, the sessions are marked by sobbing and wailing, particularly on the, part of women, as all discourse is brought back periodically to the theme of the death of the members of the household of the Prophet.

Religious practice also enters into daily life at the critical moments of birth, marriage and death as in other parts of the Islamic world and, in fact, in other religions. At the moment of birth there is the simple recitation of the 'testimony of Islam' or the Shahadah in the ear of the new-born child. In the case of boys, the rite of circumcision is perhaps even more directly connected with religious practices than birth itself. As for marriage, although it is a contract and not a sacramental act, nevertheless, since it is made valid by virtue of the Shari'uft, it is definitely a religious act. The verses binding the contract are usually read by one of the 'ulama' although any male Muslim can perform this and other functions of a priestly nature.

It is naturally at the moment of death that religious rites become most vividly remembered and seriously practised. The acts of washing the body and burial are all performed in accordance with Islamic law. Afterwards, a funeral service is held which men attend in a mosque, and another where women gather in the home of the deceased or of one of his or her relatives. Since to attend those services is a social duty and most men have many friends and relatives, attendance at funeral services in mosques is a regular event throughout one's life. The sermon delivered after the chanting of the Holy Quran is the best means available to religious authorities to reach the higher strata of society, especially those who hold political power in their hands. That is why a funeral service held for a member of the government or for a person of high reputation holds a special significance in the religio-political life of Persia. In fact, several political assassinations and attempts toward this end have been made on such occasions during the modern history of Persia.

There is also a practice called preparing sufrah, popular among women, at which a table is laid full of all kinds of food, to which friends and neighbours are invited. During the 'feast', a person specializing in performing the rawdah, called rawdah-khwan, chants the Quran and religious poems and preaches on religious, themes. The rest of the food is then given to the poor and some taken to each participant's home and given to friends and relatives, especially those who are ill, as an object possessing barakah (tabarruk). The sufrah, being especially for women, is usually connected with important events in the lives of women in the household of the Prophet such as Fatimah and Zaynab. The whole process of preparing the table, which is done with the greatest care and the best taste, is considered as a religious labour, one in which, once again, denial of the world is combined with the enjoyment of God's bounty.

The sufrah, as well as pilgrimage and many other religious acts, is often performed as a result of a vow and solemn promise to God (nadhr) in return of which the person asks something of God. The practice of nadhr is very popular in all segments of Persian society, especially among women. Women make a vow to pay so much money to the poor or "set a sufrah if they bear a child or if their daughter finds a suitable mate". Students often vow to fast or perform a certain pilgrimage if they pass their examinations. Merchants in the bazaar make the nadhr to sacrifice so many sheep if their business transactions succeed. There is continuous 'religious barter', in which Persians, like other traditional people, ask of God something in exchange for which they perform acts pleasing to Him. One can hardly understand the psychology of the Persian and the tensions of hope and fear within him without understanding his attitude toward nadhr and the 'barter' he makes continuously with the Creator. Only the saintly man lives fully according to the will of God without asking anything in return. But this highest spiritual attitude does not in any way invalidate the general exoteric religious form of it.

Besides religious practices that have been sanctioned and protected by the 'ulama'. and represent the conscious, intellectual aspects of Islamic tradition there are many popular practices which are often combined with the most in tense religious fervour and enthusiasm. During the month of Muharram, long processions are organized by men who, dressed in black, celebrate the passion of Karbala by chanting religious poems and often beating themselves until they fall into a state of frenzy. Occasionally these practices are carried to extremes, some beating themselves with chains and even swords until they faint from loss of blood. Most processions, however, march through the streets of cities to the solemn rhythm of drum beats and the harmony of human voices choking with grief. In larger cities, the sight of thousands of men and boys marching behind religious emblems and symbols of the family of the Prophet is a most moving religious experience.

There is also the passion play (ta'ziyah), which, although developed into an aristocratic art in Safavid and Qajar times, is essentially a popular religious manifestation. It is not usually encouraged by the 'ulama', although they do not oppose it since it is a medium for profound religious expression. Varying from simple versions in the villages to elaborate ones in big cities, the taziah depicts the events that led to the martyrdom of Husayn at Karbala. The climax is usually performed at high noon on the day of 'Ashwa, the tenth of Muharram, when the third Shi'ite Imam, Husayn, died and was beheaded. In a city like Qum, where several thousand people participate in the performance of the drama and thousands more flock from the countryside to join the population of the city in observing the ta'ziyah, one sees one of the most overwhelming manifestations of religious life in Persia.

Finally, among popular religious phenomena one cannot overlook the interest in omens, magic and other occult arts. Islam, on the Shari'ite level, opposes the practice of magic, but that has not prevented people, especially women, from utilizing it often in combination with specifically Muslim practices. Furthermore, there is a complete traditional science of the 'magic-like' use of Quranic phrases, that is, the recitation of formulae for appropriate occasions. Although this science is itself far from being 'popular' in the usual sense, it has a widely extended field of application in daily life. There are also prayers (du'd') connected with the names of Imams and Sufi saints which people carry about with them or recite on various occasions. Besides their purely religious aspect, practices of this kind have also acquired a kind of magical quality. The 'prayer writer' (du'a'-niwis), like the practitioner of geomancy (rammal), is a permanent fixture in the life of Persian women in both the city and the countryside. He combines strictly religious elements with all forms of fortune-telling and both occult and pseudo-occult sciences.

Rhythm of Life

The rhythm of life in Persia is determined by a number of holidays, many Islamic, some derived from ancient Persia and a few celebrating modern national events. Both the Islamic and the ancient Persian dates have a wholly religious aspect. Even the ancient Zoroastrian naw-russ or 'New Year', which marks the Persian new year to this day, has acquired a completely Islamic colour. At the moment of the vernal equinox, people place the Quran on their tables along with the seven objects beginning with the letter 's' (the haft sin or seven s's) that have survived from Zoroastrian days. Prayers are also said and benedictions invoked upon the Prophet and his family.

As for the Islamic religious dates, the festivities of adhd at the end of the hajj, 'id-i-fitr at the end of Ramadan, the date of the birth of the Prophet, the birthday of 'All and 'id-ighadir, when according to Shi'ite belief 'All was chosen by the Prophet as his successor, are widely celebrated as joyous occasions. Also of great importance is the date of birth of the Mahdi, when all crties are illuminated with countless lights.

The calendar is also dotted with tragic events, the most important being the loth of Muharram, the death of Husayn, the zist of Ramadan, the death of 'All, the 28th of Safar, the death of the Prophet and the second Imam Hasan, as well as the dates of the deaths of other Imams and of Fatimah. All these dates mark an intensification of religious life and a transformation of many aspects of daily life. The tragic element in the Persian soul expresses itself at the highest levels during these occasions, which have the effect of cleansing the individual and society from the dross of neglecting their religious vocation.

Shi'ite Teachings

There exist in Persia today a number of sects which are marked by their emphasis upon a certain aspect of Shi'ite teachings at the expense of other elements, and by their ensuing separation from the main community. Of these the Isma'ilis are perhaps the oldest, being the remnant of the much larger Isma'ili community of early mediaeval times. In religious beliefs they are close to the Twelve-Imam Shi'ites except on the question of the Hidden Imam or Mahdi. Theologically, of particular interest are the Shaykhis, centred mostly in Kirman, and founded by Shaykh Ahmad Ahsa'i two centuries ago. They emphasize the role of ta'wil, or spiritual hermeneutics, and have a special reverence for the Imams. The 'Ali-Allahi and Ahl-i Haqq have followers in Kurdistan, Mazandaran and some of the southern provinces. Some members of these sects even go to the extreme of believing in the divinity of 'All and also in re-incarnation.

The significance of these sects from the point of view of the general religious life of Persia is that most of them belittle the practice of the Sharfah, and some do not even perform the daily prayers in the usual manner. In most cases they represent Sufi orders that have become politicized or have taken on an external social character resulting in the destruction, of the equilibrium which characterizes the orthodox Muslim community, Sunnite and Shi'ite alike. They are nevertheless Islamic sects in that they are still within the total matrix of the Islamic tradition. Such is not, however, the case with Babism and Baha'ism, particularly the latter, which broke completely away from the structure of Islam and cannot in any way be considered as an Islamic movement or sect. The presence of Baha'ism in Persia today, therefore, even if limited in its membership, has a role to play in the process of secularization and in the destruction of the religious unity of the country.

In conclusion it must be noted that the Persian psyche possesses an elasticity that makes the study of religion in Persia based on external forms alone difficult. From outward signs, one sees the superimposition of a modern, Westernized class, more or less torn away from religious practices, upon the traditional Persian society, nearly all aspects of whose life are dominated by the religious spirit. Even pre-Islamic norms have become, for those living in the matrix of the traditional Persian world, totally Muslimized. But even among the Modernised who outwardly seem completely secularized there exist many traditional religious tendencies which in a people of less elastic mentality would not be conceivable. One often sees women who dress in the latest European fashions and try to act like Western women but who, at the same time, display a completely traditional religious attitude at moments of stress or sorrow or on religious occasions. Likewise, many men who present a rationalistic front indifferent to religion become totally transformed in holy places of pilgrimage or at moments of participation in religious ceremonies.

It can therefore be said that most of contemporary Persian life is still dominated in its universal principles as well as in its daily acts by the spirit and form of the Islamic revelation, which also integrated into its world view elements of older religions which were in conformity with its own principles. Moreover, whereas certain domains of life have drawn away from the orbit of traditional religious life as a result of the advent of modernism, even in these domains religious elements and attitudes persist. Of course in Persia, as in the Arab World, there are the few who have become torn a\vav completely from Islam, at least outwardly, and who possess a world-view based upon imitation of various Western ideologies and who experience constantly that tension between East and West alluded to in earlier chapters concerning

Muslims in general. But for the vast majority of Persians, the religious truths by which they have lived and died for centuries continue to dominate the horizon of their lives today, even if occasional clouds momentarily obscure the horizon from some eyes. The clouds, however, can never be permanent, and there is hardly anyone who during his lifetime does not gain some kind of vision ot that horizon which has co-ordinated and oriented the lives of Persians, as of other Muslims, throughout the ages and continues as the most abiding reality today.

18

Arab Nations Today

The Arabs were chosen as the recipients and the first propagators of the Islamic revelation, and since the inception of Islamic civilization their destiny hag remained indissolubly bound with the earthly manifestations of Islam wherever these might be. The vast majority of Arabs are Muslims, and even the few among the Muslim Arabs who have recently rebelled against the faith are nevertheless influenced in many ways by Islam's norms and spirit. Their psychic and mental make-up has been moulded and structured for too long by Islam to allow its influence to be eradicated overnight. In the lives of those Arabs who consciously practise Islam and accept its teachings, and even of the few who have wandered away from its sacred mould, Islam remains the overwhelming reality, penetrating even now into practically every aspect of their individual and collective existence.

But despite this indissoluble bond between Islam and the Arabs, events of the past century have caused the penetration of many foreign ideas, ranging from nationalism and secularism to socialism and Marxism, into the traditional universe of the Arabs, and have brought about some modifications in the understanding of the traditional pattern of religion among certain classes. These factors must, of course, be evaluated and considered in any appraisal of the situation of Islam in the contemporary Arab world, for they form the background of the complex and often bewildering scene observable today.

Present-day Religious Life

The first element to consider in studying present-day religious life among the Arabs is the shock received by all Muslims, and especially the Arabs, during the nineteenth century, from the domination of the European powers, a domination Which for Muslims posed a crisis of cosmic dimensions. For the first time in their history, except for the short episode of the Mongol invasion, Muslims experienced political humiliation at the hands of non-Muslims.The very promise of the Holy Quran to give Afusn'ms victory in the world provided they remained faithful to Islam seemed to have become negated by the experience of history itself. This shock, at once political, social and religious, was the source of a series of reactions of differing natures, ranging from the 'reform' movements, which sought to purify Islam, to various forms of Mahdism, which saw in the corruption of the times a confirmation of the teachings of the Quran about the latter days, and to out-and-out secularism, which, however, did not gain any notable followers until the present century.

Facing the Reality

The unitary nature of Islam, combined with the nature of the political shock received from Western domination, has made political considerations a major aspect of the religious thought and writing of many contemporary Arabs. Strangely enough, this emphasis has been fortified in the twentieth century by the final political humiliation of the Arabs in Palestine at the hands of a movement which is itself inseparable from religion, despite its fiercely nationalistic and often secular character. The tragedy of Palestine, which for the Arabs was the final confirmation of the immorality of Western politics, emphasized at the same time for many of them the religious aspect of political activity and the pertinence of the political expression of religious sentiments even in the modern world. Palestine has become for the Arabs at once the supreme political issue and the tracing upon the canvas of history of the image of traditional accounts of eschatological events of the greatest religious importance relating to the city of Jerusalem.

The political preoccupations of the Arabs in the nineteenth century, combined with the development of a sense of frustration and also a sense of cultural weakness vis-a-vis the West, resulted finally in the attempt to adopt Western patterns of nationalism. The fire of Arab nationalism, first lit by a group of Western-educated Arabs mostly from Syria and also mostly Christian, soon transformed the political life of the Arab World. First of all it helped to break up the Ottoman Empire, then to bring independence to various Arab states, and finally to bring about the movement to seek to unify them, this last phase remaining still in the stage of trial and experiment. But even this force, which was originally of a purely Western and secularist origin, became gradually Muslimized as it penetrated the masses, to the extent that today Arabism, or 'uribah, is identified closely by the majority of the common people almost automatically with Islam. For a simple Arab in the street, any Muslim who knows a few verses of the Quran and can perform his prayers is considered somehow to be 'an Arab', for in his mind to be Arab and to be Muslim are the same. Even in educated circles in such countries as Egypt and Algeria, many people closely identify national and Islamic bonds and affiliations. Politics remains inseparable from religion and a great deal of the religious thinking of the Arabs has been devoted during the past century to political facets of Islam and the Arab World.

Attack of the West

The attack of the West upon the Arab World, aside from its political effects, was also a direct attack against Islam as a religion. The Arab has remained conscious of the fact that ever since his political subjugation his religion and his culture have been the target of innumerable assaults, ranging from out-and-out slander by older missionaries and orientalists to much more subtle techniques of 'de Islamicizing' the minds of Muslim youth in Western-owned and directed educational institutions in the Arab World. Much of Muslim religious thought, therefore, took an apologetic turn from late in the nineteenth century, and gradually there came into being a certain type of Muslim religious thinker who had already unconsciously lost the intellectual battle to modernism and the West, and was now seeking only to defend his faith by showing that somehow every fashionable thought of the time had been Islamic before being adopted by the West. Even discoveries of modern science, which, of course, soon become stale and outmoded, were traced back to the Quran as if to show that the grandeur of the Quran resides in anticipating this or that discovery of physics or biology. The apologetic attitude became, because of the incessant attacks of the West, an almost ubiquitous aspect of the religious thought and writings of Modernised Arabs, and to this day it remains, along with the political preoccupation mentioned above, of importance in a certain type of religious writing that is read widely by the Modernised classes of society.

The attack made upon Islam hastened another tendency which had been inaugurated in the twelfth/eighteenth century in the heartland of the Arab World by Muhammad ibn 'Abd al-Wahhab and others to 'purify' Islam by returning to the sources of the religion and doing away with the later developments of the Islamic tradition, both intellectual and artistic. Had there not been the shock of Western domination, this movement would have probably developed along lines very different from those which it actually took. As it was, frustration in the face of complete domination by the West forced this movement to become more and more the rallying point for the well-known 'reformist' movement associated with the names of such men as 'Abd al-Rahman al-Kawakibi, Jamal al-Din al-Afghani (or Astarabadi) and Muhammad 'Abduh and Rashid Rida, to the extent that, with Rashid Rida, the intellectual background of the reform of the Salafiyyah—as his school was called—was nearly the same as that of the Wahhabis. In both cases there was, along with a positive emphasis upon the Shari'ah, an opposition to Sufism and the mystical life, to Islamic philosophy and to nearly the whole Islamic intellectual tradition. A 'rationalism' was developed which was combined with 'puritanism' and based upon a jurisdical and theological attitude which drew much from the writings of Ibn Taymiyyah and his students and which limited the vast horizons of Islamic intellectual life to a small portion of its traditional expanse. The effect of this type of religious thinking among the educated classes in the Arab World is still considerable, especially in the Arab Near East. The Maghrib of the Arab World, however, has been to some extent spared from this wave which swept over Egypt and Syria, not to speak of Wahhabi Saudi Arabia, during the past century.

In opposition to this fundamentalist and puritanical tendency, there developed gradually among the Arabs from the beginning of this century another mode of thought, which preached various degrees of secularism and ranged from mild defences of Western civilization to the writings of Salamah Musa and the early Taha Pusayn, who preached the complete adoption of Western culture and a total break with the sacred ambience of traditional Islam. Of course at the very moment when such men began to defend Western culture and secularism, others like Mustafa Sadiq al-Rafi'i, Mustafa Lutfi al-Manfaluti and Shakib Arsalan rose and violently attacked their writings. Nevertheless, views similar to those of the secularists have continued to be held by a certain number of influential men, and the present situation of Islam among certain classes of Arab society today cannot be understood without this background, although the present supporters of such a position are of a type somewhat different from the earlier secularists.

In addition to the tendencies and movements already mentioned, another reaction began among the Arabs, mostly after the Second World War, which has modified greatly the effect of these earlier movements. This new reaction was the disenchantment with the West and the realization of its moral bankruptcy, made so evident by the atrocities of the World War and later in the Palestine war and its aftermath. The blind admiration of the West espoused by so many of the 'leaders' of the previous generation gave way to doubt about the value of the civilization for whose sake the Arabs were asked to forsake their own religion and way of life. Some men, like Taha Husayn, even recanted openly in their later writings and expressed serious misgivings about Western civilization and its fruits. This awareness, which is still in the process of transforming the Arab image of the West, has a profound effect upon the role and function of religion among the Arabs, for it must be remembered that since the nineteenth century it has always been on the strength of arguments drawn from Western sources, and by appealing to the success of the West, that Arabs have been asked, and in fact are still being asked by certain purblind leaders of the blind, to abandon their own tradition.

Society and Economy

In the Arab World today, besides the purely intellectual and mental factors expressed in currents of thought and affecting religion on its articulate plane, there are factors of a social and economic nature and elements dealing with everyday life that have as much—if not more—effect upon religious life as philosophical and theological ideas. In fact, today in the Islamic world in general and the Arab World in particular, Islam is being corroded more by the penetration of foreign modes of everyday living than by the scientific or agnostic philosophical ideas which have affected Christianity so greatly since the Renaissance. One of the best means of gauging the intensity of Islamic religious life is to study the degree to which the Shari'ah, in its full meaning and embracing all of life, is applied in a particular ambience. In its formal and legalistic aspect, the Shari'ah is applied in varying degrees, from countries like Saudi Arabia and Kuwait, which use only Shari'ite law, to lands like Tunisia, where much of the law is derived from European codes. On the jurisdical level there is discernible a complex pattern which, for the most part, shows the attempt of most Arab governments to modify the teachings of the Shari'ah but to remain as much as possible within its injunctions and principles.

But the more difficult and profound problem is to study to what degree the mode of life, which was once dictated totally by the Shari'ah, has become secularized. Here one will discover that, surprisingly enough, even in countries where non-Shari'ite laws have been introduced, the concept of secular law or the secularization of life remains singularly alien to the mind of the vast majority of Arabs, save for a few who are thoroughly Westernized. But the encroachment of the kind of mundane and frivolous life which is characteristic of modern industrial societies is to be seen in larger Arab cities. The breaking of the injunctions of the

Shari'ah concerning such questions as adultery or the use of alcoholic drinks is an ever more frequent phenomenon in big cities, even by people who consider themselves definitely Muslim and who would protest violently if classified otherwise, but who are generally unaware of the contradictions involved in their manner of living. The Modernised Arab, like his Persian or Turkish counterpart, is drawn away from religion more through the temptation to create a sensuous and false 'paradise' around himself than by the attempt to play the role of the divinity like an agnostic Western philosopher. For Islam, the danger comes more from men so engulfed by the life of the senses and mundanity as to forget completely the sacred aspect of life taught by religion than from the type of rationalistic philosopher who in the Renaissance destroyed the unity of Christendom and weakened the hold of faith upon men. The Shari'ah continues to be respected as the concrete expression of God's Will, but more and more men in the big cities allow its hold upon their lives to be compromised by the penetration of completely un-Islamic modes of acting and living.

One of the important aspects of Islam in contemporary life among the Arabs has been the appearance of movements which stand for the re-establishment of the full and complete reign of the Shari'ah over the every-day life of Muslims. These movements range from the Istiqlal party in Morocco, which has also definite political and social programmes, to the Ikhwan al-Muslimin, the most important movement of this kind to appear during the past decade in the Arab World. The writings of the intellectual elite of this movement, such as Sayyid Qutb, are based most of all upon a renewed and vigorous application of the Shari'ah to the whole of human life. The persistence of the influence of this movement, even among the young, reveals a strong desire on the part of a significant portion of even the Modernised classes for a moral revivification and renewal. The continuing appeal of men like Hasan al-Banna and Sayyid Qutb is due not so much to their intellectual analyses of various contemporary problems, analyses which are often oblivious of the true nature of some of the questions involved, as to their firm belief in the Shari'ah and to their own personal example of adherence to the Shari'ah. The existence of movements such as that of the Ikhwan, despite its naivety vis-a-vis the problems posed by the modern world, reveals the continuing hold of religion upon public life in its economic, social and political aspects, not to speak of the inner life of men.

Contemporary Arab World

As far as political life in the contemporary Arab World is concerned, its ever greater Islamicization, in spite of existing revolutionary tendencies which bring into power alien forms of government often with anti-Islamic ideologies, is truly amazing. The nationalist leaders are usually forced to come to terms more and more with the Islamic views of the masses, who keep a constant pressure upon them. And many of the leaders themselves combine leftist political tendencies with very strong Islamic convictions. One observes in the Arab World today not only traditional rulers who are devout Muslims or at least espouse thecause of Islam publicly, but also the most revolutionary governments which combine an extreme 'leftist' policy with a degree of adherence to the Shari'ah and the Islamic tradition which seems outwardly incongruent and amazes many a Western observer who has prepared a priori criteria, drawn from his own experience in the West, to study the Arab World. The European type of nationalism, therefore, which is by nature against the universalism of Islam, which did much to weaken Islam in the early phases of Arab nationalism, and which has produced anti-Islamic tendencies in many non-Arab Muslim countries, seems after several decades to converge paradoxically enough toward the Islamic ethos within many parts of the Arab World today, although it has done much to alienate Muslim people from each other and to dissect and divide the heritage of Islam, which belongs to all Muslim people by right.

Parallel with secularizing forces of every kind, one observes forces at play which seek to re-assert Islam in the social and political field. Furthermore, in recent years there have also become discernible tendencies which seek to achieve the same on the intellectual plane. The past few decades have witnessed the turning of the interest of many men of letters to religion and religious subjects, to the extent that some of the best known among them, such as 'Abbas Mahmud al-'Aqqad and Taha Husayn, not known in their earlier writings for their interest in religion, have written later in life several biographical studies of the Prophet and the Companions, or works on other specifically religious themes. This tendency complements the continuing flow of religious literature from the religious centres, especially al-Azhar, and by graduates of such centres. It also complements a small but growing number of writings by men in other walks of life who are deeply concerned with religion. One of the best known religious works to have appeared in the Arab World during the past decades, the City of Wrong, was written by Kamil Husayn, an Egyptian surgeon.

Intellectual Interest

This revival of intellectual interest in Islam, which of course does not by any means please the Modernised and secularized so-called 'intellectuals', usually of ultra-nationalistic or Marxist tendencies, is complemented by a renewal of interest in the whole tradition of Islamic thought, especially philosophy and Sufism. Traditional Islamic philosophy was revived in Egypt by Jamal al-Din al-Afghani after centuries during which it had ceased to be taught in most Arab madrasahs and remained a living intellectual tradition only in Persia and adjacent areas. During this century, an avid study of Islamic philosophy has been carried out in the Arab World, and especially Egypt, by such men as Mustafa 'Abd al-Raziq, Ibrahim Madkour, 'Abd al-Rahman Badawi, Fu'ad al-Ahwani, Muhammad Abu Ridah, 'Uthman Amin and others. The efforts of such men must be seen not only as simple academic scholarship but also as an attempt to revive the intellectual heritage of Islam. Their work certainly possesses a religious significance and is related in this sense to the writings of men of letters and other classes of educated Arabs on religious subjects. The ever-growing interest in Islamic philosophy in the Arab World is related to the general desire for a new self-discovery on the part of the modern educated classes after the disillusionment with the West, which indeed becomes ever more intense with the rapid decline and, in fact, disintegration of modern Western society and culture as it has been known during the past few centuries.

Legacy of Past

It must be remembered that the intensity of religious life among the Arabs cannot be gauged at all by studying simply the various reactions of the Arabs to the modern world. One must also study the unchanged but ever-living traditional modes of religious life. Most Western scholars, who as already mentioned are trained by profession to study only change and who have made an a priori judgment that only that which changes is significant, have tended to neglect the permanent elements in the traditional religious life of Muslims in general and of the Arabs in particular, and have exaggerated the importance of the so-called 'reform' movement. In reality, today, the influence of the 'reformists' in the Arab \Vorid is far less than that of the traditional Muslim authorities both past and present. One would like to know, for example, which work of the modernist "reformers' compares in popularity with those of an al-Ghazzali. The heart of the religious life resides and will continue to reside in traditional forms and practices, in the inner being of individuals for whom Islam means an approach to the Divine and a sanctification of human life, and not a mere asser with which to further particular worldly causes, whether they be political, social or economic.

To understand religion in the contemporary Arab World one must also understand the meaning of the still-continuing congregational prayers held in every city, of the countless pilgrims who continue to be attracted to the spiritual pole of Mecca, and of the millions who visit sanctuaries, from Mulay Idris in Morocco to Ra's al-I,Iusayn in Cairo and the Shi'ite sanctuaries of Najaf and Karbala. One must realize the vitality and the continuous subsistence of traditional religious teaching among both Sunnis and Shi'ites. One must be aware of the continuity of the intellectual traditions of Islam among the 'ulama (religious scholars) and the traditional learned classes, and of the life of faith (iman) among the vast majority of the community, for whom prayer and devotion still constitute the celestial pattern into which human life is integrated. Any changes or reactions caused by the domination of the West and the political and cultural tragedies that have followed can only be understood in the light of the dominant presence of the still-living tradition of Islam. For every Arab, young or old, who speaks of secularism or socialism or Marxism there are many for whom no 'ism' can ever replace the all-embracing reality of Islam. To grasp the religious life of the Arabs in its fullness one must be aware pot only of the 'renovators', 'reformers' and rebels whose harm to the traditional order can hardly be over-emphasized, but also of the innumerable elements of permanence and continuity implied by the very notion of a living tradition and displayed fully by Islam in its manifestation among both Arabs and non-Arabs.

Also, in speaking of the religious life of contemporary Arabs it is not possible to overlook Sufism, which lies at the heart of the Islamic tradition and which has acted throughout Islamic history as the source for spiritual and religious regeneration, being the invisible origin of even external and social movements of a religious nature. Strangely enough, however, the majority of modern accounts of religion in the Arab World fail to take account of this basic element, and neglect the Sufi orders and their rejuvenation during the past century, with the sole exception of the Sanusiyyah Order, which has been studied more often precisely because of its puritanical and 'Wahhabi' tendencies.

Modernism and Secularism

The fact is that during the nineteenth century, along with the gradual penetration of modernism and secularism into the Arab World and the rise of the modernist 'reformers' about whom so many studies exist in European languages, there occurred also a genuine renewal of life within several of the Sufi orders by great saints who were in fact 'renewers' (mujaddid) in the traditional meaning of the word, which is very different from 'reformer' (muslih) in its modern sense. The renewal of life of the Shadhiliyyah Order and the founding of certain new branches and orders such as the Yashrutiyyah, the Badawiyyah and the Madaniyyah, mostly in the Arab Middle East, and the Darqawiyyah in the Maghrib, marked a revival of an intense spiritual life that has affected the whole religious life of the community to this day.

During this century the same forces of inner renewal can be observed. The influence of the remarkable Algerian Darqawi master, Shaykh Ahmad al-'Alawi, who founded a new branch of the Shadhiliyyah Order, spread beyond the confines of the Maghrib and even the Arab World and is felt far and wide to this day. Anyone who has frequented a gathering of the Shadhiliyyah-'Alawiyyah Order in Damascus or Aleppo has become aware of the degree of influence of this master and the extent of his living grace (barakah) within branches of the order founded by his disciples in many Arab lands as far away from each other as Syria, the Yemen and Morocco.

In Egypt also, almost contemporary with Shaykh al-'Alawi, another Shadhili master, Salamah I.Iasạn al-Radi, founded the Hamidiyyah branch of the order, which soon began to attract many into its fold. Its emphasis upon both the practice of the Shari'ah and spiritual discipline has made it one of the main spiritual forces in contemporary Egypt, attracting adepts from many walks of life, including the young in universities. Its current role in Egypt exemplifies the basic importance of Sufism in the contemporary religious life of many parts of the Arab World.

Social and Political Strains

The events of the past two or three decades have caused major social and political strains in the Arab World and have accentuated many of the tendencies alluded to above as well as causing new ones to come into being. A sense of bewilderment combined with emotional irrationality has captivated the minds of certain men as a result of the extreme despair and unbelievable stress caused by the injustice brought upon the Arabs by the Palestine tragedy and its aftermath, including all the extremist forms of government that this event helped to bring into being. Also, an ever greater degree of destruction of the religious quality of life is to be observed in the bigger cities, especially among notable segments of the youth drawn to the frivolities and trivialities of modern life. Furthermore, out-and-out secularist and anti-Islamic political ideologies have gained power in certain regions of the Arab World.

But along with the growth of all these anti-traditional forces and tendencies one can notice a marked renewal of interest in religion, especially among the youth. It is enough to compare the number of young people who used to visit a place such as the tomb of Ibn 'Arab! in Damascus or Ra's al-Husayn in Cairo two decades ago with the number who are seen there now. Both Sufism and the Shari'ite practices of Islam have been attracting numerous people of late, not only from the traditional classes in the countryside but also from urban classes that only a generation ago showed little interest in religion. Along with the young Arabs studying in the West or in Western-oriented universities in the East who are becoming infatuated with various fashions of Western thought ranging from positivism to Marxism, there are those who are searching again for their own roots and looking within their own tradition for an answer to the dilemma of human existence in an inhuman world whose overt contradictions become more apparent every day. The rise of religious interest in the Arab World during the past decade or two is a phenomenon of central importance which can hardly be brushed aside as a momentary emotional reaction before the inevitable onslaught of complete secularism, as secularist historians would wish to do.

Western Civilization

In reality, what has happened during this period is that on the one hand the blinding glitter of Western civilization has begun to fade and its innate faults and present difficulties have become more evident, and, on the other hand, the false gods for whose sake the Modernised Arabs sought to brush Islam aside have failed them in the worst way imaginable. The defeat in the 1967 war and the humiliations before and after cannot possibly be blamed in any way upon traditional Islamic institutions. It is the failure of the modern ideologies whose adoption dates back to the nineteenth century that has now come into the open. For many an Arab, recent events have only strengthened their serious disillusionment with the programme of simply aping the West. Rather, they see recent tragedies as a divine punishment for their having forsaken Islam". They have come to view all these difficulties as trials which, according to the teachings of the Quran, the individual Muslim as well as Muslim society as a whole must pass through in this world. They have also come to realize that in order to return to Islam they must re-discover Islam in all its fullness, not in its atrophied and apologetic form as presented by so many of the modernist 'reformers' during the last centuries.

On the scholarly level also, a new class, small but of considerable significance, has come into being which is traditional and at the same time well acquainted with the West without being its slavish imitator. Both on the popular and the intellectual level the awareness of the necessity of taking religion seriously is to be discerned in many circles, whose members thus return to the living stream of the authentic Islamic tradition in both its Shari'ite and its Sufi aspects.

Today the Arab World stands at a most crucial stage of its history. There are still those who would like to secularize the Arab world and separate it from Islam as much as possible. But because Arabic was chosen as the vehicle of the Quranic revelation and the Arabs as the first propagators of Islam, the destiny of the Arabs remains inseparable from that of the whole Islamic world and in fact from the earthly manifestation of Islam itself. Moreover, the future well-being of the Arabs depends upon the degree to which they are able to remember their true identity and to remain faithful to the task which their identification with Islam upon the historical scene has placed upon their shoulders. Inasmuch as it is impossible for men to remove the imprint of the Divine upon the human order, Islam continues today as the most powerful and enduring motivating force within the Arab soul and mind, and an ever-present factor in Arab life in all its aspects. It is the source to which all things must of necessity return, even if they wander away momentarily, and it continues as an objective norm which moulds the lives of, and at the same time serves as the ideal for, the vast majority of Arabs, both individually and collectively. Islam remains a living reality without which it is impossible to understand the Arabs today. To speak of the Arabs is to speak of a people whose language is that of the Quran, and the fabric of whose soul has been woven over the ages from elements of the Quranic revelation in a manner that makes their contemporary history inseparable from Islam and the Islamic universe into which most Arabs still are born and in which they live and die.

19

Science under Islam

This is no secret, the history bears incontestable testimony to the fact that Islam gave unprecedented impetus to the intellectual development of the human race and that the early Muslims held high the torch of light and learning at a time when the whole world was immersed in ignorance and barbarity. The impression prevalent in the West that Islam is an unprogressive religion, antagonistic to science and civilization, is absolutely incorrect. Perhaps, no religion has been so greatly misrepresented and misinterpreted by prejudiced and uninformed critics as Islam. Far from adequately appreciating the glorious scientific achievements of the early Muslims and gratefully acknowledging the immense debt the world owes to them, the designing critics have shamelessly calumniated Islam by completely distorting historical facts and wilfully perverting established truths. Hopefully, it may be proved conclusively that Islam, far from retarding the progress of science, the chief factor of civilization, immensely furthered its cause. In fact, it was Islam that gave birth to modern science, inaugurated a scientific era in the world's history and made the early Muslims precursors of modern scientists and pioneers of modern civilization. The subsequent intellectual stagnation that came upon the Muslim world, giving rise to a false impression regarding Islamic influence, was entirely due to certain historical circumstances similar to those that prevailed in Europe during the Middle Ages, before the Renaissance and the Reformation. The Islamic faith and its teachings were in no way responsible for this social degeneration and political debacle.

It is now being realised that modern science owes its origin to Islam and modern progress is the outcome of the freedom of thought and spirit of enquiry prescribed for the Muslims by the Holy Quran, and not a product of Christianity which for a long time relentlessly proscribed all free thinking and liberal reasoning and even scientific researches on original lines, and horribly persecuted all those who indulged in these. The impression that it was Christianity that advanced science and civilisation is, therefore, as erroneous as the idea that Islam hampered their progress. In fact, there can be no comparison between Islam and Christianity as civilising forces. While the Muslims rose to a pinnacle of learning within a few centuries of the promulgation of Islam, the Christians remained steeped in ignorance for more than a thousand years.

After a careful study of the history of Islam, Canon Isaac Taylor came to the definite conclusion that "Islam has done more for civilisation than Christianity."[1] If Europe's indebtedness to Islam for the extraordinary progress it has latterly made in science and civilisation were adequately known, it would have astounded the modern civilised world. "During the darkest period of European history," writes Bosworth Smith, "the Arabs for five hundred years held up the torch of learning to humanity." Arthur Leonard has truly said, "Islam, in fact, has accomplished a great feat. It has left a mark on the pages of human history, which is so indelible that it can never be effaced............. only when the world grows wiser will that be acknowledged in full."

That the early Muslims very largely contributed to the cultural development of the world cannot but be admitted by all unprejudiced and fair-minded critics of Islamic history. It is nothing but religious prejudice and an overweening sense of racial superiority which have stood in the way of acknowledgement and appreciation by the West of the glorious achievements of the East. Draper is perfectly justified in deploring "the systematic manner in which the literature" of Europe has continued to put out of sight our scientific obligations to Mohamedans. Surely they cannot be much longer hidden. Injustice founded on religious rancour and national conceit cannot be perpetrated for ever.

The Old School

It is a historical fact that cannot be controverted that, before the advent of Islam, the cultivation of science was condemned as heresy. The reason for this is not far to seek. The bulk of mankind could not at that time think in the abstract, and they looked upon the elements of Nature, the subject-matter of science, as sacred objects, possessing supernatural powers. They made idols, symbolizing different elements, and worshipped them as gods and goddesses, either for protection from evil or for attainment of certain objects. Thus were the sun, the moon, the stars, air, water, animals, and even trees and stones, deified and adored. It was not unnatural that in such circumstances any deviation from the prevailing belief in their sanctity should have been branded as sacrilege, and any attempt at a critical examination of their potentiality, for good or evil, stigmatised as profanity. Thus all that was useful in the heavens and the earth remained altogether unexplored, and for thousands of years man did not realise the sublime utility of the forces of Nature. It was reserved for the untutored son of the desert to open man's eye to the wonderland of Nature by bringing down her elements from the high pedestal of divinity, on which they had been placed, to the position of servants of mankind.

Practical Approach

And He has made subservient to you the night and the day and the sun and moon and the stars are made subservient by His commandment; most surely there are signs in this for people to ponder......

Al Quran.

Thus were the gods of the pre-Islamic people reduced by one stroke to man's servants. For the first time in the history of the world the Holy Quran declared in unmistakable language that the main purpose for which all objects, from the mightiest sun to the most insignificant atom, were created, was to minister to man's needs. Everything in the universe being intended for his use, man has been commanded to investigate their intrinsic properties,—in other words, to cultivate every branch of science. Thus, by declaring man the lord of the universe and everything in it subservient to him, the Quran gave a tremendous impetus to the development of scientific research. In fact the foundation of modern science was thus laid by acquainting man with the real nature of the forces and laws of Nature and by teaching him how to harness them for human service. The initiation of the conquest of Nature leading to the utilisation of its forces for the good of humanity is, indeed, one of the greatest blessings Islam has conferred upon mankind.

The Quran clearly indicated the way in which to reduce Nature to human service by contemplation and observation of four kinds, viz., *Tafaqquh, Tadakkur, Tafakkur* and *Taaqqul*. By the first a correct idea of things and their different features can be arrived at, by the second the knowledge of how to utilise them properly can be acquired, the third teaches the ways by which things have come into existence, while the fourth gives the knowledge which enables man to make the right use of different things in everyday life. It was the meditations indicated by *Tafakkur* and *Taaqqul* that actuated different kinds of scientific research among the early Muslims. This is how the Quran placed in the hands of man the key to the treasure-house of Nature, and Divine Revelation came to show him the way to material progress. Everything in the universe having been intended for the use of man, it was a virtuous act for him to conduct research into the realms of Nature in order to discover the utility of its various components. Thus, the first principle of progress, — the utilisation of the forces of Nature for the needs of man —became an article of faith with the Muslims, and impelled them to engage in scientific research.

Conquest of Universe

The Prophet of Islam went so far as to carry out explorations of the realms of Nature, the real glorification of God, and to place the acquisition of knowledge on an equal footing with His worship. Man was required to glorify God not by mere lip service, but by discovering and utilising the properties and potentialities of the things He created to meet the needs of His creatures. Realisation of the scattered bounties of God was to be the realisation of God Himself. A Muslim was to spiritualise, as it were, his whole material surroundings by seeing and feeling the evidence of God's power and love in every blade of grass and in every breath of air.

Truly, in the creation of the heavens and earth, and the alternation of night and day, there are signs for men of understanding, who remember Allah standing, sitting and while lying on their sides, and ponder over the creation of the heavens and earth (and say) our Lord, You have not created (all) this in vain. Glory be to You.

Al-Quran

Religion not against Science

Before the advent of Islam, learning was confined to the chosen few. The masses had to blindly accept whatever was placed before them as their religion and they were not permitted to use their intellect or judgment. In fact, before the promulgation of Islam, religion was synonymous with dogmas and doctrines, rites and rituals; and bigotry had placed an embargo on freedom of thought and enquiry. Whenever anyone conceived any new idea or propounded a new theory, he was condemned by his co-religionists as a heretic. Some of the most inhuman atrocities ever committed on men in search of truth were thus perpetrated in the name of religion. It was Islam that for the first time discountenanced all dogmatic teachings and made reason the test of faith. "The first thing created" says the Prophet of Islam, "was reason. God has not created anything better than reason." On another occasion the Prophet said, "Truly, a man may have performed prayers, fasts, charity and pilgrimages and all other good deeds, but he will not be rewarded save in proportion to the sense he employs." According to the Quran, "There is no piety in turning your face towards the East or the West." *Iman* (faith) means knowledge of a truth or principle with such conviction as to its truth as will incite one to live up to it. It does not signify belief that cannot be translated into action. All this unmistakably demonstrates that Islam does not regard rituals and ceremonies as essentials of religion. In fact, mere dogmatic doctrines have no significance for a true Muslim, who has to observe his religion in every deed and action, in every thought and conception. He may indulge in free thought and free inquiry concerning everything that man's intelligence is capable of apprehending. To him, science, the aim of which is truth, is the greatest ally of true religion. "Islam stands almost alone," says Guizot in his *History of European Civilisation* "among the religions in discountenancing the reliance on tradition without argument. It demands that its votaries should undertake the investigation of the great work of their faith." Miracle has no place in Islam to which nature itself is a revelation of God, and its laws His eternal miracles, demonstrating His Majesty, His omnipotence and His benevolence. In fact, man knew nothing of God except through His work in Nature. Islam thus gave to scientific research a religious aspect unknown and unthought of before.

By thus putting an end to all conflicts between religion and science, and by making the first principle of scientific progress—the subservience of nature to man—an article of faith, Islam revolutionised the human mind, imparted immense energy and initiative to it and strongly impelled it to investigate the marvels of creation. Moreover, it immeasurably enlarged the scope of religion, which had till then been regarded only as a means of man's future salvation, but now, for the first time, came to be looked upon also as an effective factor in his material advancement. Every branch of learning conducive to human wealth and progress thus came within the purview of Islam, which harmonised the esoteric and exoteric sides of man's life. Thus modern progress had its origin in the spirit of free thought and investigation engendered by Islam.

Attaining Education, a Duty

I have already stated what Islam did for two of the most important factors of modern culture and civilization. Let us now see what it did for another important factor, viz., the dissemination of knowledge. It is a historical fact that no messenger of God, from Noah to Jesus, had done anything worth mentioning for the dissemination of knowledge, which was selfishly monopolised by a few priests and theologians, anxious to retain all power in their own hands. But the Prophet of Islam, though he himself did not know how to read and write, laid the greatest stress on the acquisition of knowledge and made it essentially incumbent upon all his followers, irrespective of sex, rank, colour and country. *Talabul-Ilm Farizatun Ala Kulli Muslimin Wa Muslimatin:* "Seeking of knowledge is imperative for all Muslims, male and female." "He who has been gifted with knowledge", says the Quran, "has been gifted with an abounding blessing." Convinced that an ignorant person cannot adequately realise the greatness and goodness of God, the Prophet of Islam made acquisition of knowledge an essential of faith and did not approve of his followers being entirely absorbed in meditation upon God, "an hour's contemplation and study of His creation being better than a year's adoration." Muslims were particularly enjoined to be in constant search of knowledge "from the cradle to the grave," and they were told that "the ink of the scholar was holier than the blood of the martyr."

Thus in that dark age, when the world was enveloped in ignorance and illiteracy, Islam created an insatiable thirst for knowledge and caused a tremendous upheaval of science in realms hitherto altogether unexplored. Such an extraordinary outburst of intellectual activity was unparalleled in human history. Some undreamt of discoveries and inventions were made and these contributed immensely to the progress of civilisation and the welfare of mankind. There was hardly any science of which the Muslims did not make themselves masters. They created modern Chemistry, made most important discoveries in Astronomy, added much to the knowledge of Mathematics and Medicine and conducted very valuable research in Botany, Geology, Zoology and other branches of Natural Philosophy. The foundation of what is termed Physical Science was thus laid, and the gates of investigation into the marvels of creation were flung wide open.

The Muslims, by unravelling the mysteries of Nature and widening the scope of knowledge, introduced such blessings of comfort and happiness as were unknown in the world. It was the intellectual liberty and the spirit of scientific research inaugurated by them that brought about the European Renaissance and introduced into the modern world the arts and sciences which ennobled the heart, elevated the mind, thus making a major contribution to human happiness.

The height of scientific progress forecast by the Quran has not yet been fully attained. The world is full of materials that await man's exertion and ingenuity for their development and utilisation. There are millions of things in the realm of the seas and in the bowels of the earth and the ocean that have been created for man's use. All these have to be harnessed in order to meet the increased requirements of human society. The Quran repeatedly speaks of the subservience of the physical world and phenomena to man, whose duty it is to explore them for use.

Before the advent of Islam, the West, which nowadays claims all the credit for progress in science and civilisation, was steeped in ignorance and darkness. It was the intellectual liberty and scientific research inaugurated by the Muslims which brought about the Renaissance to which Europe owed its regeneration. Medieval Europe was a hot-bed of religious fanaticism and social conservatism; and the intellectual stagnation which prevailed there is altogether beyond conception in modern times.

Dark Age of Europe

In medieval Europe religion and science were thought to be quite irreconcilable to each other, and whoever ventured to express any opinion contrary to the prevailing sacerdotal belief was not merely branded as a heretic, but was relentlessly persecuted, inhumanly tortured and even mercilessly put to death. For his belief in the theory of evolution, Vanini's tongue was torn out of his mouth and he was burnt alive. Hypatia, the renowned commentator on Plato, had to pay the penalty for her intellectual audacity with her life. Copernicus tried to demonstrate that the earth revolves and not the heavens. Thereupon even Martin Luther denounced him as "an upstart astrologer," and Calvin most severely condemned him. He had, therefore, to end his life in disgrace. Bruno, who dared to advance the Copernican theory, was seized, imprisoned and at last put to death by a "fire made slow to increase the torture." Galileo, who supported the Copernican theory, was thrown into a dungeon, horribly tortured and forced to recant as follows: "I, Galileo, being in my seventieth year, being a prisoner on my knees before your Eminences, having before my eyes the Holy Gospel, abjure, curse and detest the error and the heresy of the movements of the Earth." Not content with mere recantation, the Holy Inquisition sent him into exile for the rest of his life. Thus many a devoted votary of science fell a victim to Christian fanaticism prevalent in the Middle Ages, and some famous libraries, containing the accumulated treasure of ages, were consigned to the flames.

All this conclusively proves that the credit given to Christianity, as a religion, for promoting the cause of science is nothing but a travesty of truth.

A Derived Civilization and Culture

It is an uncontroverted truth that modern progress in the West was not the outcome of Man's faith in Church dogmas. In fact, the West made no progress worth the name as it was in the iron grip of Christianity. This is borne out by the fact that centuries of domination of Spain, from them the utter darkness in which they were groping and the appalling ignorance in which they were immersed. The extraordinary progress made by the Christian countries during the last five hundred years is directly due to the teachings of Islam, which were promulgated six hundred years after Christianity. It was not till freedom of thought was advocated and the torch of learning was lighted by the Muslims in Spain that any progress in science and civilisation could be made in Europe, or any possibility could arise for the Renaissance and the Reformation to make their appearance in the Christian world. It was from Muslim Spain that a new life dawned upon the whole of Europe, giving birth to a new culture, which greatly stimulated the intellectual activity of its people. All that Christian Europe learnt of Greek and Hindu Philosophy and Science up to the Renaissance period emanated from the Saracenic culture of Spain.

After the conquest of Spain the Muslims established there several Universities which opened their doors to all students without distinction of creed, caste, colour or country; and also boarded and lodged them at public expense. Spain thus became the centre of European culture, and scholars from all parts of Christian Europe looked to her seats of learning. Rogers, Bacon and other pioneers of the Rationalist movements in Europe, all received their education in the Muslim University of Cordova. Even the great Emperor Charlemagne had to send his son to Spain to be educated by the Muslim teachers, for nowhere else in Europe was there any seat of learning worthy of the name.

Every branch of science was seriously investigated in Muslim Spain. Medicine achieved greater development through the discoveries of her doctors and surgeons than it had gained during all the centuries that had elapsed since the days of Galen. Astronomy, Chemistry, Geography, Natural History, all were studied at Cordova with great ardour; as for the graces of literature, there never was such a time when poetry became almost the common speech of everybody. "The taste for science and literature," writes Renan, "had by the 10th century established, in this privileged corner of the world, a toleration of which modern times hardly offer us an example. Christians, Jews and Muslims spoke the same tongue, sang the same songs, and participated in the same literary and scientific studies." All the barriers which separated the various peoples were effaced: all strove with one accord in the work of a common civilisation. The mosques of Cordova, where the students could be counted by the thousands, became the active centres of philosophical and scientific studies. "It must be owned" observes John Davenport, "that all the knowledge, whether of physics, astronomy, philosophy or mathematics, which flourished in Europe from the 10th century, was originally derived from the Arabian schools, and the Spanish Saracen may be looked upon as the father of European philosophy."

Some idea of the architectural beauty and grandeur introduced into Europe by the Muslims may be had from the Alhambra Court in the Crystal Palace in London. Stanley Lane-Pool in "The Moors in Spain" has aptly described all this; he says, "Beautiful as were the palaces and gardens of Cordova, her claims to admiration in higher matters were no less strong. The mind was as lovely as the body."

As rightly acknowledged by Gustav Diercks in his 'Europe's Debt to Islam,' there can be no denying that Europe is deeply in debt to Islam for all its scientific discoveries. In fact, it was Islam that produced scientists who anticipated Bacon, Newton, Kepler and other great scientists of Europe. But for the introduction into Europe by the Muslims of paper, gun-powder, the mariner's compass and such other instruments of progress, who knows that the condition of Europe in respect of science and civilisation would not still have been today what it was fourteen hundred years ago.

The industries developed by the Muslims during their rule in Spain were many and of farreaching consequence. Shipbuilding, horticulture, tanyards, glassware, silver mines, cotton manufactures, silks, woollen carpets, iron and copper utensils and inlaid metal work were some of these. The Muslims gave Europe the mulberry tree, the maize, the sugar-cane, the windmill and many such other items of industry. During the reign of the Spanish king, Al-Hakam, the irrigation systems were developed in Granada, Valencia and Arragon. In short, the art of war, industry, commerce and seamanship made unprecedented progress in Muslim Spain. It is a historical fact that 477 years before Columbus, the Arabs and the moors of Spain traded with the American continent.

Though the average westerner is under the impression that Europe's salvation was caused by the defeat of the Muslims at Tours (Poitiers), the real fact is that the world's progress was retarded for ages by this check on the advance of the Muslims in the West. Perhaps the darkest pages in the annals of history, dealing with the inquisition and such other disgraceful matters, would never have been written at all and Renaissance, which ushered in an era of civilisation in Europe, would have been accelerated by 700 years if the Muslims had won that battle and Islamised the whole of Europe. Anatole France who was above racial and religious prejudice, truly said in his *La Vie En Flour*. "The most tragic event in history is that of the Battle of Poitiers, when the science, the art and the civilisation of Arabia fell before the barbarism of the Franks."

It is indeed a most happy sign of the times that not only fair-minded individuals, whose illuminating observations have been quoted, but even a whole nation has at last realised that Europe's extraordinary progress in science and civilisation, which has given her a dominating position all the world over, is to be ascribed to the civilising force of Islam. As a mark of belated justice the Spanish Republic is arranging to establish an Arabic University at Madrid in order to commemorate what Islam achieved for science and civilisation during the Muslim occupation of Spain. It is hoped this will enlighten the world about the fact that the Muslims were the most zealous promoters and protectors of knowledge and culture for full one thousand years, during which other peoples were enshrouded in ignorance, bigotry and barbarism.

Muslim Contribution to Intellect and Knowledge

It is now an undisputed fact that the early Muslims made incomparable contributions to the culture and civilizations of the world. Far from proscribing free thought and enquiry, or placing any ban upon the cultivation of science, as early and medieval Christianity had done, Islam gave it a tremendous impetus by making it a part of religion itself. A Muslim was enjoined to look upon the universe as an expression of God's attributes, and he had to explore it and utilise its objects for the service of mankind as an item of worship of their Creator. It was this religious stimulus to scientific research that particularly impelled the early Muslims to exert themselves so zealously for the advancement of science. A detailed account of their numerous scientific achievements would fill many volumes. The more the world advances in civilization, the more will their inestimable services to humanity be adequately realised and appreciated.

History bears witness to the fact that it was Islam that raised some of the most backward nations to the highest pinnacle of moral and material progress. Wherever the Muslims conquered a country, instead of slaughtering the vanquished, as was done by the Israelites of old, they gave them new life, inspired them with lofty ideals and raised them to a high level of civilization. Thus, indeed, were many savage tribes transformed into civilized people. To whatever land the Arabs migrated, they made it their home; they absorbed the culture of the conquered people and they did their best for the intellectual, moral and material improvement of the land of their adoption. The people to whom the later intellectual development of the Muslims was due were, for the most part, not Arabs but descendants of those who had adopted the faith of the conquerors. Wherever the banner of Islam was carried, remarkable centres of learning sprangup in no time and produced illustrious men in the fields of literature, arts, science and industry. Thus Damascus, Cordova, Granada, Baghdad and Cairo became, in turn, reputed centres of Muslim culture and held aloft the torch of light and learning, art and science in Asia, Europe and Africa, at a time when the West was sunk in ignorance and superstition.

Europe's indebtedness to Islam for her scientific progress is much greater than she cares to admit. She remained barren of all progress as long as she was under the heel of the Church. Even the intellectual development that had taken place among the Greeks and Romans disappeared under the persecutions of the Church. During the centuries of moral and intellectual stagnation in Europe, it was the Muslim who led the vanguard of intellectual progress in the world. There was a time when learning in Europe could be obtained only through the medium of the Arabic tongue. The very Renaissance, that awakened her from her long lethargy, was brought about by the impact of Islamic culture and learning. But for the conquest of Spain by the Muslims, who knows how long she would have remained in that savage condition. All her later achievements in the domain of science, art and learning owe their inspiration wholly and solely to the influences that emanated from Muslim Spain and penetrated the rest of the continent. All knowledge, whether of Astronomy, Mathematics, Physics or Philosophy, of which the Europeans later made themselves masters, was originally derived from the Saracenic schools.

Besides, there has been hardly any reform—religious, social or political— from the time of Martin Luther to that of Lenin, which does not bear the stamp of Islamic influence. Draper has very truly said, "In whatever direction we look, we meet in various pursuits of peace and war, of letters and science, Saracenic vestiges."

Dr Campbell, a reputed British scientist, in his book *Arabian Medicine* writes, "When Europe was lying torpid in the depth of intellectual obscurity and gloom in the dark ages, culture and civilization were spread in the Islamic States under the high patronage of the Caliphs of Baghdad and Cordova, and at a time, when the Barons and Ladies of Medieval Europe could not even sign their names, almost every adolescent boy and girl in Islam could read and write freely and with ease."

In his famous *History of Human Society*, Professor Frank Blackmore of the University of Kansas writes, "In every country that was conquered, the first duty of Islam was to build a mosque in which Allah would be worshipped and his Prophet honoured. Attached to this mosque was a school where people were taught to read and study the Qur'an. From this initial point they enlarged the study of science, literature and art, and, through the appreciation of these sublime things, they collected the treasures of art and learning wherever these could be found. From imitation they passed on to the great field of creation, and great advances were made to the sum of human knowledge. Schools were founded, great universities established, and libraries were built which laid the permanent foundations of knowledge."

The Muslims made phenomenal progress in Science in a wonderfully short time. They visualised, thirteen centuries ago, many things which are being discovered today. They explored and exploited the potentialities of objects which had remained unknown and unthought of since the creation of the world. In fact, there was hardly any conceivable subject to which they did not give serious thought. They made most important discoveries in Chemistry, in Astronomy, in Mathematics, in Medicine. They specialised in History and Geography. They unearthed Alchemy and Algebra. They initiated and developed the study of Political

Economy and Sociology, which till then had been unknown sciences. They carried out valuable research in Zoology, Geology and Botany. Muslim students, accompanied by artists, travelled far and wide to study various vegetations, which were minutely described by pen and brush. Alherin, a renowned botanist, travelled to and fro in India for forty years collecting materials for his studies. Besides, Muslims investigated and wrote on various other subjects such as navigation, agriculture, irrigation, gardening, statistics, chronology and topography. Even aviation, the latest achievement of Europe and an early wonder of the twentieth century, was not left untried. The first two martyrs among the conquerors of the air were Muslims. In the reign of Khalifa Al-Mamun, a scientist named Abul Qasim invented an aeroplane, but crashed when flying and was killed.

In the eighth century, the Abbaside Khalifas established the famous academy of Baghdad, where the works of the renowned mathematicians Euclid, Archimedes and Appollonius, of the astronomer Ptolemy, and of the naturalists, Hippocrates and Diomedes were translated. In this and other Muslim centres of learning, Greek culture was kept alive at a time when, outside Byzantium, it had no abiding place in the non-Muslim world. Many were the libraries, observatories and laboratories that were established by Muslim kings. In the library attached to Baitul-ul-Hikmat, the abode of learning, a remarkable university founded by Khalifa Harun-al-Rashid, there were many hundred thousand Sanskrit, Greek, Coptic, Chaldean, and Persian books besides those in Arabic. Khalifa Al-Hakim's library was so very extensive that its catalogue had to be prepared in forty large volumes.

Chemistry: Modern Chemistry, as Humboldt rightly says, was "admittedly the invention of the Muslims" whose achievements in this sphere were of unique interest. They conclusively proved the worthlessness of ancient chemistry. They found out the chemical affinities of mercury, lead, copper, silver and gold and knew the chemical processes of oxidation and calcination. A number of words such as alembic, alkali, etc., were derived from Arabic. Jabir bin Hayyan, known as Geber in the western world, wrote some five hundred treatises on chemistry. He discovered, for the first time, nitric acid, sulphuric acid, aqua regia, silver nitrate and several compounds. The Muslims were the first to teach the world distillation, filtration, crystallisation, etc. They knew how to change a liquid into vapour. It was in Muslim Spain that chemistry was first established in Europe, and would have reached its zenith there, had the Muslims not suffered the disastrous defeat at Poitiers. Jildaki was the last great Muslim chemist. He died in 1361 A.D.

Astronomy: The Muslims may be said to have written their names on heaven itself. They identified and classified a large number of stars in their observatories. They made wonderful discoveries concerning the movements of the Solar system and other astral bodies. They ascertained the size of the earth, the variation of the lunar latitudes and the precession of the equinoxes. Averroes (Ibn-i Rushd) discovered the sun-spot: Al-Hazan (Abul Hasan) discovered atmospheric reflection; Al-Maimun determined the obliquity of ecliptic; Ibn-i-Junus, Nasiruddin Tusi and Albani constructed astronomical tables of great value. Albani's tables were translated into Latin and formed the basis of astronomical study in Europe, where that science was introduced by the translation of the works of Muhammad Farghani. Abu Junus and Al-Batan were two of the greatest Muslim astronomers. It was the Muslims who first built observatories in Europe and invented the telescope, and compass, the pendulum and many other useful astronomical instruments. The most famous of the many observatories in the Muslim Empire was that at Marghana near Taurus, built in 1259 A.D.

Mathematics: Almost every branch of higher mathematics bears the impress of Muslim genius. Many were the improvements effected by the Muslims in this important subject. The Arabic numerals, the decimal system and the art of figures, which Europe got from the Muslims, gave a great impetus to learning. By means of these the Muslims led the world in Astronomy, Mechanics and Mathematics. Algebra, Statics, Conic Sections and other branches of applied Mathematics are amongst Muslim discoveries. In Geometry the Muslims were the first of all nations to translate Euclid and use his ideas. His work was not properly translated into any European language till the sixteenth century. The Muslims for the first time applied Algebra to Geometry. They discovered equations of the second degree, and developed the theory of quadratic equations and the binomial theorem. They invented spherical Trigonometry and, by introducing the use of Sine and Cosine, they made great contributions to the science of surveying and astronomy. The Muslims were the first to use instruments of precision for the measurement of time by the use of the pendulum and the measurement of heavenly bodies by the use of the astrolabe.

Medicine: The father of the present-day European medical science was Avicenna (Ibn-i-Sina), whose *Materia Medica* is still in vogue. Aven Zoor (Ibn-i-Zoar) was a great authority on pharmacy, which was an institution of Muslim invention. He and others carefully studied the effect on the body of drugs obtained from various parts of the world, and discovered many remedies. The Muslim doctors were the first to use anaesthetics. Al-Bucasis of Cordova was an expert surgeon of world-wide reputation. There were renowned surgeons, opticians, dentists and specialists in female diseases. The science of optics owes much to Muslim research. Al-Hazan, who understood the weight of air, corrected the misconceptions of the Greeks as to the nature of vision and demonstrated, for the first time in history, that the rays of light come from the external object to the eye, and not from the eye itself, impinging on external things. He showed that the retina is the seat of vision, and proved that impressions made upon it were conveyed along the nerves to the brain. He discovered that the refraction of light varied with the density of the atmosphere and *vice versa*. In Baghdad, there were no less than 860 doctors of different classes, each class of whom made one particular branch of medicine their special study. Doctors as well as chemists had to pass an examination in order to obtain a license to practise. There were hospitals throughout the wide Muslim empire. All classes of people, irrespective of their creed, caste, colour and country, were freely admitted to these hospitals.

Geography and History: There are in Arabic many immortal works on Geography. The spherical shape of the globe was demonstrated by the Muslims at a time when the scientists of priest-ridden Europe emphatically asserted that it was flat. The great historical achievements of the Muslims are too well-known to require detailed mention. They produced several thousand books on history, ranging in magnitude from one to eighty volumes.

To sum up, for about one thousand years the Muslims made history; they held aloft the torch of light and learning and spread knowledge and culture throughout the world. But for-the vast intellectual heritage bequeathed by them to the people of the West, it would not have been possible for them to make the immense progress they have now made. The Muslims were in the vanguard of the world's advancement as long as they were true to Islam and faithfully followed the lofty injunctions of the Holy Quran. Their downfall began as they left the path of true Islam. Interestingly, there were orthodox Christians; in the iron grip of Christianity that they could make any appreciable advance in science and civilization: In one case the influence of a peaceful and progressive religion and in the other the effect of the disappearance of religious fervour and the presence of materialistic greed are clearly observable in the history of their respective notable achievements.

The pre-Islamic religions confined their operation to the moral aspect of human nature, and almost altogether ignored its worldly aspect. But Islam, in addition to morality, laid much stress on the practical aspect of man's everyday life. Under the inspiration of Islam, the chief mission of which is the service of humanity, the Muslims attended to such useful subjects as were calculated to contribute to the material welfare of mankind. Realising that man's material progress depends upon his mastery over nature, they devoted themselves to the development of useful sciences such as chemistry, astronomy, medicine, agriculture, irrigation, navigation, etc. Had the idea of man's capabilities to harness the forces of Nature to the service of humanity dawned on the human mind before the Holy Prophet of Islam taught it, the immense potentialites of Nature would have been utilised for the welfare of mankind long before the promulgation of Islam.

Most of the outstanding achievements of the people over whom religion has little influence and who are guided more by the fear of man than by the fear of God, have been in the domain of arms, ammunition, explosives, poisons—of death and destruction rather than of peace and construction. Had their religion had sufficient influence over them, the followers of Christ, who enjoin the turning of one cheek if the other is smitten, would have never been so very eager for the invention of all sorts of death-dealing instruments.

After the enjoyment of power, wealth and supremacy for about a thousand years, the Muslims became enervated and luxury-loving, and a sort of blight overtook them. Spiritual stagnation and intellectual sterility soon followed as a natural consequence. This has more or less been the case with all other religious communities. The Muslims themselves, and not Islam, are entirely to blame for this regrettable check on their progress. A glance at the condition of the world before and after the promulgation of Islam would convince one of what it is capable of accomplishing. The decadence of the Muslims must not, therefore, be thought to stem from their religion. It would be a great injustice to Islam to judge it by the life led by its present-day followers. True Islam, which is life and light, is very different from what goes by its name today—a bundle of dead rites and meaningless rituals.

It is, however, gratifying to note that Muslims are at last realising that they have strayed from the essentials of their noble religion and are now engaged in controversies over mere trifles. I believe true Islam will again assert itself. Signs of Islamic renaissance are already visible all over the Muslim world. Movements pregnant with great potentialities are afoot in Turkey, Persia, Arabia, Egypt, and Afghanistan. It is hoped that, before long, Muslims will shake off the languor and lethargy that have come upon them, and will be able to take their rightful place in the progressive movements of the world.

Islam, which means peace and submission to the will of God, is not a new religion promulgated by the Prophet Muhammad, but the oldest religion based on the unity of God, proclaimed by

Abraham, Moses, Jesus and all other Messengers whom the Lord was pleased to send at different times and in different climes for the reclamation of degraded and debased humanity. Islam simply claims to have purged that religion of adulteration and impurities which had crept into it in the course of time. It would, therefore, be a misnomer to call it Muhammedanism. A Muslim has to believe in all the Scriptures that were revealed from time to time, and he has to respect and revere all the Prophets who preceded his own. Universalism is thus the most distinctive feature of Islam, which is intended, not like other religions for a particular time or a particular country or a particular nation, but for all time, for all countries and for all peoples.

Some of the master minds of Europe and America, like the great poet Goethe, the great historian Gibbon, the great philosopher Carlyle, the great orator Ingersoll, the great socialist George Bernard Shaw, who is perhaps the greatest intellect of the present age, among others, were most profoundly impressed by the message of Islam, and all of them lauded the greatness of its Prophet. Although an atheist himself, and hardly any dogma of any religion has passed unscathed by his trenchant pen, Bernard Shaw thinks Islam is the only religion that can satisfy all intelligent people who want a religion to guide them spiritually, morally and socially. The strongest argument advanced by him to prove the universal acceptability of Islam is that it has the great power of absorbing every form of progress made by philosophy and science.

That Bernard Shaw is not beside the mark in his forecast regarding Islam's future may be judged by what Islam, which is now in its fifteenth century, has done. Its comparison with other religions in their fifteenth century may give an idea of what it is likely to be in its twenty first century. It is, in the opinion of unbiased judges, the only power that can effectively withstand the atheism, scepticism and materialism that are gradually getting a hold over the new world order.

20

Conquest of Universe

A critical question :

"Is the present day research about the moon, the sun and the planets in accordance with the Quran. There, are some people who claim that there is no inconformity between science and the Quran and the Traditions, hence everything the science presents is correct, while others say that the views of science clash with the Quran. Kindly give your comprehensive view and opinion about it ?"

Answer : An elaborate answer of this question requires comprehensive article. However, I am presenting certain things by way of principles hoping that they will be helpful to remove your doubt in this matter.

1. First of all it must be understood that the purpose of science is to explore the fundamental forces which Allah has created in this universe. If these forces are used for the welfare and well being of mankind it is not only permissible but desirable in Islam. Rather than raising obstacles in the way of such attempts Islam encourages them. In this connection Islam only demands that these forces should be used for the purpose that are permissible and useful in the eyes of Islam. In other words, science aims at discovering the hidden forces of universe but the correct use of these forces is told by religion which provides proper direction and better atmosphere for such attempts. Science and technology

can be useful to mankind only if they are used on the principles laid down by Islam. Nobody would deny the fact that whereas science can be a means to the welfare and material progress of mankind, its wrongful and misdirected use can be disastrous for us. The example is before us. In recent years science has provided mankind with the means of comfort and ease, but at the same time its wrongful use has converted the whole world into the hell of turmoil and disturbance. It is the science that invented the high speed means of travel like the jet planes but at the same time the science is responsible of creating disastrous nuclear bombs, hence true benefits from it can be achieved only when it is used according to the principles laid down by Allah.

2. The second thing to understand is that scientific discoveries are of two kinds. Firstly those which pertain to human observation. Such discoveries are never in opposition to the Quran and the Traditions. In fact, they have helped to affirm the Quran and traditions in many things which were difficult for people to understand. For example, the tremendous speed of the "Buraq" (The heavenly horse) on which the Prophet travelled from Makkah to Jerusalem on the night of Ascension, was regarded as unimaginable by the so-called intellectuals of that time. But the science has today proved that the speed is a relative entity that cannot be bound to any limits.

Secondly, there are some views that are based on conjectures and presumptions due to lack of knowledge, rather than observation and certainty. The scientists have not reached any definite conclusions on these matters so far. Such findings sometimes are opposed to the explicit views of the Qur'an and the traditions. In such situations the most proper way is to maintain firm faith in them without making new interpretation to the Qur'an. The scientific researches that clash with them should be regarded as yet inconclusive due to lack of knowledge about them. The more scientific knowledge keeps growing the more it will help to expound the realities described by the Qur'an and the Traditions.

For example, the scientists think that the "sky" has no physical existence. Obviously this hypothesis is not based on observation and definite proof but on the assumption that they have not been able to get any trace of the existence of the sky hence they do not accept its existence. In other words this hypothesis is based on "non existence of knowledge" rather than "knowledge of non -existence". Hence we, the believers in the Qur'an and the Traditions, assert with full confidence that this hypothesis of the scientists is not correct. According to the Qur'an and Tradition the skies do exist but due to its lack of knowledge science has not been able to discover it. If scientific knowledge continues to increase it is quite possible that the scientists realize their mistake and they accept the existence of the ideas, just as they have accepted many other things which they had been denying earlier.

The problem is that the tendency of looking everything in its own perspective is gradually fading away from our minds. Whenever the importance of certain thing dominates our mind we find it difficult to remain within bounds. Undoubtedly, science and technology are Very useful and essential branch of learning, and in the present times they are an inevitable requirement for the Muslim (Uammah) to survive. It is not possible to attain their due place in the world today without science. But this certainly does not mean that any hypothesis proclaimed by a scientist based on conjectures and individual ideas should be accepted as true and given the status of Divine Revelation (Wahy) and the door of interpolations and alterations in the Qur'an and the Sunnah be opened, or doubts and suspicions be given air on this basis, particularly when it is often observed that scientific views and theories are changing every day.

3. It must be remembered that the case of Islam is quite different from that of Christianity. 'The latter did not have the very force and spirit to stand against newly arising needs and scientific discoveries of man. Hence, science threatened it as a great danger. Thus, in order to uphold the prestige of the church, it was essential for Christianity either to oppose scientific achievements or make amendments in the religion itself. In the beginning Roman Catholic church adopted the first course. Having full power and authority on the people, the scientists, like Galileo, had to face tremendous

punishments. But when the authority of church was made to lose its grip they had no alternatives than to make new interpretations and fabricate the religion itself. Hence the scholars of modernism adopted this way.

It happened because the whole edifice of Christianity was erected on extremely unnatural and baseless grounds. Islam is a different religion. it is the natural religion and no sensible argument can challenge it. It is fully capable of fulfilling the needs of the time and to satisfy the demands of new circumstances without making any changes in the religion. Our belief is that the truth of Islam will flourish more and more with the advancement of science and scientific knowledge, provided that his point of view remains scientific in the real sense of the word and he does not give his conjectures the status of certainty and observation.

This is what the religious scholars of Islam think. It implies that everything must be looked in its true perspective. It will not be wise to cross the limits misled by sentimental slogans.

How strange it is that due to this moderate and absolutely reasonable attitude some people are constantly propagating that the scholars of Islam are opposed to science and technology and they do not like any progress in this field. We can only pray to Almighty Allah to bless them with common sense. Ameen!

Man in Space

In the last few years the historical achievements attained by American scientists in the field of space technology, particularly the incident of man's landing on the moon, has attracted the attention of the entire world. Undoubtedly, the amazing journey of Apollos in the space have presented a wonderful exposure of human intellect. The success achieved by them is extremely valuable and a historical marvel from the scientific point of view. They have indeed demonstrated the highest accuracy of mathematical calculations and technological implementation of the scientific ideas. They are able to make predictions of extraordinary circumstances.

The first time man has examined the moon from so near through these spacecrafts. If a century ago somebody claimed that man had reached the moon by flying in the space or that he had seen the earth rising from the horizon of the moon, it would have been considered a fabulous story of the Arabian Nights. It is a reality today.

Every phase of this journey, right from the "take off' of the spacecraft to its successful landing on the earth, is an extremely amazing feat for the common man. From the purely scientific point of view this journey is an achievement that can never be forgotten. But this is only one side of the picture. Taking in view the end result of this wonderful journey reminds us an incident that occurred at the time of Caliph Haroon-al-Rasheed.

It is stated that a certain person sought the permission of Caliph to present an astonishing performance in his court. When the permission granted he erected a needle upright on the floor and himself stood at some distance with a few needles in his hand. Then he took one of those needles in the other hand, aimed at the needle on the floor, and threw the needle in his hand toward it. People saw that this needle passed through the eye of the needle on the floor. He repeated this performance several times and never missed the target even once.

On seeing this astonishing feat the Caliph ordered, "Give him ten dinars, and punish him with ten lashes!" The courtiers asked for an explanation of this equally astonishing reward. The Caliph said, "He gets ten dinars for his accuracy of aim, truthfulness and ambition, as a reward. But he will get ten lashes as a punishment for spending his capabilities in a thing that is of no benefit to any one materially or spiritually."

Incident of the Prudence

This incident of the prudence and wit of Haroon-al- is fully applicable to the space-race of the present times. In fact one feels obliged to commend and praise the scientists on the remarkable feat of landing on the moon who have set unique records of their technical and intellectual skill and their courage and endurance. But when we see how much mental, financial and physical energy of mankind has been spent on this and what humanity received in return, this very achievement becomes an international crime.

Since there are several misunderstandings, perplexing the minds of the people we would discuss the matter in some detail.

There is a group of simple people who think that all these attempts to conquer moon and space are contradictory to the views of the Qur'an and the tradition and (God forbid) they are a challenge to the authority of God. So much so that, some people have been heard saying, purely out of love for Islam, that all the news about landing on the moon are fictions and they cannot be relied upon. But the fact is that if the scientists of America or Russia or any Other country reach the moon or mars or any other planet, it does not in any way clash with the Qur'an and the traditions, nor does it affect the supreme authority of God. There is not a single verse of the Qur'an or narration of the Prophet which denies the ascent of man to moon or M ars or any other planet.

On the contrary, if those travelling in the space keep their eyes open to realities they will find clear signs of the truth of the Qur'an and the traditions. They will observe with their naked eyes the realities of many Islamic concepts which are made more comprehensible through the progress of the scientific knowledge, and which were previously mocked at by the blind followers of Rationalism. For instance, the description of the incredible speed of the "Buraq" in the Holy Traditions, with refierence to the Ascension, was regarded as fairy-tale by the socalled pioneers of rationalism. But the astronauts of today have circled around the world in less than an hour and thus proved that speed is something that can not be confined to any limits. So when the American scientists and astronauts can exhibit such an astonishing super speed through the limited powers of their mind why can't the unlimited power of the Cherisher and Sustainer (Allah) of this universe give even a higher speed, to any of His creatures.

In short, we have firm belief, and there is nothing to shake it, that man is bound to salute and acknowledge the realities of the Qur'an and the Sunnah with the ever increasing progress of science and technology, if, of course, he remains within the bounds and does not claim his calculations to be scientific observations.

The religion brought by the Holy Prophet Mohammed (PBUH) is not like the religion of Christianity which should be frightened by the progress of science. This is the religion which is the most symmetrical with human nature. It had openly proclaimed fourteen centuries ago,that:

> "We shall soon show them Our signs in the horizons and within themselves, until it becomes clear to them that this is the Truth". (Ha Mim As Sajdah: 53)

Imam Razi has quoted earlier commentators to say that the signs in the "Horizons" means the wonders of skies, moon and stars and the elements. The phrase "We will show our signs" means that these wonders have no limits. Thus Allah will continue exhibiting new wonders in every era of time.

On the other side there is a group among the Muslims who are so much dazzled with the grandeur of science that they see nothing more valuable, more important and worth following than throwing rockets on the planets. The overawed tone and longing with which these people talk of this type of scientific advancement gives an impression that for them the most fortunate and exalted and benefactor of mankind is the nation that has performed this wondrous feat, and most deprived are those who have lagged behind in this "sacred" race.

Discarding the Old Views

You must have heard people saying— "the world has entrapped the moon and planets but the Muslims are still entangled in the problems of Salah, fasting, marriage and divorce"-. This expression actually depicts the same mentality that the Western nations, have surpassed all other nations in every walk of life by inventing the rockets and satellites, and hence the solution to all our problems must be sought by following the footsteps of the West.

In fact both these trends are dangerous. We have no hesitation in acknowledging that this is an amazing achievement, and from the scientific point of view, it is a great success of man. But the question arises whether this "achievement" was worth attempting in view of the price man had to pay for it? There are many who take pleasure out of the success of space explorations but very few know what quantity of wealth was spent in each of these space journeys? The expenses incurred on Apollo-8 were one trillion and twenty billion rupees (*Jang*, Karachi, 14 January 1969). This amount was equivalent to at least twenty annual budgets and six years of national income of Pakistan. In other words the amount spent by Pakistan in twenty years and the money earned by 100 million people of Pakistan in six years was spent on only one space journey. It is the amount spent only on the journey of the Appollo-8. The journey of Appalo- 10 must have cost far more money than the Appollo-8. It is equal to the money that could be spent by Pakistan in 80 years.

Compassion for Mankind

The question arises can it be the act of any one having slightest compassion for mankind to spend billion of trillions rupees in space journey in a world where people are massacred by hunger and poverty, where millions of people are begging for a loaf of bread, where countless people die for not being able to get the medicines required for their ailment, where about half the population remain deprived of education facilities? In America itself which has the "honour" of performing the "great achievement" a report was published in the same month in which one trillion and twenty billion rupees were spent on Apollo-8, that one out of every nine persons is destitute, and that:

> "Poverty is the greatest material problem of today" (Weekly "Time" New York, 24 January 1929, p29)

This huge expenditure on the useless probe of space in a country like America cannot be justified for a nation who claims to be sympathetic to mankind. It seems that Sa'adi had been addressing the astronauts of today when he said:

> You have well solved the problems of the earth That
> you are going to play with the heavens.

If a man from the East tries to show the other side of the picture of space-race, it may be said that lie is saying it due to his jealousy for Western advancement. Hence we present the comments of a renowned historian and thinker of the West itself on this subject. A very thoughtful article of distinguished historian and philosopher of England Dr. Arnold Tyne Bee has been published. We are presenting herewith a summary of its excerpts. After admitting the wondrous feat of space achievements he writes:

> "Even today 10% or 20% of American population comprises of indigent people. Looking at the world as a whole only one third of its increasing population is such as is getting proper food. Hence utilisation of the economic resources of mankind is in the foolish pursuits of erecting the Pyramids of Egypt or landing on the moon, which, in themselves, are included in the list of the crimes.
>
> "The world of today is involved in three wars. Individual strikes are getting frequent. students are protesting everywhere and different ways of terrorism are being adopted. All this is happening under the disgraceful feeling that use of force is the only way to attract attention of people when one is offended."
>
> "People of Russia and America had been congratulating each other on their space achievements although the main cause of this "stupidity- had been their own rivalries. If these two political powers had not been in combat with each other on the small planet of Earth this "stupidity" would not have occurred.
>
> "From the very early days of history of human activities, the technical advancement and moral degradation of man are becoming inseparable. The history of our science and technology is indeed a wonderful "Tale of achievernents" but the history of our mutual relations has been proved to be a story of grief and regrets on our failures. This is the moral "gap" which after 1945 A.D. has widened to the extent that it has opened a vast channel for disaster to enter.
>
> In this atomic age, the priority must be given to save ourselves from the crime of wasting the lives of other

human beings For, this, it is essential that a Supreme government should be formed on the universal level and all local governments be placed under it. But this is becoming even more difficult than landing on the moon because at present Nationalism has become as sacred as an idol. To part with a false deity need greater courage and bravery in this world than is needed by the astronauts.

"Next in the list of priority comes making effective arrangements to produce food for the population on this earth. We do not know the extent to which world population would have gone by the time the movement of' family planning gains popularity throughout the world However we do know that we should not waste a single moment to increase the supply of food. The fast moving technological progress should equally speed up the productivity in every field.

These are the two most important targets before mankind while space adventures can not be of any service to any of them.

Hence, the fact is that the conquest of space is an absolutely wasteful exercise, and by spending out energies in this direction we are intentionally imposing on ourselves huge economic liabilities. We cannot, and should not ignore our econornic problerns at a time when human race is heading fast toward starvation

As to the question that in case we put the space programme at the bottom of our agenda, delete the preparation of war from it, what alternate use of the scientific knowledge of our inventor be?

The question has already been answered by the Japanese government. The researches of scientists should be directed to explore the resources hidden in the sea instead of wasting them in space and war strategies

The sea is within the reach of man as against the nearest planet from the earth. The two-third area of our planet is water and it is a huge treasure of' the unknown resources. It has been estimated that there exists the greatest store of natural resources in the sea which remains yet unexplored.

This is a vast field of research for man and in addition to satisfying the desire for research it may also provide a surety that the population will not die of starvation even if it increases ten-fold of the current population.

A yellow female fish lays one million eggs during its life span, but under ordinary circumstances only three fully grown fish can be produced that would be capable of laying further eggs. But when Japan's "sea-farmers" tried to enhance the ability of these eggs artificially and nurtured the stock of eggs and protected them from other animals it resulted in the production of 100,000 fish from the eggs of one fish.

When Apollo-8 returned after its victorious flight I received a telephone call from across the Atlantic a few hours after it, "Do you think this is a revolutionary incidence in the history of mankind?" My answer was 'NO'.

"My answer could have been 'Yes' if the news of that day had been that humanity has suddenly regained its consciousness and it has formed a universal central state, and their researchers have discovered from the depth of the sea things that can be used by mankind for its collective purposes." We have yet to achieve this revolutionary aim, and for that the first step of the world powers should be to divert their resources towards the collective advancement of human beings instead of wasting them in space adventures and war weapons. If this is achieved the population of the entire world can be brought to the standard of living now enjoyed by 80% of American people.

> This will indeed be a 'Revolutionary incidence' but this will not be achieved through technology alone. If one wants to reap fruits through the power of technology the essential condition for it is a spiritual revolution. This spiritual surgery is our dire need and without it all our recently discovered' material resources would be useless. Even if we land on the moon without the spiritual revival the dust and ashes obtained frorn there will mock at our spiritual bankruptcy from which we could not get rid of in our motherland."

In this article Dr. Tyne Bee has made a wise diagnosis of the disease, and if you give a little thought you will know that the root cause of this disease is that the people tracking the heavenly bodies have no definite aim nor any exalted motto of life. All the ways of their struggle have been lost in their childish desire of surpassing others. The result is that they have not been able to utilise their unlimited capabilities for the conquest of this universe that could lead mankind to the goal of peace and tranquillity. All their energy is being spent in combating with each-other, in surpassing or defeating each other, and in this struggle they have overlooked to note what great harm they have inflicted on themselves.

A race between the two parties, no matter how fast and speedy it is, cannot be of any benefit to humanity if it is not in the right direction. Tyne Bee was right in saying that spiritual surgery was needed to take full advantage of science. But what he does not know is that such a surgical treatment cannot be possible without submission to the gireatest benefactor of mankind. Muhammad (Peace of Allah be upon him) had made the return trip to heavenly destination far beyond the moon, Mars, Venus and Plato and which is beyond the scientific imagination. Instead of directing his followers to conquer the moon he asked them to conquer the hearts and souls of the people. Unless the world kneels down to his feet and seeks guidance from Him, it will never be able to acquire peace and tranquillity, though it may launch numerous artificial satellites or plant its rags on the Moon or Mars or any other planet.

After the landing on the moon all further advancement of science in this direction will prove more disasterous for mankind and only add to the uneasiness and darken the clouds of suffering and distress over mankind.

Dr. Iqbal, the great philosopher-poet of East has rightly said:

> "The one who is seeking the paths of heavenly bodies, could not travel in the world of his own thoughts. He captured the rays of the sun, but could not turn his night into the dawn of life. He was so much involved in the perplexities of his logic that he remains unable to decide between gain and loss."

Conquest of Planets

This is no secret : The Holy Qur'an has expounded the fact in many places that the entire universe has been created for mankind and every particle has been placed for the service of human beings. It stated:

> He is (Allah) Who created for you all that is in the earth. (2:29)
>
> And He (Allah) has subjugated to you all that is in the heavens and all that is in the earth, altogether from Him. Surely in that are signs for a people who reflect. (45:13)

In these verses, while describing His bounties, Allah has made subtle indication that since all these things have been created for man, it is man's duty to get knowledge and explore them by applying his logic and wisdom bestowed on him by Allah, for the benefit of mankind. He should put to his use all resources that Allah has stored in the universe. There are two kinds of bounties of Allah created in the universe. The things that are general which man uses in his life, yet there are some bounties which can be acquired by the use of knowledge and wisdom. The Qur'an said:

> Have you not seen how Allah has subjugated to you whatsoever is in the heavens and whatsoever is in the earth, and He has perfected His blessings on you, (both) open and hidden?

In other words, Allah has indeed subjugated the universe to man yet it does not mean that he shall get all these blessings without striving for them and using physical and mental talents for achieving them.

At another place the Holy Qur'an said:

> Allah is He, who has subjugated the sea to you that the ships may sail through it by His cornmand- and that you may seek of His bounty and that you may offer thanks. (Q.45:12)

Subjugation of Sea

In this verse the cause for subjugation of sea has been described as providing it as a means of seeking Allah's blessings and bounties. In the Qur'an "seeking Allah's bounty" generally means "striving for earning the livelihood". Hence, one meaning of this verse may be that mankind has been given authority and power of navigation on the sea so that he may trade through it. Some commentators have, however, stated that "seeking Allah's bounty" in this verse does not mean trade but research and exploration of countless other bounties that He has created in the sea. The verse then means: "We have subjugated the sea for you after creating in it innumerable useful things so that you may seek for them and make use of them". Thus, every now and then the discoveries of modern science are making it apparent that the treasures of mineral and botanical products hidden in the sea are far more than those on the earth.

> The Qur'an has explicitly pointed out at various places that even new bounties of this universe will get exposed as often as man would march forward in the way of research and exploration. For example, where the Qur'an has mentioned horses and mules as means of transport, it has further pointed out that in future there will come out such means of transport which man did not know at that stage.
>
> (Allah has created for you) horses, mules and donkeys that you may ride on them, and (in future) He will create such things which as yet you don't know.

In this manner the Qur'an has pointed out to all kinds of means of communication to be invented till the Last Day.

At another place it said:

> We shall show them Our signs, in the universe and also in their selves until it is clear to them that this (Qur'an) is the Truth.

This verse signifies that the exposition of Allah's attribute of creation will never cease to create. The new blessings and productions will keep appearing in every-era of time till the Last Day.

Prophetic Traditions

Many more statements frorn the Qur'an and prophetic traditions can be produced on this subject, but even if these few verses are positively reflected upon, the reality will be exposed as broad daylight that if access through research, investigation, experiments and discoveries is made to the hidden powers of the universe with rightful intentions and rightful methods, it is not condemnable in the eyes of the Qur'an. Rather, it is desirable, and not only that Islam has not laid down any restriction on such scientific experiments, it has, in fact, encouraged them: This is the reason why Muslims have left lasting impressions of their scientific endeavours which will continue to serve as guidelines for mankind.

Concept of Exploration

However, it must be remembered that the concept of conquering the universe as presented by Islam is quite different from the materialistic concept of the West. The West has also undertaken the task of conquering it, and indeed in the last few years they have attained extraordinary successes in this field. But the first and fundamental difference of Islam with the West is that their restricted material visualisation of things have deprived them of seeing the vast world beyond matter. Hence whatever new inventions are made by them are regarded as the fruits of their own power, intellect and labour. They do not perceive the active hand of the Creator or Master behind these discoveries. But the vision of Islam sees things beyond the investigations. experiments and discoveries and it observes the supreme power of creation of Allah behind them. Allah has subjugated the entire universe for mankind on one hand, and on the other hand it has bestowed man with intellect, wisdom, power and energy through which he has been able to dominate the forces of this universe. Hence the teaching of Islam is that after the success gained in the process of subjugation of universe he should kneel down before his Creator and Master in humble submission rather than be proud and arrogant. It is Allah who awarded him with the honour of ruling over the entire universe. According to the Qur'anic teaching the call of a true Muslim on such occasions is:

> "Glorified be He Who has subjugated (all) this to us and we ourselves were not capable to do it, and surely to our Lord we shall return. "

The second fundamental difference between Islam and the West with regard to the conquest of the universe is that the ultimate object of the Western efforts in this direction is the conquest of the universe itself According to them the aim of man's life is nothing more than gaining the maximum benefit and pleasure out of the universe, and depart from this world. Contrary to this, subjugation of universe, in the eyes of Islam, is not final aim by itself, but it is a means to achieve the goal, and only a milestone on the path of man's destination. Islamic point of view is that man gets the right to utilize the services of this universe only when he fulfils the purpose of his creation and discharges his duties rightly and sincerely. Almighty Allah has not subjugated this universe to man without purpose and the purpose is that man should perform the duty imposed on him with precision and honesty. This duty is worship and submission to Allah.

Allah said:

> "And I have not created the Jinn and mankind but to worship Me". (51:56)

The third fundamental difference between the West and Islam is that any new force or power which man comes to possess as a result of his struggle for dominating the universe can be applied or used for any purpose that is allowed by human reason. But Islam teaches that the purpose of its use is determined by Almighty Allah, who has bestowed that power upon man, hence these inventions and discoveries can be used only for the objectives permitted by Him. When man determines by himself the purpose without the guidance of Divine Revelations, these bounties of the universe may sometimes lead him to the path of destruction instead of giving any benefit to mankind. This results in the fact that despite hoisting his flag on the Moon and Mars his own life seems to fall into the abyss of darkness. Thus the Islamic concept of subjugation of the universe is more universal and comprehensive than of the West and more beneficial for mankind. May Almighty Allah give us the ability to recognise its true values and to practise them in the right directions. (Amen)

Bibliography

Abul Hassan Ali Nadwi, *Saviours* of Islamic Spirit, trans. by M. Ahmad, Lucknow, 1971.

Ahmad, Aziz, *Studies in Islamic Culture in the Indian Environment,* Oxford, 1964.

Arberry, A.J., *The doctrines of the Sufis, tr., of Kalabadhi's Kitab alta, Aruf,* Cambridge, 1935.

Arnold, Sir Thomas, *The Calilhate, rev. edn.,* London, 1965.

Bagley, R.R.C. (tr.) *Ghazali's Book of Counsel for Kings,* Oxford, 1964.

Boyle, J.A. ed., *The Cambridge History of Iran,* Cambridge, 1968.

Brohi, A.K., *Islam in the Modern World,* Karachi, 1968.

Burckhardt T., *Alchemy,* trans. by W. Stoddart, London, 1967.

Burckhardit, Titus, *Introduction to Sufi Doctrines,* Lahore, 1959.

Corbin, H., *LKe livre des pénétrations métaphysiques,* Tehran-Paris, 1964.

Czaplicka, M.A., *The Turks of Central Asia in History and the Present Day,* Amsterdam, 1973.

De Laet, *Description of India* and *Fragment of Indian History,* New York, 1963.

— *Dimensions of Islam,* trans. by P. Townsend, London, 1970.

—- *En Islam Iranien,* Paris, 1971-72.

E. Zolla (ed.), *Eternitá e storia. I valori permanenti nel divenire storico,* Florence, 1970.

Faruqi, Bherhan Ahmad, *The Mujaddid's Conception of Tauhid, Lahore,* 1940.

— *Fes, Stadt des Islam,* Lausanne and Freiburg, 1960.

Field, Cland H., *Al-Ghazali : The Alchemy of Happiness,* London, 1910.

Foster, W., *The English Factories in India,* 13 Vols., Oxford, 1906-27.

Frykenberg, R.E., *Land Control and Social Structure in Indian History,* Wisconsin, 1969.

Gibb, H.A.R, *Islamic Society and the West,* London, 1960.

Guénon, R., *The Reign of Quantity and the Signs of the Times,* trans. by Lord Northbourne, Baltimore, 1972.

Halepota, A.J, *Philosophy of Shah Waliu'llah,* Lahore.

Haqq, En'amul, *Muslim Bengali Literature,* Karachi, 1957.

Hasrat, B.J., Dara Shikoh : *Life and Works,* reprinted, New Delhi, 1982.

Hodgson, *G.S. The Order of Assassin,* The Hague, 1955.

Husaini, S.A. Q. *The Pantheistic Monism of Ibn al-'Arabi,* Lahore, 1970.

Iqbal 'Ali Shah, Sardar, *Islamic Sufism,* London, 1933.

— *Ideals and Realities of Islam,* London, 1966; Boston, 1972.

Irfan Habib, *The Agrarian System of Mughal India,* Bombay, 1963.

— *Islamic Studies,* Beirut, 1967.

Izutsu, T., *The Concept and Reality of Existence,* Tokyo, 1971.

Izutsu, Toshihido, *A Comprehensive Study of the Key Philosophical Concepts of Sufism and Taoism, Tokyo,* 1966-67.

Ja'far Sharif, *Islam in India,* Oxford, 1921.

J. Servier, *L'homme et l'invisible,* Paris, 1964.

Khan, Khaja, *Studies in Tasawwuf, Madras,* 1923.

Landau, R., *The Philosophy of the Ibn'Arabi,* London, 1959.

Lewis, Bernard, *Islam,* New York, 1974.

— *Light on the Ancient Worlds,* trans. by Lord Northbourne, London, 1965.

Lings, M., *Ancient Beliefs and Modern Superstitions,* London, 1965.

Lings, Martin, *A Sufi Saint of the Twentieth Century,* 2nd edn., London, 1971.

— *Logic and Transcendence,* trans. P. Townsend, New York, 1975.

— *Looking Back on Progress,* London, 1971.

MacDonald, D.B., *The Religious Attitude and Life in Islam,* Beirut, 1965.

Maryam Jameelah, *Islam versus the West,* Lahore, 1968.

Mayne, P. *Saints of Sind,* London, 1965.

Mir Valiuddin, *Love of God,* Hyderabad, Deccan,1968.

Mohiuddin Ahmad, *Saiyid Ahmad Shahid,* Lucknow, 1975.

Moreland, W.H., *India at the Death of Akbar,* London, 1920.

Mujeeb, M., *The Indian Muslims,* London, 1969.

Nasr, Seyyed H., *Three Muslim Sages,* Cambridge, Mass., 1964.

Nasr, S.H., *The Encounter of Man and Nature, The spiritual Crisis of Modern Man,* London, 1968.

Needleman, J. (ed.), *This Sword of Gnosis,* Baltimore, 1974.

Nicholson, R.A., *The Mysteries of Islam,* London, 1914.

Northbourne Lord, *Religion in the Modern World,* London, 1963.

Nyberg, H.S., *Kleinere Schrifteu des Iban 'Arabi,* Leiden, 1919.

Petersen, E.L., *'Ali and Mu'awiya in early Arabic Traditions,* Copenhagen, 1964.

Qanungo, K.R., *Dara Shikoh,* Calcutta, 1935.

Rafiqi, A.Q., *Sufism in Kashmir,* Delhi, 1977.

Richards, J.F. *Mughal Administration in Golkonda,* Oxford. 1975.

Rizvi, S.A.A., *Muslim Revivalist Movements in Northern India in the Sixteenth and Seventeenth Centuries,* Agra, 1965.

Russel, Ralph and Khurshidu'l Islam, *Three Mughal Poets,* Cambridge, Mass., 1968.

Sadiq, M., *A History of Urdu Poetry,* London, 1964.

Saksena, R.B., *A History of Urdu Literature,* Allahabad, 1927.

Schacht, J., *The Origin of Muhammadan Jurisprudence,* Oxford, 1950.

Schuon, F., *Islam: the Perennial Philosophy,* London, 1976.

— *Science and Civilization in Islam,* Cambridge, 1968; New York, 1970.

Sharif, M.M., *A History of Muslim Philosophy,* Wiesebaden.

Sharma, R.S. and Jha, V. *ed., Indian Society : Historical Probings,* Delhi, 1974.

Sharma, S.R., *Mughal Government and Administration,* Bombay. 1951.

Shehadi, F., *Ghazali's Unique Unknowable God,* Leiden, 1964.

Shemesh, A.B., *Taxation in Islam*, Leiden, 1958, 1965.

Siddiqi, M.Z., *Hadith Literature*, Calcutta, 1961.

Spear, P., *Twilight of the Mughals*, 2nd edn., Cambridge, 1969, reprint, New Delhi, 1970.

Storey, C.A., *Persian Literature: A Bibliographical Survey*, London, 1927-58.

Subhan, J.A., *Sufism : Its Saints and Shrines*, 2nd edn., Lucknow, 1960.

— *Sufi Essays*, London 1972, trans. J. Peter Hobson, Albany (N.Y.), 1973.

Sufi, G.M.D., *Kashmir*, Lahore, 1940-9.

Tarachand, *Influence of Islam on Indian Culture*, Allahabad, 1963.

Tavernier, Jean-Baptiste, *Travels in India*, London, 1925, reprinted, New Delhi, 1977.

Temple, R.C., *Legends of the Punjab*, London, 1893-1901.

— "The Force of Traditional Islamic Philosophy in Iran Today", *Studies in Comparative Religion*, 1968.

Thomas, R.C., *Legends of the Punjab*, London, 1893-1901.

Titus, M., *Indian Islam*, Milford, 1930, reprinted, New Delhi, 1979.

Trimingham. J.S., *The Sufi Orders in Islam*, Oxford, 1971.

Tritton, A.S., *The Caliphs and their non-Muslim Subjects*, Oxford, 1930.

— *Understanding Islam*, trans. by D.M. Matheson, London, 1963; Baltimore, 1972.

Vaudeville, *Charlotte, Kabir*, Oxford, 1974.

Wahed Husain, *Administration of Justice during the Muslim Rule in India*, Delhi, 1977.

Walker, B., *Hindu World*, London, 1968.

Watanmal, L., *The Life of Shah' Abdul Latif*, Hyderabad, Sind, 1889.

Yusuf Iblish and Peter Lambron Wilson, *Traditional Modes of Contemplation and Action*, Tehran, 1977.

Zaehner, R.C., *Hindu and Muslim Mysticism*, London, 1960.

Ziadah, N.A., *Sanusiyah : A study of a Revivalist Movement in Islam*, Leiden, 1958.

Index

□□□